Agnieszka Bron, Michael Schemmann (Eds.)

Language – Mobility – Identity

Bochum Studies
in
International Adult Education

edited by

Agnieszka Bron and Michael Schemmann

volume 1

LIT

Agnieszka Bron, Michael Schemmann (Eds.)

Language – Mobility – Identity

Contemporary Issues for Adult Education in Europe

LIT

Printed with support of the Ruhr-University of Bochum

Managing Editor: Marcus Reinecke

Manuscripts for publication may be submitted directly to the Editors,
Prof. Dr. Agnieszka Bron and Dr. Michael Schemmann.

Address: Lehrstuhl für Erwachsenenbildung
Institut für Pädagogik
Ruhr-Universität Bochum
Universitätsstr. 150
D-44780 Bochum

Die Deutsche Bibliothek – CIP-Einheitsaufnahme

Language – Mobility – Identity : Contemporary Issues for Adult Education in
Europe / Agnieszka Bron, Michael Schemmann (Eds.). – Hamburg : LIT, 2000
    (Bochum Studies in International Adult Education ; 1.)
    ISBN 3-8258-4364-5

NE: GT

© LIT VERLAG Münster – Hamburg – London
    Grindelberg 15a 20144 Hamburg Tel. 040–44 64 46 Fax 040–44 14 22

Distributed in North America by:

Transaction Publishers
New Brunswick (U.S.A.) and London (U.K.)

Transaction Publishers
Rutgers University
35 Berrue Circle
Piscataway, NJ 08854

Tel.: (732) 445 – 2280
Fax: (732) 445 – 3138
for orders (U.S. only):
toll free 888-999-6778

CONTENTS

PART I: EDITORIAL

PART II: KEYNOTE

PART III: A NOTION OF A EUROPEAN DIMENSION

PART I

EDITORIAL

Bochum Studies in International Adult Education
Introduction to the Series

With "Language – Mobility – Identity. Contemporary Issues for Adult Learning in Europe", the first volume of *Bochum Studies in International Adult Education*, we are launching a new series of publications from the Chair of Adult Education at the Ruhr-University of Bochum. In announcing this new publication series we would like to replace the usual solemn, ceremonial comments with a clarifying statement – on the one hand explaining the intention and structure of *Bochum Studies in International Adult Education*, on the other hand commenting on its underlying understanding of international adult education.

First, the structure of the publication involves some particularities. Each volume will be organised around one topic or issue which is of interest, of importance or of particular relevance for adult education in general. This particular topic will be considered from various points of view, i.e. comparative, historical, gender, socio-political and cultural. In that way each volume will exist as a closed unit in itself. This means that the collection of individual books can be seen, on the one hand, as a series of publications on adult education which in the long run will be a useful collection of articles about adult education. On the other hand, each individual publication can be used by those interested in the characteristics and in an the overview of the particular topic within the field of adult education focused on in that issue.

Second, *Bochum Studies in International Adult Education* addresses not only researchers, university teachers and students of adult education but also those from related disciplines. Adult education as a discipline is becoming more and more interrelated with other disciplines of social sciences and *Bochum Studies in International Adult Education* acknowledges this by its employed perspectives. While not explicitly addressing practitioners, except for providing them with up-to-date research overviews, each issue will also address politicians and policy makers. In this respect we hope to establish a forum for a discourse and a debate around adult education that brings together research from different disciplines and encourages a broader public of adult education.

Third, the fact that adult education is becoming more and more inter-related with other disciplines influences the general understanding of adult education implied in *Bochum Studies in International Adult Education*. We are aware of the shifts in the terminology of our discipline that seems, for example, in the English discourse to favour the term 'lifelong learning' after long years of using 'continuing education'. This same priority can be seen in the European Union discourse. By contrast, in the context of UNESCO the term 'adult learning' has been put at the centre of documents and publications since CONFINTEA V was held in July 1997 in Hamburg. We could give other examples from other countries disputing the terms 'andragogy' and 'adult education', letting alone the German debate about the terms 'Erwachsenenbildung' and 'Weiterbildung'.

Considering this ongoing debate, we felt it made sense to stick to the – as it seems – rather traditional term 'adult education' when referring to our discipline in its broadest sense. By doing so we hope to combine the stability and historical side of our discipline with the innovations and new tendencies which have meanwhile developed.

Fourth, the underlying perspective for *Bochum Studies in International Adult Education* will be an international one. Nevertheless our concept of internationality will be both geographically and culturally restricted to a more European-focused perspective. There are many definitions and understandings of the concept of 'Europe'. For our purposes we will define 'Europe' in the broad sense, disregarding political, religious, economic or cultural divisions; its borders will encompass all countries from the Canary Islands to parts of Russia, from Norway and Iceland to Malta, Cyprus, also Turkey and Israel. What we refer to here is a simple concept of 'Europe' – always bearing in mind an openness and a responsibility towards the other regions of the world. Our ambition, thus, is to showcase the voices of experienced researchers from various European countries, as well as new adepts, i.e. those involved in preparing their doctoral thesis. In this way we hope to make the research results and debates of these researchers an internationally common knowledge.

Fifth, one further important aspect about this new series of publications is its editorial policy in terms of authors. *Bochum Studies in International Adult Education* particularly encourages those researchers who normally do not publish in English due to language barriers. Those researchers should feel encouraged to send their articles to this publication. Submitted texts will have to be in English, preferably proof-read by a native speaker. However, some editorial proof-reading will be provided by the editors. Of course, researchers with a good command of English or who are themselves native English speakers are equally encouraged to contribute.

Sixth, we must also mention that *Bochum Studies in International Adult Education* uses a referee system to judge contributions. All articles will be reviewed for acceptance by a selected group of invited specialists. At the same time, responsibility for the contents of the article remains that of the authors and not that of the editors. We would like here to formally state that opinions formulated in individual articles are not necessarily those held by the editors.

Finally, we would like to stress that *Bochum Studies in International Adult Education* will try to foster the scientific community in Europe, maybe even bringing those people a little more to the centre who have thus far been marginalised due to language reasons. We hope that *Bochum Studies in International Adult Education* enforce a new culture of scientific communication and discourse in Europe, a communication that really deserves the attribute 'European'.

The Managing Editor of *Bochum Studies in International Adult Education* is Marcus Reinecke. This series of publications is funded by the Ruhr-University of Bochum, for which we are extremely grateful.

Agnieszka Bron   Michael Schemmann
(Editor-in-Chief)   (Editor)

BRON, A., SCHEMMANN, M. (eds.) (2000). LANGUAGE, MOBILITY,
IDENTITY. CONTEMPORARY ISSUES FOR ADULT EDUCATION IN
EUROPE. MÜNSTER, pp. 12-19.

Kjell Rubenson

DO WE NEED A NEW PUBLICATION?

At a time when the future of adult education as a field of study is under
threat, and many adult education journals struggling to survive as print-
media are replaced by electronic journals Bochum announces a daring new
initiative by launching *Bochum Studies in International Adult Education*.
The focus of BSIAE is to provide a forum where important European social
issues can be discussed from an adult learning/education frame of reference. The audience is the university community, professionals and policy
makers. Do we need BSIAE? Rather than answer with a simple yes or no I
would like to briefly provide a very personal view on how BSIAE can
make a valuable contribution and address some of the weaknesses in the
field of international and comparative adult education. I will point to three
main areas where BSIAE can fill a vacuum:

• the need for a European focus;
• the need to better integrate research, professional practice and policy
  analysis;
• the need to revitalise comparative adult education.

A European Perspective

The fall of the former Communist Block and the integration of Europe currently taking place within the context of the European Union is having a
profound effect on the nation state. These changes effect how decisions are
made regarding economic and social policies and perhaps most impor-
tantly, have an impact on the 'European psyche'. The *Amsterdam Treaty*
commits the member states to developing the citizenship of the Union, not
just in a legal sense but also through the fulfilment of the ideal of a Europe
close to its citizens. The development of European citizenship education

and training offers – as stated by *DG XXII-Education Training Youth* – a privileged vehicle for the promotion of active participation in Europe's rich diversity of cultures, economies, polities and cultures. Consequently our understanding of adult education is to no small extent being shaped in the context of European cooperation with programs like Socrates, Erasmus, Leorardo and soon to be, Grundtvig. Common in projects funded under these umbrellas are the European content of the activities, and the transnationality of cooperation and dissemination of project results.

BSIAE has an important role to play as an arena for critical debates on the outcomes of these projects as well as to enrich our understanding of the linkages – or the lack thereof – between research and development projects and strategic policy initiatives. Thus, at a time when skills are trumpeted by national governments and EU as a generic response to the economic problems facing Europe a serious discussion from and adult education/learning perspective has much to offer. The economic imperative, although dominating, is not the only force driving the interest in adult learning. In Eastern and Central European countries there is a struggle to build a new system following the collapse of the old order. This involves a search for a new identity, establishing democratic institutions and recreating civil society. Touraine notes that while it is understandable that Eastern Europe places much of its trust in the market, this is not enough to build a future (Touraine 1995). In the Western World the status of civil society and democracy, the ecological crisis and the status of women and minorities are being debated. Giddens notes that in the post-traditional order individuals more or less have to engage with the wider world if they are to survive (Giddens 1994). He continues:

> Information produced by specialists (including scientific knowledge) can no longer be wholly confined to specific groups, but becomes routinely interpreted and acted on by lay individuals in the course of their everyday actions (Giddens 1994, 7).

Using the European Union program on *Education and Active Citizenship* as a vehicle BSIAE can play a crucial role in enhancing the understanding of the relationship between various forms of adult education and learning and the fostering of democratic citizens.

BSIAE can also play a major role in the 'Europification' of the adult education map. Until quite recently the evolution of adult education as a field
of study has to a large extent been driven by developments in North
America. Assumptions and perceptions of the territory that governed the
efforts to accumulate knowledge on the education of adults were rooted in
North American traditions and circumstances. However, in recent years
there has been a concentrated effort to build a European profile. The creation of the *European Society for the Research on the Education of Adults*
(ESREA) – with its vibrant research networks and biannual European Research conference – has the potential to build a European map. ESREA
brings together researchers from various parts of the continent working
within different paradigms and traditions but with a shared interest in the
scholarly aspect of adult education processes. ESREA's strength, its informal organisation with loosely linked networks, is also its weakness. BSIAE
can function as a vehicle to bring together and integrate the scholarly activities taking place under ESREA and make them visible to a larger audience.

Integration of Research, Policy Analysis and Professional Practice

Two criticisms are generally launched against adult education research.
First, it is of no use to practitioners and policy makers, and second it is not
of the same standard as social science research in general. Looking from
within academia, adult education research does not seem to be able to compete for funding from high status social science and humanities research
councils. As Duke notes, this makes adult education departments vulner-
able, as they need to win research standing to hold their place in today's
competitive university climate (Duke 1994). Clearly some of the criticism
is unfounded but at a time when issues that have traditionally been the pre-
rogative of adult education scholars are becoming of such interest that other
disciplines are also showing an interest in them. There is no time for com-
placency.

ESREA's reviews of trends in adult education research in Europe (Hake
1994, Jelenc 1994) show that not only has practice-related research dominated the research agenda but also there is a general move towards a predominance of applied research. This is linked to changes in the funding

structure for research with funds being shifted to contract research in specific areas defined by government bodies and councils for adult education. Jelenc observes that research in adult education in Central and Eastern Europe, after the fall of the Communist Block, has become rare and the focus today is almost exclusively on the narrow applicability of research (Jelenc 1994). However, there are doubts about whether this practical research actually reaches out to those working in the field of adult education (e.g. SOU 1999). Furthermore the usefulness of policy research in adult education has been questioned not only with regard to policy making, but also with regard to its contribution to scholarship (Hake 1992, 1994). This criticism reflects the dominant situation where policy research is done in the form of contracts and is narrowly instrumental in character.

Is it reasonable to ask BSIAE to fix this problem? Probably not. But the stated intention of the publication gives some promising indications. In this respect I would like to point to some hobby horses of mine. What I see as a major obstacle to theoretical development within adult education as well as the production of 'useful knowledge' is the often sharp separation that exists between theory development and empirical (qualitative as well as quantitative) research. This is not to deny the developments that have occurred in connection with the introduction of critical theory and later post-structural perspectives into adult education research. The problem, however, with much of the so-called critical literature is that it is confined to introducing social theorists to an adult education audience, or the analyses are purely theoretical, addressing issues related to various positions of leading social theorists. Valuable as it might be, it does little to inform the empirical research and, more problematic is that knowledge production as such is hampered by a lack of fruitful interplay between empirical research and theory development. Without this interplay the scholarly literature in our field continues to primarily put forward normative positions without an interest in, or the capability to study, the conditions under which the ideals could be realised. However, as BSIAE intends to do focus on critical social issues in the European society and to bring a broad body of adult education research into the debate we have a promising start. This will help adult education move towards the 'conceptual position' of policy research, which is one step to remedying some of the above problems facing the knowledge production in adult education (Rubenson 1994). Here the role of research is not primarily seen as coming up with a solution and/or answer to a specific issue but rather helps develop a broader understanding of the underlying problem. This involves widening the debate, reformulating the problem, clarifying goals, and analysing eventual conflicts between multiple goals. Instead of being of direct instrumental use, the primary function of research is conceptual. Naturally a development towards policy-oriented research of the proposed nature will to a large extent depend on the availability of funding for these kinds of critical activities. However, BSIAE can help foster an understanding that it will also require a willingness to change the way we do research in adult education departments. Without long-term research programs, integration of empirical studies and theory development, and a willingness and capability to attack 'real problems', Duke's sensible recommendation to give more attention to how development projects can be used as research will not be a fruitful direction to pursue (Duke 1994). Thus, BSIAE can through its publication policy help to realise Jackall and Vidich classical understanding of social theory (Jackhall, Vidich 1995) namely that: "Theory is the historically informed framing of intellectual problems about concrete social issues and the resolution of those problems through the analysis of empirical data" (Jackhall, Vidich 1995, viii).

Revitalisation of Comparative Adult Education

There is a strange paradox in adult education. There has existed – since World War I – a strong international movement of adult educators who come together in meetings like the recent CONFITEA V held in July of 1997. Adult education policy is also extensively discussed at the intergovernmental level by organisations like OECD, UNESCO and EU. At the same time, comparative adult education is not very prominent within the adult education research community. By addressing major social issue facing Europe from a comparative perspective BSIAE can over time have a major impact on the field of adult education.

Now that lifelong learning is promoted as a solution to all kinds of problem facing the European society, whether economic, social or cultural, there is a danger of accepting slogans about the evolving Learning Society too readily and uncritically. For example, despite the gradual rise in levels of educational attainment in Europe, a large number of Europeans still find themselves at the tail end of the skills distribution. And while higher-skilled workers will share in the knowledge economy's wealth, they still face frequent job changes, high turn-over rates, and a need for continuing access to education and training. For the many others tied to dormant economic sectors, dead-end jobs with low pay and poor benefits, few opportunities are offered for acquiring new skills or qualifications. Skills and educational qualifications are powerful factors in determining access to wealth created by the knowledge economy. Formal schooling and adult education and training must be considered necessary elements in any strategy for improving the life chances of disadvantaged populations. Hence, an important issue is the extent to which adult education and training is presently reaching such populations.

From this perspective recent results of participation in structured adult education are disturbing. Despite a rhetoric of *Lifelong Learning for All* (OECD 1996) little has happened in terms of extending adult education to disadvantaged groups. Results from *The International Adult Literacy Survey* (IALS) indicate a noticeable relationship between social background, educational attainment, and participation in adult education in all 12 countries in the study (OECD 1997). In the context of BSIAE's mandate, it is particularly interesting to note that the relationship is stronger in some countries than in others. The IALS study suggests that public policy can be effective in moderating inequality in adult education participation. These findings point to the relationship between the state and its citizens. As Carnoy points out, there are crucial differences in what adult education attempts to do and what it can do in different social-political structures (Carnoy 1990). He states:

> Ultimately, these differences depend heavily on the possibilities and limits of the state, since it is the state that defines adult education and is the principal beneficiary of its effective implementation. These possibilities and limits of the state are, then, a key issue under standing the form and content of adult education (Carnoy 1990, x).

Thus, work presented in BSIAE can help to highlight the links between the state and adult education practices and show how the realisation of lifelong learning for all derives different positions from differences in underlying, often implicit, theories of the state.

I want to showcase *The International Adult Literacy Survey* as it represents new possibilities for advanced comparative policy oriented research made possible by the availability of better data. It is of interest to reflect on what Heyneman stated in his *Presidential Address* to the Comparative and International Education Society (Heyneman 1993). His message was that in order to make significant progress in comparative education and be able to adequately answer the kinds of question now being posed by public authorities, we need more resources devoted to educational statistics and educational research (Heyneman 1993, 382). With IALS and similar initiatives, like the Life Skills Survey, there are new opportunities to address crucial policy issues around the development towards lifelong learning in Europe that should be reflected in what BSIAE publishes.

In summary, I believe there is an important role to be played by a new publication like the *Bochum Studies in International Adult Education*. However, as discussed above, we do not need just any publication but one that provides a strong European focus and in a new way integrates research, professional practice and policy analysis while revitalising comparative adult education. This is no small task. But under the very capable and experienced leadership of Agnieszka Bron and Michael Schemmann we have every reasons to have high expectations for BSIAE.

References

Carnoy, M. (1990). Foreword: How Should We Study Adult Education. In: Torres, C. A. (ed.). *The Politics of Nonformal Education in Latin America.* New York.

Duke, C. (1994). Funded Research and the Management of Innovation. In: *Studies in the Education of Adults,* 26 (2), pp. 219-235.

Elzinga, A. (1987). Internal and External Regulative in Research and Higher Educational Systems. In: Premfors, R. (ed.). *Disciplinary Perspectives on Higher Education and Research.* Stockholm.

Garrison, R. (1994). Preface. In: Garrison, R. (ed.) *Research Perspectives in Adult Education.* Malbar, Florida.

Giddens, A. (1994). *Beyond Left and Right*. Stanford, California.

Hake, B. J. (1992). Remaking the Study of Adult Education. The Relevance of Recent Developments in the Netherlands to the Search for Disciplinary Identity. In: *Adult Education Quarterly*, 42 (2), pp. 63-78.

Hake, B. J. (1994). *Adult Education Research. Trends in the Western European Countries*. Montreal: Paper presented at UNESCO International seminar, 6-9 September, 1994.

Heyneman, S. P. (1993). Quantity, Quality and Source. In: *Comparative Education Review*, 37 (7), pp. 372-388.

Jackall, R., Vidich, A. J. (1995). Series Preface. In: Stanford, M. L. (ed). *Social Movements. Critiques, Concepts, Case-Studies*. New York.

Jelenc, Z. (1994). *Research on Adult Education in the Central and Eastern European Countries*. Montreal: Paper presented at UNESCO International seminar, 6-9 September, 1994.

OECD (1996). *Lifelong Learning for All*. Paris.

OECD (1997). *Literacy Skills for the Knowledge Society*. Paris.

Rubenson, K. (1994). The Functions and Utilisation of Policy Oriented Research. In: Garrison, R. (ed.). *Research Perspectives in Adult Education*. Malbar, Florida.

SOU (1999:39). *Vuxenutbildning för alla? Andra året med kunskapslyftet*. Stockholm.

Touraine, A. (1995). *Critique of Modernity*. Oxford.

Language – Mobility – Identity
Introduction to the Topic

The changes that people, Europeans in particular, have experienced over the last decade are remarkable. Only eleven years ago an incredible upheaval forced the world to completely change its frame of thinking. The East-West dichotomy which had dominated for more than forty years was broken up with the fall of the Berlin Wall.

At the beginning of the new century we are once again forced to restructure our thinking. For the future the phenomenon of globalisation will be the major issue. Even though the concept of globalisation is by its nature a phenomenon affecting the whole world it is actually only possible to experience the consequences in the local environment. That is why it plays an important role and very much effects local, national and European politics.

In the European context it is the European Union that is on the way to prove to be most successful in coping with the consequences of globalisation. Besides having established and guaranteed more than fifty years of peace in Europe the EU also shows its strength in the global economic competition. Globalisation has forced the EU member countries to come together and form an alliance rivalling the U.S. and Japan. Its attraction is reflected by the striving of the Central and Eastern European states to join its ranks, a tendency that became particularly obvious prior to the European Council in Helsinki, Finland, in December 1999.

However, whereas the economic side of the European integration process seems to be very successful, its policies for social integration remain problematic. Despite several provisions towards social integration the EU has yet to take the final steps necessary for its full realisation. Of course, the Treaty of Amsterdam guarantees European citizenship to all those already entitled to citizenship in one of its member states. This, however, automatically raises questions around our thematic triangle of language, identity and mobility, such as: Is it possible to develop and establish a concept of European citizenship based on several differing or overlapping identities? What role does language play in this context? Finally, is mobility a means to strengthen a concept of European identity and citizenship? And if so, are the people of the EU really mobile?

The first issue of *Bochum Studies in International Adult Education* intends to look closely at the topics Language – Mobility – Identity and attempts to discuss these issues from the point of view of adult education. There is also a personal reason to begin *Bochum Studies in International Adult Education* with this particular topic. At the Chair of Adult Education at the Ruhr-University Bochum we currently have a Swedish scholar of Polish origin as head of a Chair in Germany. The personal learning and reflection processes initiated as a result of this situation for everybody working in the team have been very interesting and have given these topics a very prominent place within the work of the Chair.

The intention of this volume is to create a compilation of different viewpoints and critical analyses on the three topics which together form an overview of their interrelation and their relevance for European development, adult education and adult's learning. This will be achieved not only by looking at the interrelation of the topics with each other and the particular roles played by adult education but also by addressing the issues from different perspectives, i.e. from a micro, meso and macro perspective.

This issue of *Bochum Studies in International Adult Education* contains several distinct sections: Following the Editorial introducing this new series of publications there is a keynote article by Zygmunt Bauman questioning the role of institutions, in this particular case of universities. But it is the emphasis he places on the issue of non-formal education that make his ideas important for adult education and for this particular publication. Due to its underlying principles of plurality and subsidiarity the adult education sector is the least formalised compared to the primary, secondary or tertiary sectors of the educational system in the European context. Adult education therefore has the potential of creating both self-reflexivity and awareness of the risks in life. According to Bauman it is the sector most likely to provide the 'deutero-learning'. Moreover, in a post-modern society individuals take biographical risks and are overwhelmed with information. In such a situation the self-directed learning provided by adult education can be a means to come to grips with the struggle with one's own identity or identities as well as with making choices in the labyrinth of knowledge.

The third part of the book takes up "A Notion of a European Dimension". As has been stated before, it is actually the adult education sector of the whole educational system that is most likely to develop a European dimension and in that way to contribute to higher mobility within Europe. This thesis is put forward in the contribution of John Morgan and Albert Tuijnman and is mostly seen from a macro perspective. Their article also inquires into the tasks lying ahead of adult education in Europe. The joint contribution of John Field, Lars Grundström, Mieczysław Malewski and Ewa Solarczyk-Ambrozik takes up the issue of a European dimension from a meso perspective. Their research tried to clarify what impact 'Europeanisation' has on adult education practitioners and thus on the practice of teaching. The multiple implications of APEL (Accreditation of Prior Experiential Learning) to the topic Language – Mobility – Identity are considered in the article by Barbara Merrill and Christina Lönnheden starting from geographical and social mobility and ending with reflections on biographical implications and the potential of APEL in terms of shaping an individual biography. This section concludes with an overview of the European dimension within the national education systems of two countries under transformation, Slovenia and Hungary.

Part four inquires into the meaning of language, language policy and the European dimension in a more practical sense. Consequently the two contributions focus on language in particular and only marginally consider the aspects of identity and mobility. The first article is a policy analysis of European language policy by Michael Schemmann, the second contribution by Wolfgang Jütte is a study concentrating on one country and examining the role of minority languages in relation to a majority language as well as the resulting political implications.

The fifth part deals with "Language as a Means of Constructing Identities". Here the role of language in identity construction is considered from different points of view. Etienne Bourgeois takes up the issue from a psychological point of view and the issue of constructing identity in a cross-cultural context is taken up by Tordis Dahllöf. Her analysis refers to both cross-cultural encounters as well as to biographies of immigrants and their identity-building. However, language and identity are not only an issue of minority and majority problems, but are also important when taking a more sociological perspective and when looking at gender construction pertaining to these issues. Cecilia Almlöv's article, as well as the contribution of Elżbieta Oleksy, take up the gender issue underlying completely different concepts of language. The genres of fiction literature and fiction movies as sources of sociological knowledge are demonstrated in this part.

The book is concluded by a selected bibliography compiled by Marcus Reinecke. This bibliography covers books to the topic published between 1995 and 1999 as well as articles in Journals of the years 1997-1999. We hope that the bibliography is useful for further reading.

When the individual articles are taken together as a whole, it becomes clear that the topic Language – Mobility – Identity is closely related to the concept of 'Civil Society'. Therefore, we have already decided to choose 'Civil Society' as the leading topic for volume two of the *Bochum Studies in International Adult Education*.

Agnieszka Bron   Michael Schemmann
(Editor-in-Chief)   (Editor)

PART II

KEYNOTE

Bron, A., Schemmann, M. (eds.) (2000). Language, Mobility,
Identity. Contemporary Issues For Adult Education in
Europe. Münster, pp. 27-43.

Zygmunt Bauman

EDUCATION UNDER, FOR AND DESPITE POSTMODERNITY

Summing up dozens of years dedicated to the study of the ways of life practised by many and different, distant and near societies, Margaret Mead reached the following conclusion:

> The social structure of a society and the way learning is structured – the way it passes from mother to daughter, from father to son, from mother's brother to sister's son, from shaman to novice, from mythological specialist to aspirant specialist – determine far beyond the actual content of the learning both how individual's will learn to think and how the store of learning, the sum total of separate pieces of skill and knowledge ... is shared and used (Mead 1964, 79).

In the quoted statement Mead did not invoke the concept of "deutero-learning", or "learning to learn", forged a quarter of a century earlier by Gregory Bateson, her life-companion, yet she clearly pays tribute to Bateson's vision when assigning the primal and decisive role in the process of teaching and learning to the social context and the mode in which message is conveyed, rather than to the contents of instruction. The contents – the subject-matter of what Bateson calls "proto-learning" (primary learning or the "first degree learning") can be seen with the naked eye, monitored and recorded, even designed and planned; but deutero-learning is so to speak a subterranean process, hardly ever consciously noticed and even less frequently monitored by its participants and only loosely related to the ostensible topic of education. It is in the course the deutero-learning, seldom by the appointed or self-proclaimed educators consciously controlled, that the objects of educational action acquire the skills incomparably more important for their future life than even the most carefully pre-selected bits

and pieces of knowledge which combine into the written or contrived curriculum. They acquire

> ... a habit of looking for contexts and sequences of one type
> rather than another, a habit of 'punctuating' the stream of
> events to give repetitions of a certain type of meaningful
> sentence... The states of mind which we call 'free will', in-
> strumental thinking, dominance, passivity, etc., are acquired
> by a process which we may equate with 'learning to learn'
> (Bateson 1973, 140).

Later Bateson would dot the i's and cross the t's, asserting that the
deutero-learning, that "learning how to learn", is not only unavoidable, but
an indispensable complement of all proto-learning; short of deutero-
learning, the "first degree learning" would result in a desiccated and ossi-
fied mind incapable of assimilating a changed, or simply un-thought of in
advance, situation. Later still, much later, as a kind of afterthought, Bateson
would feel the need to cap the idea of the "second degree learning" with the
concept of the "learning of a third degree", "tertiary learning" – which consists in the acquisition of skills to modify the set of alternatives which the
subject of education learns to expect and handle in the course of the
deutero-learning.

Deutero-learning retains its adaptive value and renders all the necessary
service only as far as the learners have good reason to expect that the con-
tingencies they encounter do plot themselves into certain stable patterns; to
put it differently – the usefulness or harmfulness of the habits acquired in
the course of the deutero-learning depends not so much the diligence and
talents of the learners and competence and assiduity of their teachers, as on
the attributes of the world in which the former pupils are bound to live their
lives. In Bateson's view, the first two degrees of learning concord with the
nature of the human species, as it has been formed in the course of the
evolution, and so they appear in one shape or another in every known culture; the third degree learning however may have, and often does have,
pathogenic consequences, resulting in a listless, drifting, schizophrenic
personality.

One can say about our times, described, by now, with many names like
"late modernity", "reflexive modernity", "sur-modernity" or "post-modernity", that they elevate to the rank of the norm what Bateson in the last

years of his life still view, or rather adumbrate, as abnormality – a kind of condition dissonant with the inherited and innate equipment of the human species and from the point of view of human nature pathological. Every single orientation point which made the world look solid and favoured logic in selecting life strategies: the jobs, the skills, human partnerships, models of property and decorum, visions of health and disease, values thought to be worth pursuing and the proved ways to pursue them – all these and many more once stable orientation points seem to be in flux. Many games seem to be going on at the same time, and each game changes its rules while played. Our times excel in dismantling frames and liqui-dising patterns – all frames and all patterns, at random and without advance warning. Under such circumstances the "tertiary learning" – learning how to break the regularity, how to get free from habits and prevent habitualisa-tion, how to re-arrange the fragmentary experiences in heretofore unfamiliar patterns while treating all patterns as acceptable solely "until further notice" – far from being a distortion of the educational process and deviation from true purpose, acquires the supreme adaptable value and moves fast to the centre of indispensable "equipment for life". The post-modern humans are denied the luxury of assuming, with the Shakespearean hero, that "there is a method in this madness". If they expect to find a cohe-sion and coherent structure in the mangle of contingent events, they are in for costly errors and painful illusions. If the habits acquired in the course of training prompt them to seek such cohesive and coherent structures and make their actions dependent on finding them – they are in real trouble. The postmodern humans must therefore be capable not so much of un-earthing the hidden logic in the pile of events or concealed in random collections of colourful spots, but of the un-doing their mental patterns at short notice and tearing down artful canvasses in one sharp move of mind; briefly – to handle their experience the way a child plays with a kaleido-scope found under the Christmas tree. Life success (and so the rationality) of postmodern men and women depends on the speed with which they manage to get rid of old habits, rather the quick acquisition of new ones. Best of all not to bother at all with the business of patterning; the kind of habit acquired in the "tertiary learning" is the habit of doing without the habits...

The deutero-learning, as we remember, is only obliquely and in part under control of the professionals of education, the "people in charge", the composers of curricula and the teachers. And yet the conscious over deutero-learning and its purposeful management seem straightforward and easy when compared with the flow of the "tertiary learning". Margaret Mead was fully aware of the certain degree of intransigence and unruliness of the deutero-learning, but this knowledge did not stop her from con-sidring the phenomenon of education in terms of "from to" – from mother to daughter, from the master to his apprentices. Whatever is being trans-mitted in this picture of the educational event, has clear labels with the addresses of the sender and the recipient; the division of roles is not in question. What is missing in Margaret Mead's perceptive analysis is a situation in which it is far from clear who acts as the teacher and who acts as the pupil, who owns the knowledge to be transmitted and who is placed at the receiving end of the transmission, and who decides, which knowl-edge to be passed over and is worth appropriating. In other words, a situation devoid of structure, or another situation with equally confusing consequences – one marked by the excess of structures, overlapping and criss-crossing, mutually independent and uncoordinated structures, a situa-tion in which educational processes are anything but neatly separated from the rest of life engagements and intercourse a so no one is truly "in charge". Education having been understood since at the least the Age of Enlighten-ment as tightly structured setting with its supervisors firmly in the saddle and having all the initiative, the ungoverned and in all probability un-governable setting cannot but give the theories and the practitioners of edu-cation pause and be seen as the cause for worry. A sketchy, yet vivid description of such an educational context, ever more prominent, noticeable and acknowledged by the analysts of our times, was provided a few years ago by Cornelius Castoriadis. Having first observed, that "the democratic society is one huge pedagogical institution, the place of an unstoppable self-education of its citizens", Castoriadis points out, sadly, that "an exactly opposite situation has now arisen":

> City walls, books, spectacles, events educate – yet now they
> mostly miseducate their residents. Compare the lessons,
> taken by the citizens of Athens (women and slaves includ-
> ing) during the performances of Greek tragedies with the

kind of knowledge which is today consumed by the spectator of *Dynasty* or *Perdue de vue* (Castoriadis 1996, 73).

It seems that the overwhelming of crisis we all – the philosophers, the
theorists and the practitioners of education alike – experience in a greater or
smaller measure, that current version of the 'living on the cross-roads'
feeling, the feverish search for the new self-definition and, ideally, a new
identity as well – have little to do with the faults, errors or negligence of
the professional pedagogues or failures of educational theory, but quite a
lot with the universal melting of identities, de-regulation and privatisation
of the identity-formation processes, dispersal of authorities, polyphony of
value-messages and the ensuing fragmentation of life which, characterise
the world we live in – the world I prefer to call 'postmodern' (though, I repeat, I would not mind calling it late-, reflexive-, sur-modern, or by any
other name that matter, providing we all agree on what the name stands
for). The postmodern condition has split the one big game of modern times
into many little and poorly co-ordinated games, played with the rules of all
the games shortened sharply the life-span any set of rules. Beyond this
slicing and splicing one can sense the crumbling of time, no more continuous, cumulative and directional as it seemed a hundred or so years ago;
postmodern fragmentary life is lived in an episodic time, and once the
events episodes they can be plotted into a cohesive historical narrative only
posthumously; as long as lived, each episode has only itself to supply all
the sense and purpose it needs or is able to muster, keep it on course and to
see it through. All in all, the world in which postmodern men and women
need to live and to shape up their life-strategies put a premium on the "tertiary learning" – a kind of learning which our inherited educational
institutions, born and matured among the modern ordering bustle, are ill
prepared to handle; and one which the educational theory, developed as a
reflection on modern ambitions and their institutional embodiments, can
only view with a mixture of bewilderment and horror, as a pathological
growth a portent of advancing schizophrenia.

The present educational crisis is first and for most the crisis of inherited
institutions and inherited philosophies. Meant for a different kind of reality,
they find it increasingly difficult to absorb, accommodate and hold the
changes without a thorough revision of the conceptual frames they deploy,
and such a revision, as we know from Thomas Kuhn, is the most

overpowering and deadly of all the challenges thought may encounter. Short of designing different frames, philosophical or orthodoxy can only set aside and dismiss the rising pile of new phenomena as so many anomalies and deviations.

The postmodern crisis afflicts all established educational institutions from the top to the bottom, yet at each level, given the peculiarity of the assigned tasks and educational briefings, it gives birth to somewhat different misgivings and worries. Let me focus the more detailed analysis on the problems that arise in the universities as an example of institutional levels of education in general. Such a focus is all the better justified by the role of the education pacesetter and the tune-caller assigned to, claimed and to some extent carried by the universities throughout modern history.

Though roots of European universities are sunk deep in the Middle Ages, our received idea of the university and its role in society is a modern creation. Among many aspects distinguishing modern civilisation from other modes of human cohabitation, the marriage between knowledge and power is perhaps the most conspicuous and seminal. Modern power seeks enlightenment and guidance in scholarship, while modern knowledge follows August Comte's succinct yet precise recipe *savoir pour prevoir, prevoir pour pourvoir* - to know in order to have the power to act. And since modern civilisation has been all along mostly about acting, about making things different from what they were and about using power to enforce change – the marriage placed the practitioners of knowledge, the discoverers of new truths and disseminators of the old ones, either close to or in competition with the rulers, but in both cases in the very centre of the institutional network and in a top rank of spiritual authority.

The institutional centrality of knowledge and its practitioners was anchored, on one side, in the state-national reliance on legitimation (Max Weber), ruling formula (Gaetano Mosca), or central cluster of values (Talcott Parsons) for the translation of domination into authority and discipline; on the other, in the practice of culture (education, *Bildung*) meant to shape up individual members of society into social beings fit to perform, and willing to abide by, the socially assigned roles. Both anchors were service by the universities – the crucial sites where the values instrumental social integration were generated, and the training ground where the educators meant to disseminate them and translate into social skills were

trained. Both anchors, though, are today afloat. This is why the recent os-
tensibly programmatic statement of the *Magna Carta of European Universities* – that the universities be 'autonomic institutions in the centre of
society' – is redolent of nostalgia for a fast disappearing state of affairs, and
why the image of the university painted with the brushes of historical
memory inclines us to define the present realities as pregnant with crisis.
After all, both the autonomy, and the centrality of the universities and the
scholarship as such are today in question.

The list of social/cultural/political transformations which brought the
crisis about is long. The most decisive among them, however, are inti-
mately related to the rapid weakening of the orthodox institutional
bases/guarantees of the universities' authority.

On the one hand, contemporary nation-states all over the globe and on
both sides of the recent global divide have all but abandoned most of the
integrative functions which the paradigmatic nation-state claimed in modern times, and ceded them to the forces which they do not control and
which stay by and large outside the reach of the political process. Having
done that, the present-day states lose interest in ideological conversion and
mobilisation, in cultural policy, in the promotion of cultural patterns
stamped as superior to other patterns, which because of their inferiority are
condemned to extinction. By the same token, they leave the formation of
cultural hierarchies (or, indeed, the very question of their feasibility) to the
mercy of diffuse and uncoordinated market forces. As a result, also the pre-
rogative to distribute and apportion knowledge-generated authority upon
individuals active in the production and dissemination of knowledge a pre-
rogative once bestowed by the state exclusively on the universities has been
challenged and successfully contested by other agencies. Reputations are
made and unmade by and large outside the university walls, with di-
minishing role assigned to the once crucial peers' judgement. In shaping
hierarchies of influence, notoriety replaced fame, public visibility elbowed
out scholarly credentials, and so the process is not so much controlled, as
buffeted by agencies specialising in the management of public attention.
Régis Debray speaks of 'mediocracy'; the pun entailed is clearly intentional
(Debray 1979). It is the media value of the news, rather than the orthodox
university standards of scholarly significance, which determined the

hierarchy of authority – and as unstable and short living as the 'news value' of the messages.

On the other hand, with the prospect of cultural universality receding and no more arousing enthusiasm nor dedication, and with cultural plurality having no serious adversaries while enjoying ample institutional support – the monopolistic, or even privileged role of the universities in value creation and selection is now no more tenable. Universities have to compete on allegedly equal terms with numerous other agencies, many of which are much more skilful in 'getting their message across' and much more in tune with the cravings and fears of contemporary consumers. It is not clear why individuals attracted by the assumed 'enabling' capacity of skills and knowledge and thus wishing to acquire them, should look for assistance to the universities, rather than to their competitors.

As if it was not strong enough a blow to the status and prestige of the university, institutions at every level of learning, once the unquestioned arbiters of professional skill and competence find this slipping out of their hands. At time when everyone – students, teachers, and teachers' teachers alike – has equal access to the internet, when the latest thoughts of science are bowdlerised, where there are trimmed curriculum requirements, as well as user-friendly and tamely interactive experiences are available in every game shop; and where access to the latest fads and foibles of scholarship depends on money, rather than the degrees, who can claim that his or her pretence to instruct the ignorant and to guide the perplexed is his or her natural right? It was the opening of the information super-highway that revealed, in retrospect, just how much the claimed, and yet more the genuine, authority of the teachers used to rest on their collectively exercised, exclusive control over the sources of knowledge and the no-appeal-allowed policing of all roads leading to such sources. It has also showed to what extent that authority depended on the unshared right of the teachers to up the 'logic of learning' – the time sequence in which various bits and pieces of knowledge can and need be ingested and digested. With those once exclusive properties now deregulated, privatised, floated on the publicity stock-exchange and for grabs, the claim of the academia to be the only and the natural seat for those 'in pursuit of higher learning' sounds increasingly hollow to everybody's ears except of those who voice it.

This is not, though, the whole story. The permanent and continuing technology revolution transforms the acquired know-how and learned habits from assets into a handicap, and shortens sharply the life-span of useful skills, which often lose their utility and 'enabling power' in less time then it takes to acquire them and certify them through a university diploma. Under such circumstances, the ad-hoc, short-term professional training administered by the employers and oriented directly to the prospective jobs, or flexible courses and (quickly updated) teach-yourself kits offered through the market by the extra-university media become more attractive (and, indeed, more reasonable a choice) than a fully-fledged university education which is no more capable of promising, let alone guaranteeing, a life-long career. The burden of occupational training is shifting gradually yet steadily away from the universities, which is reflected everywhere in waning willingness of the state to subsidise them from the public purse. One is inclined to suspect that if the university intake is not yet falling sharply, it is to a large extent due to this unanticipated and un-bargained-for role of a temporary shelter in a society afflicted by structural unemployment; a device allowing the newcomers to postpone for a few years the moment of truth that arrives when the harsh realities of the labour market need be faced.

Like all other value-adding monopolies, the monopoly of institutional 'commodification' of acquired or assumed skills also needs a regulated environment to be effective; but the kind of regulation required here, like tango, takes two. In the case under discussion, the condition of effectiveness is a relatively stable coordination between job descriptions and skill descriptions both stable enough to be measured by the average time-span of the 'pursuit of higher education'. In our increasingly 'flexible' and thoroughly deregulated job market this condition is seldom met, and all prospects of arresting the rot, let alone restoring the fast vanishing framework of prospective planning, grow bleaker by the hour. The process of higher learning historically institutionalised by university practice cannot easily adopt the job-market pace of flexible experiment and even less it can accommodate to the all too apparent normlessness and thus unpredictability of mutations which the drifting called flexibility cannot but spawn. Besides, the type of skills required to practice flexible occupations does not on the whole demand long-term and systematic learning. More often than not, it transforms a well profiled, logically coherent body of acquired skills and habits from an asset it used to be into a handicap it is now. And this severely dents the commodity value of the degree certificate. The latter may find it difficult to compete with the market value of in-job-training, short courses and weekend seminars. The loss of its after-Robbins universal availability and relative cheapness deprived university education of one more even – perhaps decisive – competitive advantage. With its fast growing fees and living costs it is not entirely fanciful to suppose that the university education may soon be discovered as not offering, in market terms, value for money – and even price itself out of the competition altogether...

In a world characterised by the episodicity and fragmentation of social and individual time, the universities burdened with the sense of history and linear time fit ill and must feel ill at ease. Everything the universities have been doing for the last nine hundred academic reputations, public fame and influence are made and unmade. Those grounds used to be the cooperative property of academic peers, but already in the first half of this century had been transferred to the administration of the publishing houses. The new owners did not manage their property for long, tough; it took just a few dozen, of years for the property to shift again, this time to the ownership of mass media. Intellectual authority, says Debray, was once measured solely by the size of the crowd of disciples flocking in from far and wide to hear the master; then also, and in a rising degree, by the number of copies sold and the critical accolade the *œuvre* received; but both measurements, though not entirely extinct, have been dwarfed now TV time and newspaper space (Debray 1979). For the intellectual authority, the appropriate years made sense either inside the time of eternity or the time of progress, if modernity got rid of the first, postmodernity put paid to the second. And the episodic time hovering among the two-tiered ruins of eternity and progress proves inhospitable to everything which we grew up to treat as the mark of the university, that according to the OECD 'coming together in pursuit of higher learning'. Not just to the life-long academic tenure, but to all those ideas which used to underpin it and justify: that *auspicium meioris aevi*; that experience, like wine, acquires nobility with age; that skills, like houses, are built floor by floor; that reputations can be accumulated like savings and, like savings, yield more interest the longer they are kept.

Régis Debray pointed out the gradual, yet relentless grounds on which version of Descartes' cogito would be today: I am talked about, therefore I am (Debray 1979).

Let us note that this is not just a story of property changing hands and new controllers taking over. The property itself could not emerge unscathed from the change of management and the shift in control could not but transform the controlled object beyond recognition. Publishing houses cultivate a kind of intellectual authority quite different from that sprouting on university private plots; and the authority emerging out of the information-processing plants of the mass media bears but a vague resemblance to either of its two predecessors. According to the witty remark of a French journalist – if Émile Zola was allowed to state his case on TV, he would be given just enough time to shout 'J'accuse!' With public attention turning now into the scarcest of commodities, media have noting like the amount of time required to cultivate fame – what they are good at growing is the fast harvested and fast disposed of crop of notoriety. "Maximal impact and instant obsolence", as George Steiner put it, has become the most effective technique of its production. Whoever enters the game of notoriety, must play by its rules. And the rules do not privilege the intellectual pursuits which once made academics famous and the universities imperious; the relentless, but slow and circumspect search of truth or justice is ill fit for being conducted under public gaze, unlikely to attract, let alone to hold, public attention and most certainly not calculated for an instant applause. Once notoriety takes over from fame, college dons find themselves in competition with the sportsmen, pop stars, lottery winners, terrorists, bank robbers and mass killers – and in this competition they have little, if any, chance of winning.

The very titles of academia and its members to superior prestige and exclusive treatment are being gnawed at the roots. One of the most resplendent feathers in the modern universities cap used to be the assumed link between the acquisition of knowledge and moral refinement. Science – so it was believed – was a most potent humanising factor; so was the aesthetic discernment and culture in general; culture ennobles the human person and pacifies human societies. After the scientifically assisted horrors of the twentieth century the faith seems laughably, perhaps even criminally, na-ive. Rather than entrusting ourselves gratefully to the knowledge-carriers, we are inclined watch their hands with growing suspicion and fear. The new apprehension found its spectacular expression in Michel Foucault's ex-ceedingly popular hypothesis of the intimate link between development of scientific discourse and the tightening of the all-penetrating surveillance and control, rather than praised for promoting enlightenment, techno-science has been charged with responsibility for the new, refined version of constraint and dependency. The 'mad scientist' bugbear of yesteryear is now casting a gigantic shadow on the popular image of science as such. Most recently, and with a world-wide acclaim, Ulrich Beck proposed that it is the metastatically and chaotically self-propagating technoscience that stand behind the most awesome, terrifying risks mankind is facing today on a scale never faced before. The equation mark put traditionally between knowledge, civilisation, moral quality of human cohabitation and (social as well as individual) well-being has been brutally effaced; a most crucial ar-gument in the universities bid for social resources and deference has been thereby made invalid.

This is, roughly, the gist of the present crisis: with virtually all ortho-dox grounds and justifications of their once elevated position either gone or considerably weakened, universities (at least in the developed and affluent countries; in the 'modernising' countries they may still play the traditional role of the factories supplying the heretofore missing educated elite) face the need to re-think and articulate a new role in a world that has no use for their traditional services, sets new rules for the game of prestige and influ-ence and views growing suspicion the values they stood for.

One obvious strategy is to accept the new rules and play the game ac-cordingly. In practice, this means submission to the stern criteria of the market and measuring the 'social usefulness' of university products by the presence of 'clearing demand', treating the know-how universities may offer as one more commodity that still has to fight for a place on over-crowded supermarket shelves, as one more commodity among other commodities, still to be tested for quality by its merchandising success. Many an academic embraces the new reality with gusto, looking forward to making the university into a business enterprise and spying out an exhila-rating opportunity where previously threats were sighted. Particularly the

US, but also to extent in Britain and less blatantly in other European countries the ranks of the university professors praising the salutary effects of market competition for money and positions grow unstoppably. The entitlement of the knowledge-bearers to claim superiority for their explicit judgements over those emerging implicitly from the supply-and-demand game are questioned and detracted from the inside of academia. In a desperate attempt to make a virtue out of necessity, or to steal the thunder, the intellectuals collectively downgraded by the market competition convert into zealous promoters of market criteria in university life: this or that course or project is good and sound since it stands a good market chance, it sells well – and the saleability ('meeting the demand'; 'satisfying the manpower needs'; 'offering the services industry requires') is to be elevated as the supreme criterion of open curricula, courses and degrees. Spiritual leadership is a mirage; the task of the intellectuals is to follow the world out there, not to legislate for the standards of propriety, truth, and good taste.

The opposite strategy, counting no less supporters and practitioners, is to burn the bridges: to withdraw from the no-win situation of the market into the fortress built of esoteric language and obscure, impervious theory; to hide behind secure walls of a competition-free mini-market if the supermarkets are out of bounds or unpromising. The withdrawal and implosion, rather than outward movement and explosion, may be a viable strategy in a country which, like the United States, is densely populated with academic professionals to the extent of supporting a well-nigh self-sufficient and self-feeding (one is tempted to say incestuous) producing/consuming milieu for the products too obscure and nebulous for the wider public, exposed to the 'general' market. In such a country, yet in such a country only, there may be no limit to incomprehensibility and social irrelevance beyond which a product would find no clients and, therefore, no publishers or distributors.

Each in its own way, both strategies renounce the traditional role which the universities claimed, were assigned, and tried to fulfil throughout the modern era. Both spell the end to 'autonomy' of the university activity (note that the splendid isolation from all engagement with the world, preached by the second strategy, is not autonomy, but irrelevance) and to the 'centrality' of intellectual work. Both strategies, each in his own way, mean surrender: first strategy, the acceptance of a servant, subordinated, derivative position in a hierarchy of relevance shaped up and presided over by the market forces; the second, the acceptance of social/cultural irrelevance imposed by the unchallenged rule of those forces. Both strategies make the prospect of the *Magna Carta of the Universities,* signed recently in Bologna, becoming anything more than a pious wish, look bleak indeed.

The present-day version of the theory of evolution tells us that the 'generalistic', that is the un-choosy species have much greater survival capacity than the species splendidly accommodated to a particular ecological niche, and thus environmentally selective and whimsical. It is tempting to say that the universities fall victim of their own perfect fit and adjustment; it just happened that what they adjusted to was a different, now vanishing, world. That was the world marked first and foremost by a slow, sluggish, present standard flow of time. A world in which it took quite a while for the skills to become obsolete, for specialisms to be relabelled as blinkers, for bold heresies to turn into retrograde orthodoxies, and all in all for the assets to turn into liabilities and for the spade to stop being a spade. Such a world, let me repeat once more, is now vanishing and the sheer speed of vanishing is much in excess of the re-adjustment and re-deployment capacities the universities have acquired over the centuries. Besides, it is not just that the situation in which the universities operate is changing; the most difficult thing to cope with adequately is, so to speak, the 'meta-change' – the change in the fashion in which the situation is changing...

The world to which the institution adjusts leaves its imprint on the shape of the institutionalised routine, on the monotony of pattern reproduction. But it also shapes up the institution's way of coping with crises, reacting to the environmental change, articulating problems and seeking solutions. Whenever in crisis and well before the nature of the crisis has been fathomed and understood, institutions tend to resort instinctively to the repertory of tried and thus habitualised responses. This is one, the insider's, way of putting it; another, an outsider's, way would be to observe that crises are joint products of the perception of the situation as critical, and proceeding to act in a fashion jarring with what the situation renders possible and/or desirable. What the outsider' a perspective reveals therefore is the sad yet all-too-real suicidal tendency of any evolutionary success story. The more successful an institution has been in fighting off certain kind of crises, the less apt it becomes to react sensibly and effectively to crises of a different and heretofore unexperienced kind. I suppose that if applied to the universities this rather banal rule would go some way towards better comprehension of their present-day predicament – not a small part of which derives from their institutionalised reluctance or learned incapacity to recognise the present environmental change as an essentially novel event – novel enough to call for a revision of strategic ends and rules of their pursuits.

The chance of adjusting to the new post-modern situation, that paradoxical situation which renders a perfect adjustment a liability, lies precisely in the selfsame all-too-often bewailed plurality and multi-vocality of the present-day collection of the 'gatherings for the sake of the pursuit of higher learning', which jar with the legislators' love of cohesion and harmony and which they, the legislators, approach with the kind of disgust and contempt with which one treats public threats and personal offences. It is this multi-vocality that offers the universities the chance of emerging successfully from the present challenge. It is good luck for the universities that there are so many of them, that there are not two of them exactly alike, and that inside every university there is a mind-boggling variety of departments, schools, styles of thoughts, styles of conversation and even the styles of stylistic concerns. It is good luck for the universities that despite all the efforts of the self-proclaimed saviours know-betters and well-wishers to prove the contrary, they are not comparable, not measurable by yardstick and – most of important off all – not speaking in unison. Only such universities have something of value to offer to the multivocal world of uncoordinated needs, self-procreating possibilities and self-multiplying choices. In the world in which no one can (though many do, with consequences ranging from irrelevant to disastrous) anticipate the kind of expertise that may be needed tomorrow, the debates that may need mediation and beliefs that may need interpretation – the recognition of many and varied ways to, and many and varied canons of, higher learning is the condition sine qua non of the university system capable of rising to the postmodern challenge.

What has been said here of the universities, applies to present-day education as a whole. The co-ordination (perhaps even the pre-ordained harmony) between the effort to 'rationalise' the world and the effort to groom rational beings fit to inhabit it, that underlying assumption of the modern educational project, seems credible no more. And with the hope of rational control over the social habitat of human life fading, the adaptive value of 'tertiary learning' becomes more evident. 'Preparing for life' – that perennial, invariable task of all education – must mean first and foremost cultivating the ability to live daily and at peace with uncertainty and am-bivalence, with variety of standpoints and the absence of unerring and trustworthy authorities; must mean instilling the tolerance of difference and the will to respect the right to be different; must mean fortifying the critical and self-critical faculties and the courage needed to assume the responsi-bility for one's choices and their consequences; must mean training the capacity for 'changing the frames' and for resisting the temptation to es-cape from freedom which brings the anxiety of indecision alongside the joys of the new and the unexplored. The point is, though, that such qualities can hardly be developed in full through that aspect of the educational pro-cess which lends itself best to the designing and controlling powers of the theorists and professional practitioners of education: through the verbally explicit contents of the curricula and vested in what Bateson called the "proto-learning". One could attach more hope to the "deutero-learning" as-pect of the education, which, however, is notoriously less amenable to planning and to comprehensive, all-out control. The qualities in question can be expected to emerge, though, primarily out of the 'tertiary learning' aspect of educational processes, such as is related not to one particular cur-riculum and the setting of one particular educational event, but precisely to the variety of criss-crossing and competing curricula and events.

In as far as the above observation holds true, educational philosophy and theories[1] face an unfamiliar and challenging task of theorising a for-mative process which is not guided from the start by the target-form designed in advance; a mode without the model to be arrived at in the end being known or clearly visualised; a process which can at best adumbrate, never enforce, its results and which builds that limitation into its own structure; in short, an open-ended process, concerned more with remaining

---

[1] Much more than the educational practice, which cannot but follow, in each of its concrete manifestations taken apart, the traditional urge to pattern and structure, the centre of gravity lies, after all, not in separate educational events, but in their variety and, indeed, in their lack of coordination.

open-ended than with any specific product, and fearing all premature clo-sure more than it shuns the prospect of staying forever inconclusive.

This is perhaps the greatest challenge which the philosophers of educa-tion, together with the rest of their philosophical colleagues, have encoun-tered in the modern history of their discipline.

References

Bateson, G. (1973). *Steps to an Ecology of Mind.* Frognore.

Castoriadis, C. (1996). *La monée de l'insignifiance.* Paris.

Debray, R. (1979). *Le pouvoir intellectuel en France.* Paris.

Mead, M. (1964). *Continuities in Cultural Evolution.* New Haven.

PART III

A NOTION OF A EUROPEAN DIMENSION

Bron, A., Schemmann, M. (eds.) (2000). Language, Mobility, Identity. Contemporary Issues For Adult Education in Europe. Münster, pp. 47-62.

W. John Morgan / Albert C. Tuijnman

The Challenges of Adult Education in Europe Deconstruction and Reconstruction of Nations and States

Introduction

What are the challenges that lie ahead for adult education and its practitioners in contemporary Europe? Essentially, they are faced with the paradoxes and tensions that have beset the European ideal during the past decade. These concern growing uncertainties over the European identity. What are its defining characteristics and culture? Who are its peoples? Where do its boundaries lie and should they be exclusive or open? Again, although the principle of European unity is widely, if not universally, accepted, the form that such unity should take, and the degree of sovereign power that goes with it, remain a source of debate and dispute. At the heart of these unresolved tensions lies the fact that the political patterns that appeared to define the template on which the new Europe could be designed, has changed dramatically – and even violently. This new political geography is accompanied by the renaissance of a social psychology that, once again, emphasises ethnicity and nation while economic integration continues, accompanied by the continuing rhetoric of the original post World War II idea of European unity. How did this situation arise and what can adult education do to help resolve it to the benefit of the peoples of Europe and their neighbours?

Europe and Nationalism

Modern Europe has been shaped by the ideological force of nationalism which as a political movement dates from the French Revolution of 1789. It was called upon to provide a fresh legitimacy for government with the essentially democratic and secular '*la Patrie*' replacing the Monarchy and the Church. Among the most influential and resilient of political ideologies, nationalism has however remained one of the most difficult to categorize. Consider the definition offered by the French historian Renan in 1882.

> A nation is a soul, a spiritual principle. Two things which are really one, go to make up this soul or spiritual principle. The one is the possession of a rich heritage of memories. And the other is actual agreement, desire to live together and the will to continue to make the most of a joint inheritance. The existence of a nation is a daily plebiscite, just as that of an individual is a continual affirmation of life (Friedman 1965, 67; Morgan 1973, 10).

Renan is clearly describing a 'community', a social grouping which involves attitudes of natural friendship and attachment. It does not need to have a previously specified purpose for existence, nor need it be deliberately organised. The close ties that are produced by a shared life in a community and the common possession of sentiments and aspirations combine to produce a sense of group loyalty. The nation may be regarded as such a community and the group loyalty felt for the national community described as patriotism. But there is another form of social grouping, the 'association', which is defined as one formed for the pursuit of a specified common purpose. For example, a number of householders may form an 'association' to campaign against industrial development in their neighbourhood. This requires an agreed objective, rules of action and rational decision whether or not to participate. The State is such an association and is the most highly organised of all its forms. State formation might arise from a sense of national community and, in today's world, the state is usually still a nation-state. By this is meant the national 'community' organised as an 'association', though the nation and the state do not necessarily coincide in this way.

The essence of nationalism, as it came to be manifested in modern Europe, was that the nation represented an end in itself. The nationalism of revolutionary France had been motivated by belief in liberty, equality and fraternity. However, as early as the Napoleonic era it had degenerated into an aggressive and undemocratic ideology of national domination. The two world wars of the first half of the twentieth century are seen by many as the logical consequences, with the nationalist era represented as a terrible aberration which had, among other tragic results, the effect of splitting up a common cultural heritage, a special quality of being European. The importance given to Franco-German 'rapprochement' and the cause of economic and political unity are the results.

The Idea of European Unity

At a series of lectures given at the State University of Leiden in 1959, the distinguished Dutch historian Pieter Geyl reflected on the historical background of the idea of European unity, commenting in a manner which connected his remarks to those of Renan:

> European unity. We hear the cry on all sides. Everyone agrees that the times demand its realization and implementation. This can be argued on political or political strategic, as well as on economic grounds... Yet at the base of it all there lies the fact of a spiritual affinity which, across distinctness and discordance, reaches far into history (Geyl 1963, 363).

After reminding his audience that European civilisation sprang from two historic roots, the Graeco-Roman tradition and Christianity, Geyl focussed on the significance of the French Revolution for the problem of European unity. The French Revolution, as the American Revolution before it, was the political expression of the Enlightenment, the thinking of which was both rationalist and universalist. The preamble to the celebrated *Declaration of the Rights of Man and of the Citizen* of August 1789 spoke not only for the French citizen, but humanity. All European nations were to be liberated and all united in equality and fraternity. The paradox of the Revolution was that the revolutionary sense of mission also stimulated in the French the opposing tendency of nationalism. The Napoleonic period saw nationalism displace universalism as the dominant ideology, with unity of Europe being effected through domination and conquest. Ultimately, the paradox proved too great to be sustained as the realities of Napoleonic rule stimulated the other European peoples into a multiple expression of national resistance which, despite the intentions of the Congress of Vienna of

1815, led to the consolidation of nation-states and to the triumph of nation-alism. The same outcomes, though for somewhat different reasons, followed the Treaty of Versailles of 1919, with the concept of European unity still lacking the precise definition and consensus that would make its achievement possible. Worse, the triumph of National Socialism saw the idea of Europe renounced "not only politically, but culturally and morally" (Geyl 1963, 389). Europe did have a place in National Socialist ideology, but as in the Napoleonic period, only as the vehicle for domination and conquest.

The end of the World War II saw Europe divided politically and eco-nomically by the ideological divide of the Cold War, though retaining the formal structure of the nation-states. In Western Europe this led to a con-sensus on the merits of democracy and to the building up of associations for common purposes such as the Council of Europe, the European Parliament, the Organisation for European Economic Cooperation and the North Atlantic Treaty Organisation, while the leading part played by the United States in the process must not be ignored. A parallel process was underway in Central and Eastern Europe under the direction of the Soviet Union. It is against this historical background that the most recent attempts at European unity have taken place. Unfortunately, the nature of that unity has continued to give rise to bitter controversy and dispute.

The Treaty of Rome in 1957 aroused alarm among those, such as Geyl, who believed that "under cover of a devout use of the name 'Europe', a dangerous division of Europe" (Geyl 1963, 394) was being prepared. He raised also fears for the interests of small countries such as the Netherlands, saying that in an "association with states of so much greater strength, their wishes can already be seen to count for little" (Geyl 1963, 394). This was a fear aggravated by President de Gaulle's rejection of British affiliation in his press conference of January 14, 1963. Over thirty years on, the exclu-sivity of the original European Economic Community has given way to the inclusive and universalising aspirations of the European Union. However, the criteria for membership remain strict, as Turkey has found, while the enthusiasm of the still distinctive peoples of Europe for a unitary state rather than an association of nations remains doubtful to say the least. The idea of European unity is still only partially fulfilled and, as the new cen-tury looms, is in fact beset by renewed contradictions and tensions.

The Deconstruction of European States

Chief among these contradictions is that the sovereignty of the nation-states that emerged in Europe in the two centuries after the French Revolution is now being challenged from below as well as from above. The formation of states was accompanied by a massive educational and cultural effort to achieve uniformity within their legal boundaries (Green 1990, Morgan, Preston 1993). France may be taken as the classic example in which the formation of the state had to be followed by the formation of the French (Weber 1976). The same pattern was followed throughout Europe, with varying degrees of success. Some states still comprise more than one national group whose sense of identity remains intact.

The United Kingdom of Great Britain and Northern Ireland, for example, contains at least four nations, the English, the Scottish, the Welsh and the Irish. The recent referenda on political autonomy and legislation for a Scottish parliament and a Welsh National Assembly show the strength of feeling on this issue, while the differences that exist over the future of Northern Ireland rest upon interpretations of "nation" and "state" (Morgan 1997). This is to say nothing of the presence of ethnic minorities who have immigrated to the United Kingdom. Similar examples may be found throughout Europe as the concept of ethnicity coincides with a sense of local identity and community and a consequent rejection of the centralising state. Paradoxically, the development of the European idea has assisted in this process, giving rise to a regional awareness of community needs and self confidence to over ride the so called nation state. This process has not been free of violence, as the campaigns of the various factions of the Irish republican movement and of the Ulster unionists have shown in Ireland and as ETA or the military arm of Basque nationalism have shown in Spain. These are not exceptional cases, though they are the most intense and best known.

Eastern Europe has given way to the same centrifugal tendencies, but in a far more dramatic and violent fashion. It is now ten years since the fall of the Berlin Wall inaugurated the national re-unification of Germany. It signalled also the end of the Soviet dominance of Central and Eastern Europe and the renaissance of nations, such as the Baltic countries, Poland, Hungary, Bulgaria, the Czech Republic, Slovakia and Romania, that had long been either submerged in the Soviet Union or consigned to satellite status. The end of state socialism in Eastern Europe had a further and tragic consequence in the disintegration of Yugoslavia in chaos and war in an atmosphere of savage ethnic conflict. There has also been the uneasy and still incomplete break up of a Russian empire begun by the Tsars and maintained by the Soviets. This has seen the national re-emergence not only of the Ukraine and of Belarus, but also of Armenia, Georgia and the several republics of the Caucasus and of Central Asia which are culturally and historically Islamic. This process has been accompanied by the violence and mutual hostility that has usually accompanied the retreat from colonialism and empire.

The consequence throughout Europe is that the ideal of a common European identity is being countered by the re-emergence of local ethnicity, with its emphasis on cultural identity and political autonomy.

Citizenship and Ethnicity

Such a situation creates what D. D. Raphael has called the concepts of "legal" and "personal" nationality (Raphael 1970). The former may be described briefly as citizenship, the latter as ethnic identity. This raises the original question of how the ethnic group identifies itself. What is it that the members of an ethnic group have in common that makes them believe that they are of the same nationality and distinct from other national groups? It consists of an emotional appeal to place, to language, to a common history or folk memory and to a shared culture. Such a sense of "personal" nationality is a subjective thing, a frame of mind. People form a nation when they recognise each other as fellow members of such a community. However, the difference in character between "nation" and "state" remains. The nation is a community the membership of which depends on sentiment and an emotional sense of belonging.

Membership of the state, although citizenship is fundamentally important, is essentially a matter of legal status. The implications of this distinction for ethnic relations both between the nations of Europe and between those nations and the now significant numbers of immigrants from outside Europe are enormous. European unity through association in a centralised state is not likely to be a solution to the problems that are emerging, even if a mechanism could be found which registered a majority in favour.

The dissident voices would remain loud and intransigent. Again, pious exhortations to adopt a European attitude are not likely to have much effect on national identities which have developed over centuries and, in many cases, survived domination and oppression. The sad fact is that the European identity is felt most strongly in the rejection of immigrants from outside Europe. Australians and Argentinians, for instance, are recognised as culturally Europeans in a way that Moroccans and Turks are not. A centralised European state, historically favoured as an antidote to nationalism, might have the dangerous effect of establishing it on a continental scale.

Globalisation and the Borderless World

The other paradox and tension that needs to be considered is the phenomenon of globalisation and the possibility of a borderless world. The fundamental idea is that wealth is created in an open market place, rather than in colonies or through the exploitation of national resources. It aims at an 'interlinked' economy that depends for its success on the free flow of information, capital, goods and services, as well as the free migration of corporations and people, and the knowledge and ideas they represent.

Developments are spurred by four main factors: the ageing of populations, market deregulation, the integration of financial markets, and the widespread diffusion of information and communication technologies. Collectively, these factors have altered the social and economic policy landscape of nation-states and placed a new premium on the value of human and social capital. This is because neither national nor provincial governments can rely on the same range of instruments they traditionally used to regulate the economy and cushion any adverse effects of capital flows on the industrial welfare state. A global economy requires governments to formulate a new approach not only to trade, monetary and fiscal policies but also structural policies. As the scope for intervention in the macro-economic sphere has become more limited, policy makers attempting to secure comparative national advantage increasingly focus on the 'residual' factors in the productivity equation: technological innovation, human capital and civil society.

The international business consultant Kenichi Ohmae is one of its most persuasive ideologues. In his book *The Borderless World. Power and Strategy in the Interlinked Economy*, Ohmae argues that "[t]raditional governments will have to establish a new single framework of global governance" (Ohmae 1990, xiv). Such a framework would ensure the end to protectionism necessary for the interlinked economy to succeed. European Union protectionism would also come under attack as an example of what Ohmae regards as "archaic nationalistic sentiments" (Ohmae 1990, 269). He recognises that the interlinked economy is not yet a reality, but believes that the paradigm for economic behaviour is shifting in the direction of the "weave of economic and intellectual dependence of nations" (Ohmae 1990, 269).

This is evidenced in the geometric progression of networking of individuals, institutions and corporations across the globe as a direct consequence of the revolution in information and communication technology. The danger of this is that, as electronic networks encompass the world, business and intellectual elites, powerful or influential in the new corporations, will establish first a continental and then a global identity that will enable them to favour their own interests. The mass of people will remain effectively excluded or stratified in the new knowledge economy and society. Many will remain surplus in the global labour market, unless willing to migrate, consumers of a mono culture that deludes them into thinking they participate in the global society and yet is superficial in its recognition of human values. As with the idea of European unity, Ohmae's vision of a borderless world is a compelling and attractive utopia with the dangerous capacity to mutate into dystopia because of its failure to take into account social realities and deep rooted human preferences. Chief among these is the need for roots.

The Need for Roots

Simone Weil has observed that to be rooted is one of the most important and yet least recognised needs of the human soul. A human being, she says, has roots by virtue of

> ... real, active and natural participation in the life of a community which preserves in living shape certain particular treasures of the past and certain particular expectations for the future. This participation is a natural one, in the sense that it is automatically brought about by place, conditions of birth, profession and social surroundings. Every human

being needs to have multiple roots. It is necessary for him (sic) to draw well nigh the whole of his moral, intellectual and spiritual life by way of the environment of which he forms a natural part (Weil 1987, 41).

She sees uprootedness as a moral and social disease, an unhealthy condition of alienation which, in any society will undermine vitality and growth. Among its causes she lists wage capitalism, warfare and conquest and the break between the so-called 'people of culture' and the mass of the population. Anthropologists recognise, if with heavy hearts, the following:

> Ethnocentricity is the natural condition of mankind. Most peoples of the world do not, in their conservative heart of hearts, like foreigners and display feelings of hostility (often tinged with fear) towards them. This indeed is one of the most widespread ways in which people declare and affirm their identity - by saying who they are not (Lewis 1985, 15; Levi-Strauss 1987).

Yet, as Weil emphasises, "[i]f one's native land is regarded as a vital medium, there is no need for it to be protected from foreign influences ..." (Weil 1987, 155), asking by way of example, "wouldn't it be a natural thing for Brittany, Wales, Cornwall and Ireland to feel themselves, in regard to certain things, to be part of the same environment?" (Weil 1987, 156). Yet such exchange, whether within or across political frontiers is "only possible where each preserves his own genius and that is not possible without liberty" (Weil 1987, 156). Because of the security and equanimity it brings the nurturing of roots in such a way that it is in fact an antidote to aggressive hostility, to exclusion and xenophobia. These are the paradoxes and tensions facing the peoples of Europe as they make their way into the new century. They are aggravated by the fact that, as Salman Rushdie has commented, the century they are leaving has been

> ... the century of the migrant as well as the century of the bomb, perhaps there have never been so many people who end up elsewhere than they began, whether by choice or necessity, and so perhaps that's the source from which this kind of reconstruction can begin (Rushdie 1987, 63 quoted in Bottomley 1992, 3).

These tensions and particularly the importance of roots are at the core of the Report to UNESCO provided by the International Commission on Education for the twenty-first century, chaired by the former President of the European Commission, Jacques Delors (Delors 1996). As Delors pointed out:

> People today have a dizzying feeling of being torn between a globalization whose manifestations they can see and sometimes have to endure and their search for roots, reference points and a sense of belonging. Education has to face up to this problem now more than ever as a world society struggles painfully to be born (Delors 1996, 16-17).

In order to design and build our common future it will be necessary to resolve fundamental tensions, central to the problems of the twenty-first century. Delors identified these as the tensions between the global and the local, between the universal and the individual, between tradition and modernity (and now post-modernity), between long-term and short-term considerations and between the need for competition and concern for genuine equality of opportunity. As he says:

> Culture is steadily being globalized, but as yet only partially. We cannot ignore the promises of globalization nor its risks, not the least of which is the risk of forgetting the unique character of individual human beings; it is for them to choose their own future and achieve their full potential within the carefully tended wealth of their traditions and their own cultures which, unless we are careful, can be endangered by contemporary developments (Delors 1996, 15).

The Implications for Adult Education

Thus the peoples of the European sphere, defined geo-politically, are groping with a split identity. On the one hand there is the search for a 'common' European identity, which paradoxically may well be less Eurocentric than the former ones, dominated as they were by military blocs and the carefully guarded provincialism of nation-states. On the other hand there are the re-emergence of local ethnicity, the affirmation of cultural

roots and the quest for political autonomy for nations of regional communities residing both within and extending beyond the borders of post-1989
nation-states. Although they are not necessarily opposed to each other,
there are obvious tensions between these two tendencies, which involve the
making of political choices about the shaping of nations, societies and
communities.

As the Europeans are searching for new identities in response to
changes in the political economy and geography of the region – and
perhaps, in anticipation of even more drastic change still to come – it is
only natural that thought be devoted to the question of the implications for
adult education (Husén, Tuijnman, Halls 1992).[1]

The first implication concerns the relationship between adult education
and the state. To the extent adult education has been invented, promoted
and used as an instrument of nation-state building, and has been defined,
structured, financed and regulated by these nation-states, there is the question of dependence and even of loyalty. How does adult education relate to
the economic and political movements that seek to build both the 'larger
Europe' and new 'nations of regional communities', both of which may
well weaken the nation-states as we know them today? Many of the structures and institutions that had characterised adult education in the formerly
socialist Central and Eastern European states collapsed, withered or were
purposefully dismantled in an amazingly brief time span following the fall
of the Berlin Wall. The reconstruction of adult education has been going on
ever since. To what will these newly invented structures of adult education
pay allegiance – to the nation-states of Poland, Slovenia, Ukraine, to new
regional entities, or to the notion of a larger Europe? Or in the case of the
United Kingdom, how will devolution impact on adult education, and vice
versa?

The second implication concerns both the state and the role of their
governments. In a larger Europe with stronger common institutions and
more effective structural policies - and with the regions asserting their
newly found political power - how will national governments relate to their
national systems of adult education? National economies are no longer the

---

[1] The *Academia Europaea* Council, in February 1990, set up an international study
group to examine the implications for school education of economic and social
change in Europe following the fall of the Berlin Wall in November 1989.

unique framework for economic decisions to be made, and governments increasingly have to balance their policies in a broad international setting. The question of what Europe is at present, and what it may well become, is central to a range of decisions about fiscal and monetary policy, industrial and labour market policy. Because education systems interact with political, social and economic systems, it must be assumed to have some relevance also for adult education. But in which respects, and to what extent?

Compared to the conditions prevailing in the traditional industrial welfare states, governments today have fewer instruments and less scope for intervention in, for example, capital and labour markets, and hence fewer possibilities to cushion the adverse effects on social welfare. Ironically, perhaps, the movements towards new nations of communities within a larger European sphere have not much weakened the powerful hold of governments over school education. Schooling is concerned with the preservation, transmission and enlargement of culture, with the role of schools being principally to pass on the heritage and cultural patrimony of the state and prepare the young for life and for earning a living in the local milieu.

Education, by its very nature, tends to be ethnocentric and national in a provincial sense. Each country has an education system closely tied to its predominant culture and traditions. Compulsory schooling played an important role in nation-state building and industrialisation. Safeguarding the linguistic and cultural heritage of the nation has therefore long been a key goal of government policy.

Europe is far from a homogeneous cultural entity, and a majority of its citizens question whether closer educational integration is possible or even worth achieving. They argue that cultural richness thrives on diversity, and that national governments should remain responsible for schools, health and social services. It is mainly for this reason that education policy has not been a priority issue on the common European agenda. It is also on this premise that intergovernmental organisations such as the Council of Europe and OECD have traditionally concerned themselves with school education and the education of adults. It is therefore significant to note that there are some recent signs of change in this position in the context of EU space.

Whereas governments remain firmly in control over school education, this is no longer to the same extent the case in adult education. Recent treaties negotiated by EU member states and the Commission have effectively opened up new and wider dimensions in decision-making, financing and even the regulation of contents and qualifications. How can this divergence in the purposes and mechanisms of control over school education and adult education be explained? Is it because schools first and foremost teach the dominant literacy and glory of the nation state, whereas much – if not most – of adult education has become closely tied to jobs and therefore to the evolving European market place?

Over and above the imperatives of market orientations in adult education for work, it is also quite natural to see adult education as a means for promoting international understanding and solidarity. Adult education, traditionally, provides a natural ground for the teaching of foreign language learning, European history, human rights and environmental and political education. Perhaps the answer is simply that governments care less about their national systems of adult education than they do about controlling the curricula of primary and secondary schools, because the latter largely determine what today's youth will be taught about the sovereign nation's dominant language, history, geography and politics.

Whatever the reasons, it is apparent that market integration in the European sphere brings pressures to bear on national power centres to consider adult education in a broader, international context. Provincialism in policy making will likely be called into doubt in the emerging Europe-wide human capital markets. Will the objectives of national policy such as ensuring linguistic and cultural homogeneity and safeguarding national interests in education conflict with the economic and political objectives pursued by others, whether multinational corporations or 'regional nationalists' engaged in the construction of new nations of communities, as in Scotland or Wales? Clearly, there is a potential conflict of interest over the purposes of adult education between the nation state, newly emerging nations of regional communities and larger geo-political entities.

A further, rather obvious implication for adult education relates to language policy. History shows that, until recently, the nation-states of Europe could not care less for their local or regional languages. Spain and France are examples of countries where regional languages were not recognised, and hence could not be used in official communication or, for example, in education. Countries such as the United Kingdom also demonstrate that the maintenance of a political balance between a majority and small linguistic minorities is precarious, and that the temptation of the nation-state to defer to the values of the majority population is strong.

Developments demand that the need for roots and for local belonging, are balanced by the need for tolerance and accommodation: of migrants, guest workers and tourists, students and teachers, but also of science and technology, new economic activities, and new attitudes, tastes and values. Communication, and thus language, is at the heart of successful accommodation and the internationalisation of adult learning.

Conclusions

In this article, Europe is approached not primarily as a geographical concept covering a well-delineated territory. Rather, it is an imagined space identified by a diverse yet in certain respects common history, patterns of social, cultural and political interaction, and distinctive values and national identities – with the latter defined both in terms of nation-states and 'nations of regional communities'. Behind our reluctance to define nations as states in a Europe delineated in strictly geographical terms is the realisation that our ideas about what is, or should be, a European community are constantly subject to change.

We argue that to ensure peace, justice and prosperity in Europe over the coming decades it is necessary to recognise the importance of roots to the cultural health of a community and of the need also to tolerate diversity. The peoples of Europe need to be reassured that their multiple identities are not to be erased by an European super state, but can form instead the basic elements in the mosaic of a new European society, founded upon freedom, openness and autonomy. Fundamental to this is the evolution of a European and global civil society that will act as a shock absorber between the individual, the local community and the nation on the one hand and the state and business corporations on the other. Adult education and particularly the concept of lifelong learning have a major contribution to make to this process. Indeed, it could be argued that the evolution of civil society and the practice of lifelong learning are necessarily complementary. Such a civil society, to be meaningful, must be independent of state authority or commercial domination and present at all levels and in all sectors of public life. In the same way that it maintains public and community autonomy, it must also respect and protect the individual's right to freedom and to privacy.

The great challenge of the twenty-first century, and one to which adult education can make its contribution, is to reshape education from being overburdened with national concepts and ideas to becoming both 'global European' and 'local' at the same time.

References

Bottomley, G. (1992). *From Another Place. Migration and the Politics of Culture.* Cambridge.

Delors, J. (International Commission on Education for the 21th Century) (1996). *Learning: The Treasure Within.* Report to the UNESCO, Paris.

Friedman, W. (1965). *An Introduction to World Politics.* London.

Geyl, P. (1963). *Encounters in History.* London.

Green, A. (1990). *Education and State Formation. The Rise of Education Systems in England, France and the United States.* Basingstoke.

Husén, T., Tuijnman, A. C., Halls, W. D. (1992). *Schooling in Modern European Society. A Report of the Academia Europaea.* Oxford.

Levi-Strauss, C. (1987). *The View from Afar.* London.

Lewis, I. M. (1985). *Social Anthropology in Perspective. The Relevance of Social Anthropology.* Cambridge.

Morgan, W. J. (1973). *The Welsh Dilemma. Some Essays on Nationalism in Wales.* Carmarthenshire.

Morgan, W. J. (1997). Devolution. The End or the Beginning? In: *The University of Nottingham Magazine*, 3, p. 14.

Morgan, W. J., Preston, P. (eds.) (1993). *Raymond Williams. Politics, Education, Letters.* Basingstoke.

Ohmae, K. (1990). *The Borderless World. Power and Strategy in the Interlinked Economy.* London.

Raphael, D. D. (1979). *Problems of Political Philosophy.* London.

Rushdie, S. (with Grass, G.) (1987). Writing for a Future. In: Bourne, B., Eichler, U., Herman, D. (eds.). *Writers and Politics.* Nottingham.

Weber, E. (1976). *Peasants into Frenchmen. The Modernization of Rural France 1870-1914.* London.

Weil, S. (1987). *The Need for Roots. Prelude to a Declaration of Duties towards Mankind.* London.

BRON, A., SCHEMMANN, M. (eds.) (2000). LANGUAGE, MOBILITY, IDENTITY. CONTEMPORARY ISSUES FOR ADULT EDUCATION IN EUROPE. MÜNSTER, pp. 63-85.

John Field / Lars Grundström / Mieczysław Malewski
Ewa Solarczyk-Ambrozik

THE INTERNATIONALISATION OF LIFELONG LEARNING
A COMPARATIVE STUDY OF POLAND, BRITAIN AND SWEDEN

Background

Globalising tendencies are affecting all areas of education and training. Political and economic circumstances have combined to ensure that these tendencies are particularly acute within the EU and on its borders. As internal borders break down and labour markets become more international in nature, so education and training systems are being challenged to consider the European dimension to their provision. While the EU poses important learning challenges in its own right, it is also an increasingly important player in the field of education and training (Field 1998). The European Commission, moreover, is increasingly keen to promote lifelong learning in a range of policy areas. Lifelong learning was defined as central in the 1995 White Paper on *Education and Training* (CEC 1995). In the early 1990s, the European Commission also emphasised the place of lifelong learning within its policies for social affairs, research and technology development, regional affairs, and above all employment and economic growth, as well as in confronting the challenges of European integration more generally (CEC 1994). In 1996, the Commission added adult education explicitly to its SOCRATES programme of funding for transnational partnerships, and from 2000 adult education was given its own sub-programme, named after the Danish folk high school founder and cleric, Nicolai Grundtvig.

These developments have been mirrored in the growth of transnational professional networks. The early 1990s witnessed the creation, among others, of the European Universities Continuing Education Network

(EUCEN), the European Distance Education Network (EDEN), the European Society for Research in the Education of Adults (ESREA), and the European Conference for Educational Research (ECER) which has a thriving network on vocational education and training. In the same years, the long-established and somewhat stagnant European Bureau of Adult Education reorganised itself into the European Association of Adult Education (EAAE). The extent to which these supra-national networks impinge upon the work and interests of adult education professionals in the field varies widely, however. EAAE remains very much a network of national umbrella agencies, and has no means of communicating directly with professionals in the field. ECER and ESREA are scholarly bodies; they have to date made no attempt to engage with the professionals who might be end users of research. EUCEN and EDEN, albeit with a growing membership of professionals concerned with practice and policy, are somewhat specialist agencies. Yet despite these limitations, their emergence testifies to the growing interest in European collaboration.

How much impact have these tendencies had on adult education at local level? While there is growing interest in the different adult education systems of other European nations (Jarvis 1992), relatively little is known about the existing attitudes and interests of adult education professionals towards the European dimension. This report outlines the findings of a survey undertaken in 1995 and 1996 of adult education professionals in Britain, Sweden and Poland. These three countries represent respectively a well-established EU member state; a relative newcomer to EU membership; and an applicant nation that is currently treated as having 'association status' with the EU. The aim of the survey was to identify the perceptions, aspirations and competencies of adult education professionals in respect of the ongoing process of Europeanisation. While the findings are hardly definitive, they do indicate that in all three nations, adult education professionals see the European dimension of their work as at least potentially important, and have positive suggestions for links and partnerships with other European colleagues; however, they are poorly equipped when it comes to putting these ideas into practice.

Context

Relatively little research has been undertaken into the extent to which adult education professionals – that is, those working in the education and training of adults – have been affected by these developments. Analysis of policy has tended to confirm the hypothesis developed by Ryba, who argued that relatively little progress had been made in developing a European dimension within the national education systems of the EU's member states (Ryba 1992).

While Ryba's work was mainly focused on schools systems, similar findings have emerged in studies of specific areas of continuing education. Thus Liétard and Beaumelon, reflecting on French experience in the context of PETRA (the EU's programme for vocational training initiatives affecting young adults), concluded that although EU funding had stimulated many initiatives, there remained a substantial gap between intention and realisation (Liétard, Beaumelon 1989). Reviewing EU programmes in distance open learning, Lloyd concluded that they had failed to address the realities of the market, and had made little or no sustained impact on training and education systems (Lloyd 1993). Recent overviews of the impact of EU policies and programmes on women have reached slightly different conclusions. Plesser-Löper has emphasised the growing share of places on European Social Fund programmes taken up by women, and notes the stress upon equal opportunities policies within the framework of SOCRATES and its predecessor programmes (Plesser-Löper 1994). This is also the view taken by Barbara Springer, who has argued that the EU's policies and programmes have provided a degree of leverage for women to use in securing more favourably treatment in the member states (Springer 1993). Rees more cautiously notes the limitations to current equal opportunities measures in the field of vocational training, arguing that the instruments for oversight and management of the programmes are not sufficiently robust significantly to alter the prospects of women within the labour market (Rees 1995). Studies of specific programmes suggest, then, that while EU policies and programmes have had some impact, it has often been limited in nature; where it has been more substantial, this is because the EU's measures have supplied added leverage to domestic pressure groups.

More general analyses of EU programmes and policies have, for the most part, been largely speculative. Little systematic empirical research has been undertaken into the relationships between EU initiatives and national adult education systems. A recent survey of significant policies and changes across western Europe as identified by adult education specialists tended to take their awareness of the EU's role for granted. The survey included the European dimension, and the report for England and Wales notes a wide range of responses from adult education specialists favouring an active role for EU policy in areas such as the general provision and expansion of adult education, equal and universal access, and pan-European standards of provision. Of the 60 responding to the question on the scope of EU policy, only ten thought that the EU should have a relatively restricted role, or no role whatever (Dubelaar, Jarvis 1995, 54). A clear majority of the 79 respondents were themselves involved in European activities; most commonly these involved the exchange of know-how (76%) and developing networks (73%); significant numbers were involved in developing common programmes (45%) or seeking finance (42%) (Dubelaar, Jarvis 1995, 57). There was general support for direct European involvement in such activities as European credit systems, collaborative research, or a European Curriculum Centre (Dubelaar, Jarvis 1995, 58). The survey suffered from a number of methodological limitations, including the difficulties of translating a lengthy and detailed questionnaire into a number of different languages (Künzel 1997). With a response rate at best of under 25% in England and Wales (against a reported 47% in Germany (Künzel 1997, 341)), the Leuven/Ghent survey is probably best taken as a rough guide to views in the field. As respondents to the Leuven/Ghent survey were frequently senior professionals (Dubelaar, Jarvis 1995, 10), the findings can provide a basis for comparison with the present study, which attempted to survey the workforce more broadly.

Methodology

The present study was concerned with the attitudes and skills in respect of the European dimension of professionals involved in the education and training of adults at local level. It took the form of a small-scale comparative inquiry in Poland, Sweden and Britain. The research team believed that these three societies were likely to provide interesting points of both contrast and comparison. While all identify themselves as belonging to Europe (they are represented on the Council of Europe, for instance), Britain had joined the EU in 1973 while Sweden had just embarked on entry into the EU at the time of our survey; Poland, while expected to enter in the next round of enlargement, was able to participate in a large number of EU programmes while not yet being in membership of the Union.

Externally, Poland has always needed to pay close attention to its immediate neighbours (particularly Germany and Russia), but has close links with a number of western nations through emigration; Sweden remains an active member of the Nordic Council and has retained its links with Norway and Iceland as well as with those Scandinavian nations that chose to enter the EU; Britain's traditional ties to the Commonwealth and United States both complement and compete with its membership of the EU. Poland is ethnically and especially linguistically homogeneous; minority groups mostly comprise relatively recent arrivals, many of them able to speak at least one Slavonic language; Britain and Sweden by contrast are increasingly multi-ethnic societies (including significant communities with Polish connections in several cities); in Britain, English is a second language for significant minorities. In Poland and Britain, the adult education system has undergone restructuring; but the consequences for continuing education and training of the Polish transition to a democratic market society are considerably greater than the much more modest shifts in Britain. Thus although these three nations are in many ways comparable, there are important differences.

An important element of the research was to discover whether these differences affected teacher attitudes towards the European dimension. A brief questionnaire was piloted with an opportunity sample, and amended with advice from a consultant not involved in the project. The questionnaire focused on three main areas:

1. professionals' attitudes towards the European dimension;
2. professionals' language skills and awareness of the EU;
3. professionals' interest in specific links.

The study was envisaged as a low-cost and small scale exercise. Of course, communicative competence and a positive orientation towards transnational cooperation involve more than technical linguistic skills and basic factual awareness (Fairclough 1999). Within the inherent limits of this study, the aim was to provide a baseline for more detailed and in-depth studies.

It was decided to issue the questionnaire primarily through employing organisations. Organisations were selected from those public and voluntary bodies that have, as a primary aim, the provision of educational opportunities for adults. The sample in each case included both larger national bodies and smaller and more localised agencies. Two further key characteristics were used in designing the sample: geographical spread and field of work. The fields of work were:

- vocational training of adults,
- teachers' professional development centre (Poland only),
- general adult education,
- liberal adult education,
- basic adult education.

Geographically, it was important to ensure representation from across all countries; and from both rural and urban areas. For organisational and national political reasons, it was not in the end possible to include Scotland, leaving something of a gap in the British study. In Poland, the study comprised the city of Wrocław and the mixed urban and rural region of Wielkopolska, both of which are in the western part of the country. In Sweden, a random sample was undertaken of every second folkhighschool and every fourth municipality. Response rates were generally high. In Sweden, there was a response rate of 83%, in Britain of 74%, and in Poland of 48%. The lower Polish response rate is not easy to explain; while it may reflect the uncertainty surrounding adult education in provision in Poland at a time of transition, other scholars have noted low response rates in other former communist states, leading to the suggestion that this may have to do with low levels of trust in public information activities such as research (Maxwell 1996, 114-115). Be that as it may, the response rates were in all cases sufficiently high, particularly for postal questionnaires, to allow reasonable confidence in the findings as at least an approximate indicator of attitudes, orientation and competence among professionals in the field.

Involvement and Attitudes: Poland, Britain and Sweden Compared

Attitudes towards European cooperation were favourable in all three cases. Generally speaking, most adult educators in these countries appear to favour active engagement with the European project. A majority in all three cases were in touch with adult education in at least one foreign country; for most people, though, such contacts appear to rely on access to printed materials rather than exchanges and visits. These findings imply that despite a favourable attitude towards the European dimension in principle, many adult educators in Poland, Britain and Sweden tend to have only limited personal knowledge of another country's system.

There were also some significant variations between the three samples. Polish and Swedish adult educators were more likely to have some informed involvement with partners abroad. Over two-thirds of the Polish and Swedish respondents and over one half of the British respondents claimed some involvement in European links at present (table 1).

Table 1: Involvement in Adult Education Contacts with Other European Countries

Extent of Involvement	Britain	Poland	Sweden
Not at all	42.5%	31.9%	31.1%
Look at press reports	39.6%	37.8%	58.7%
Correspond with colleagues	21.6%	7.6%	9.1%
Read professional materials in the language occasionally	6.7%	16.0%	30.1%
Participate in exchanges	23.1%	11.8%	13.8%

However, the pattern of involvement varied between the three samples. One fifth of the British sample said they corresponded with colleagues abroad, compared with under 8% of Polish respondents and under one-tenth of the Swedes. Just over one tenth of the Polish sample took part in exchanges, roughly half of the proportion reported by the British and Swedish respondents. Swedish and Polish adult educators were far more likely than the British to read professional materials in the language of another country.

Most respondents in our survey said that they personally saw the European dimension as important (table 2).

Table 2: Views of the Importance of the European Dimension in the Education and Training of Adults

Importance	Britain	Poland	Sweden
Quite important	84.2%	75.6%	79.9%
Not important	11.3%	11.8%	18.3%
Distraction at present	4.5%	10.9%	2.0%

Well over four-fifths in Britain and Sweden and three-quarters in Poland agreed that it was 'quite important'. Some 3% in Sweden, 5% in Britain and 11% in Poland agreed that it was 'a distraction at the present time'. The latter question was included following piloting in Britain, during which it was forcefully pointed out that there were other far more pressing priorities including (in the context of a sustained recession) 'economic survival'. Nevertheless, few trainers and educators of adults took the view that European issues had little or no relevance to them; only in Poland did the proportion reach ten per cent. Here the results of the three samples show a remarkable degree of convergence.

There was less certainty that employing organisations recognised the importance of the European dimension (table 3).

Table 3: Priority of the European Dimension for Respondent's Own Organisation

Priority	Britain	Poland	Sweden
Very high	13.4%	9.2%	10.1%
Quite high	38.1%	36.1%	40.0%
Not a priority	44.8%	52.9%	45.0%
Actively discouraged	0.0%	0.0%	4.9%
Don't know	3.7%	0.8%	0.0%

Around one half (45% in Poland, 50% in Sweden and 51% in Britain) believed that their organisation ranked the European dimension as either a 'very high' or 'quite high' priority, but virtually the same proportion said that it was 'Not a priority' for their organisation (45% in Britain, 40% in Sweden and 53% in Poland). Of course, experience of closer contact can also provide a basis for critical comparison: one respondent from a British residential centre commented: "Our German colleagues seem to have more staff resources, it is also as though this type of work is seen as no more than a nice frill and not part of our work unless we can make money out of it".

Offered the opportunity to comment in greater detail, some respondents indicated reservations about current EU policies. Some voluntary sector respondents criticised the EU for favouring the larger and more professional continuing education providers in its programmes. In statutory organisations, on the other hand, the EU programmes may also constrain local initiative: one British respondent working in a further education college commented that "European contacts are determined by the bidding procedures for European funding. There is no real opportunity to establish links outside this procedure."

Any reservations, though, were outnumbered by a factor of about five to one by the number of respondents expressing positive views about the EU (sometimes combined among British respondents with negative comments on current UK policies towards the EU).

Findings: Orientation towards European Cooperation

Respondents showed a wide interest in establishing closer links with European colleagues. When asked to nominate up to two countries with which they would like links, only 12 British and 4 Polish respondents did not identify any. The other British respondents identified a total of 22 countries while the Poles identified a total of 14; the Swedes identified 19. Preferences however varied somewhat, with a particularly strong focus in Sweden upon the UK and other Scandinavian nations (table 4).

Table 4: Countries Where Closer Professional Contacts Are Desired

Country	Britain N=134	Poland N=119	Sweden N=533
France	66	39	27
Germany	56	71	48
United Kingdom	—	50	234
Netherlands	28	19	6
Spain	24	0	12
Italy	19	1	8
Sweden	9	5	—
Ireland	7	0	4
Denmark	5	7	48
Austria	3	7	0
Portugal	3	0	0
Switzerland	3	5	1
'Scandinavia'	3	0	7
Poland	2	—	5
Belgium	1	2	4
Russia	0	8	4
Baltic States	1	2	13
Norway	1	0	25
Finland	1	0	9
Romania	1	0	2

(From British respondents one each for Bulgaria, Czech Republic, Greece, Wales; from Sweden, one for Hungary. NB Respondents could identify up to two countries)

For Polish respondents, the most frequently named countries were Germany (selected by over half of the sample), the UK, France and Netherlands, followed by Austria, Russia and Sweden. British respondents' choices were not quite so concentrated as in the other two nations. For the British, France and then Germany were the clear front-runners, followed by Holland, Spain, Italy, Sweden and Ireland. Most respondents in these countries therefore were primarily interested in building links with the larger states of north-western Europe. Sweden's orientation towards western Europe and particularly Britain is marked, as is the Polish preference for developing links with Germany. British preferences were more dispersed.

In response to a request for additional comments, several respondents expanded on these answers. In Britain this included several respondents who work with disadvantaged groups. One, who serves as chair of a WEA branch, said that "I am particularly interested in knowing of any work being done in enabling black/white people to work together as allies. We are developing programmes in this and would welcome exchange of views."

Similar interests were expressed by an adult literacy teacher working in London. However, a larger number of respondents working with disadvantaged adults expressed a contrary view. One trainer commented that "my involvement is with unemployed adults and therefore it is only if people wish to work abroad (which is rare) that closer contacts with European countries occurs or is relevant."

Another working with refugees noted that "many of my students speak French and France could offer them a new dimension but as African refugees they have chosen to avoid France". Another, who works mainly with students from Yemeni, Asian and Afro-Caribbean backgrounds, saw the European dimension as less important than for other colleagues.

Polish respondents frequently expressed a desire to learn from others' experiences. Thus one Wrocław teacher said that:

> To my mind cooperation with other European countries might result in the eventual reform of the old-fashioned model of adult education in Poland which, as for now, does not correspond to market demands because it is mainly based on general education... It seems to me that we can, up to a point, take the pattern of the English system, which lends itself to necessary temporary changes and is based on open learning which introduces the syllabuses in the form of modules.

He also expressed interest in the ideal of European integration:

> Mutual contacts, Cupertino between educators, the exchange of students among European countries may also contribute to the destruction of certain national prejudices which stem from the past and may serve the idea of building a united Europe.

However, the European ideal was sometimes combined with the wish to learn from western European colleagues. Another Wrocław respondent said that

> My innermost professional dream is to have a Europe with-
> out borders here in Poland. Thanks to it, many of the well-
> educated, outstandingly intelligent and clever people might
> constitute a positive potention for enterprise for my country.

These Polish respondents therefore tended to emphasise their desire to tap into the experience of other European countries in adapting to a market-led system. Many of the Wielkopolska respondents placed this perspective in the wider context of a need for stronger economic Cupertino between Poland and other European nations.

The questionnaire asked respondents to say why they had selected the two countries nominated. In giving reasons for their choice, a number were somewhat instrumental in nature (linguistic skills, proximity, ease of or-ganisation, for instance, and in Poland the presence of relations). Never-theless some intriguing differences emerged in the other reasons given. Those British respondents selecting Italy and Spain were most likely to cite cultural or personal reasons for their choice, as were Polish respondents interested in France or Britain. Those selecting Germany tended to give political reasons (usually Germany's powerful role within the EU or her economic strength); those selecting Sweden and other Scandinavian nations tended to refer to educational factors. Polish respondents often justified their choice in terms of their subject specialism. Those selecting Germany were often economics or business studies teachers who emphasised the strength of the German economy; Britain was favoured by those teaching health sciences or agricultural subjects (some of whom also expressed an interest in Denmark). Beauty instructors tended to opt for France. Such tendencies indicate a high understanding of conditions elsewhere in Europe and a commitment to European integration. If anything, this pattern seemed stronger among Polish than among British respondents.

Findings: Skills and Knowledge

A positive attitude towards the European dimension may not always be combined with the capacity to develop that dimension in any meaningful fashion. The survey suggests that many adult educators in all three countries see themselves as lacking the information they need. And although Polish adult educators were more likely to speak and read at least one foreign language than were the British, the majority in both countries reported limited language skills. In Sweden on the other hand, virtually everyone claimed to have a reasonable degree of competence in English, and over half had some ability in German.

Respondents were asked to assess their awareness of EU policies and programmes in the field of education and training (table 5).

Table 5: Awareness of EU Programme

Awareness	Britain	Poland	Sweden
Well informed	8.2%	5.9%	13.4%
Some knowledge	28.4%	32.8%	32.1%
Limited knowledge	37.3%	47.1%	37.0%
No knowledge	26.1%	13.4%	17.5%

Only 6% in Poland, 8% in Britain, and 13% in Sweden described themselves as 'well-informed', while over a quarter of British respondents and rather smaller number of Swedes and Poles said they had no knowledge of the EU's initiatives. Polish awareness therefore appears relatively high for a non-member of the EU; we need to remember that, although few will have detailed knowledge of the wider education and training policies of the Union, the TEMPUS initiative in particular, as well as the Europeanisation process more widely, has been widely debated among educational circles in Poland (Kozek 1990). This left the majority – 80% in Poland, 69% in Sweden and 66% in Britain – describing themselves as having either 'some' or 'limited information'. Of course, these are self-assessed degrees of expertise and must therefore be treated with caution. On the whole, though, this suggests that few professionals in any of these nations possess sufficient awareness of EU initiatives to act effectively unless they are able to call on significant levels of specialist support.

Several respondents gave more detailed comment on what they saw as a regrettable lack of awareness. One who works for the WEA said that

I feel that although I teach on courses funded by ESF I know very little about how other countries in Europe are working in continuing education... I hope to attend conferences etc. where colleagues from other parts of Europe will be present.

Another WEA respondent said that "I have never given this a thought - but the prospect would be exciting". A third WEA respondent said "This is the first time I have had the opportunity to give some thought to the issues raised in this questionnaire ... on the whole it must be a priority that we encompass a European dimension". A respondent who works for an Further education college replied that "completion of this questionnaire has highlighted my personal lack of awareness... I do feel however that the European dimension is important".

Respondents were also asked to assess their linguistic competence in three major European languages. Those selected were French and German for all respondents; Spanish was added for British and Swedish respondents and English for the Polish and Swedish samples (table 6). Courses in all three languages are widely available in adult education programmes in the respective countries. In Sweden, adult education professionals lived up to the national stereotype of linguistic proficiency. In Britain and Poland, relatively few professionals claimed more than a basic competence in any other language than their own.

Table 6: Self-Judged Ability to Work in Another European Language
(Percentage completely unable to communicate professionally in named foreign languages)

	French	German	English	Spanish *
Britain	30.9 %	73.8 %	—	86.8 %
Poland	63.9 %	31.1 %	62.2 %	—
Sweden	68.1 %	29.8 %	2.1 %	89.4 %

* Option for "Spanish" not offered in Poland

In Poland, barely one half of the teachers were capable either of reading a professional text or participating in a discussion conducted in another language. The proportion able to deliver a prepared class in a foreign language varied from 13% in German to 3.4% in French; 9% said they could deliver a prepared class in English. Just over one half of respondents mentioned competence in a language other than these three, however. This reflects Polish educational history, with Russian being for some decades the main second language in the schools and adult education systems; the rapid expansion of foreign language teaching after 1990 had yet to make much impact at the time of our survey.

In Britain, only 30% were unable to operate in any of the three speci-fied languages. However, many of the remainder could function only at a fairly superficial level. A majority of respondents claimed to be able to speak French: 46% of the British sample could engage in a simple conver-sation in French, 12% could also read a professional text, and 6.5% could also engage in a seminar debate. Under 30% are able to speak German and 13% speak Spanish, in both cases mainly at the lower levels of compe-tence. One respondent commented that language barriers were particularly important for teachers from working class backgrounds, but in fact such barriers were apparently widespread. Pedagogic skills were considerably more limited among British teachers than among their Polish colleagues. Those who could deliver a prepared class in another language were very much in the minority: 6.8% said they could do so in French, and under one per cent in German or Spanish.

In Sweden, by contrast, foreign language skills were both widespread and at a high level. Well over half said that they could join fully in a dis-cussion held in English, while a further fifth were confident in their ability to deliver prepared teaching in English. In German, 15% of the Swedes were confident that they could join in discussions and one tenth felt able to deliver prepared teaching. This finding is clearly related to the high pro-portion of Swedish adult educators who said they consulted professional materials in other languages than their own.

Respondents were also asked to identify barriers to developing links with their chosen nations (table 7). In both Poland and Britain, language deficits were the most frequently mentioned barrier to more active in-volvement in European links and partnerships. One WEA tutor felt that languages were a particular problem for staff from working class back-grounds. Another WEA tutor, referring to experience in teaching sugarcraft to non-English speakers, said that this was less of an issue in craft subjects, where demonstration was more important than speech. In complete contrast to Britain and Poland, linguistic difficulties were hardly mentioned at all in Sweden.

Table 7: The Most Significant Barriers to Closer Cooperation

	Britain N=120	Poland N=119	Sweden N=533
Language	1st	1st	0
Cost	2nd	2nd	1st
Time	3rd	0	2nd
No prior contacts	4th	3rd	3rd
Culture/politics	5th	4th	4th
Poor information	6th	0	0
Distance/communications	8th	6th	0
Own country 'not interesting'	0	5th	0

As a barrier, language was followed by cost. This was the largest single barrier for Swedish adult educators, and was mentioned by around 43% of our sample. Well over one quarter of the Poles also maintained that financial barriers were particularly important.

In Poland, the lack of prior contacts was the third most frequently mentioned barrier. The lack of any tradition of Cupertino, and the absence of models of institutional partnership, may have been compounded both by Poland's history and – if unintentionally – by the nature of the EU's TEMPUS programme. Individual respondents' comments exemplified a typically passive attitude towards overseas contacts – they and their institutions appear to wait for offers of Cupertino rather than actively reaching out themselves. This was followed by such political factors as the perceived lack of interest in Poland among western Europeans. This opinion calls for further analysis, given Poland's reputation in the west as a focal point for resistance to communism and centre for the political transformations of the 1980s. With the democratisation of Polish society, a number of the sample believed that western European institutions were now more interested in developing contacts with more prominent regions such as Russia or Ukraine. Just over a tenth of the Swedish and British respondents also mentioned this factor.

Information deficits and time constraints were not mentioned by any Polish respondents. By contrast, time constraints were the second most important barrier in Sweden, while in Britain time constraints were the third most frequently cited barrier, followed by lack of contacts, lack of information, educational or cultural differences, and political attitudes in the UK ('insularity' or some similar term being used in these cases). A number of the barriers deemed important, such as languages and lack of information, are skills and knowledge gaps among professionals. Significantly, these are in the power of providing organisations themselves to resolve.

Discussion

The evidence in this survey suggests that in both countries teachers favour the European dimension but feel that their potential to contribute at present is limited. On the one hand, interest in the European dimension and recognition of its importance are relatively high. Particularly in Poland but also in Britain, the questionnaires abounded with comments; respondents themselves seem to have found the issues interesting ones, which may account for the relatively high response rates. Certainly there is no evidence here of isolationist thinking. On the basis of the present survey, we conclude that the vast majority of continuing education professionals in all three countries are interested in developing new links with and learning from colleagues in other European countries, and see the EU as an important player in their field. On the other hand, awareness of EU policies and programmes appears to be limited; linguistic skills are often narrow and low-level; even basic information and contacts with other European providers seem to be rare.

The degree of convergence between Britain and Poland requires some explanation. Superficially, one would expect to find substantial differences between two countries whose recent history has been so different. What we found, though, was a remarkable degree of common ground. Teachers and scholars in both countries have access to information and advice on European Union policies on education and training; in Poland, which is not as yet a member of the Union, a number of conference presentations and articles have sought to present and analyse the educational aspect of European integration.

Moreover, the EU's involvement has not yet made much impact on the curricular thinking of most European states. Whether full members or associates, the bulk of funding – which in the member states is drawn from the Structural Funds, which account for around a quarter of all EU spending – directly supports the national education and training system. Although many British teachers and trainers will be affected in one way or another by the European Social Fund, for example, its role is to subsidise training for the unemployed rather than inject a transnational dimension into the curriculum. In Poland, much EU support before the late 1990s came in the form of infrastructural aid (computers or audio-visual materials), and advice from western European consultants or teachers on adjusting educational structures to meet the needs of a deregulated market economy.

So far as the European dimension to teaching and learning is concerned, the EU has provided sufficient financial resources to interest institutional managers but not to influence national systems, even in the hard-pressed nations of Central and Eastern Europe (Kozek 1993). Indeed, in certain key respects EU policies on education and training are inconsistent, and are pursued through mechanisms that have limited their impact on providers and national education and training systems (Field 1998). Education and training remains primarily a matter of national sovereignty, and European policies have as yet not permeated the system to any depth; in this respect at least the experiences and perspectives of practitioners in a well-established member state like Britain and a relatively new applicant like Poland are not too dissimilar.

Nevertheless, very important differences remain, and these are reflected in a number of our findings. Many of the barriers identified by the British sample are open to remedy by employing institutions or even individuals: it is within the grasp of most people to learn another language or improve their knowledge of other European societies, and the larger providers – e.g. further education colleges or the Workers' Educational Association – are in a position to reallocate resources to support the European dimension if they wish so. Even though some of the barriers are similar, Polish teachers and trainers face a somewhat different set of underlying problems. Low salary levels mean that the cost of language classes and overseas travel is prohibitive for most teachers and trainers, particularly if they work in the public sector. Public sector institutions and voluntary providers can neither afford to reallocate scarce resources nor turn to what is inevitably a limited market place to generate the additional income, at least not under present circumstances. To this could be added the apparently passive approach of many Polish institutions – itself best seen as a rational response to that country's challenging political and financial situation.

Sweden, meanwhile, demonstrates a larger number of distinctive features. By comparison with their British and Polish counterparts, Swedish adult educators were far more likely to portray themselves as skilled in other European languages, and were also more likely to report reading professionally-relevant materials in other languages than their own. Language barriers simply did not feature in the list of obstacles to closer cooperation with other European countries. Yet in Sweden too, most respondents felt poorly-informed about current EU policies and programmes, and did not believe that their own organisation much values the European dimension of its work.

In many respects, these are not surprising findings. First, most British and Polish continuing education professionals received their own schooling some time ago, and their knowledge and skills may in some instances be dated. It is noticeable for example language skills are commonly in the languages most widely taught in schools in the past. Particularly in Poland, there has been a sharp rise in recent years in the numbers enrolling in foreign language programmes; however, many of these take place not in public sector adult education bodies but in the private sector. Second, teachers in continuing education in all three countries may find it difficult to see a wider picture on a European canvas. Some respondents struggled to relate the European dimension to their own subject, particularly where it was primarily practical. One British cake icing teacher, for instance, could only relate to the Dutch. Several others only saw the implications in terms of their own discipline (for example, fine arts), with no broader perspective. Third, some respondents in all three samples reported that there are serious resource challenges, as indeed there are across much of the continuing education field. This is manifested both in a strong sense among some respondents that other priorities are more pressing, and issues such as the European dimension are a luxury; and the much more common view, that the costs of developing links are beyond the means of most providing organisations. It is then fairly easy to identify possible explanations for the contrast between desire and capacity.

Is this apparently contradictory picture one which should cause concern? If it is true that the economic well-being and cultural future of European citizens lie increasingly with an ability to benefit from and operate in the new Europe, then adults as well as young people need to be given access to the skills, knowledge and attitudes that will help them thrive in this wider, more international context. In such areas as labour market, though, the significance of European integration for ordinary citizens has yet to be proven: so far the number of workers, other than the unskilled, who either wish or are being required to move across national borders is relatively small (Marsden 1994). This being so, the political demand for a European dimension to vocational preparation and development is somewhat ahead of the economic demand. Nor have the EU's policies and programmes in the field of education and training been as consistent and clear in their pursuit of lifelong learning as some Commission policy statements have suggested, despite the important symbolic declarations of the European Year of Lifelong Learning. EU mobility schemes are often criticised for excluding most categories of adult learner, while others have deplored the way that the Treaty on European Union has institutionalised divisions between vocational training and general education, as expressed in the lack of linkage between SOCRATES and LEONARDO. Only more recently has adult education itself been identified as a significant area of activity within SOCRATES. Of course, it is possible that professionals will adopt a stronger orientation towards the European dimension in future, particularly as the Grundtvig programme evolves. But in a field that is dominated to a large extent by consumer demand, an active strategy of Europeanisation depends on the extent to which adult learners themselves place pressure on the providing organisations.

A sceptical view of the EU's likely influence in the coming years is probably justified, then, and may moderate any concern over the findings in this survey. Nevertheless, if organisations choose to increase the priority they accord the European dimension, the study does help identify a number of practical areas where action might be taken, much of it at modest cost to organisations. Much staff development could be undertaken at minimal marginal costs: wider access for staff to language training within institutions that have their own foreign language programmes, for example. Raising awareness about EU programmes need not involve a flurry of newsletters and mailshots, but the circulation or posting of freely available publicity materials. Contacts and links can be developed at minimal cost, for instance by associating relatively informally with an existing international programme at another and possibly larger institution. Informal links are often maintained once initial contact and trust is established; thus a London trainer who had been associated with a joint programme in Germany in 1990 had continued to communicate. One respondent from an further education college suggested the formation of language associations among students and staff, while another teacher suggested that language classes in different countries should correspond with and perhaps visit one another (more ambitiously, this teacher also suggested the creation of a European Language Exchange as a facilitating mechanism). While developing links, raising awareness and updating skills and knowledge need not be a costly process, a lack of resources will impose important constraints.

Conclusion

This paper has shown that the Europeanisation process has so far made relatively little impact upon adult education professionals in studied countries. While there exists a considerable reserve of goodwill towards the idea of European cooperation in adult education, most professional adult educators do not feel themselves well-informed about the EU's policies and programmes, and they believe that their organisations do not particularly emphasise this aspect of their work. In two of the three countries studied, the relevant linguistic skills are lacking. While some of these difficulties could easily be tackled through staff development and other measures, there is also a strong belief among the professionals that funding is insufficient to allow for any substantive change. We conclude that, while adult education professionals may be broadly sympathetic towards the European project in general terms, the European Union has yet to exert a concrete impact on their thinking and practice at local level. This creates the risk that adult education providers will respond in a simplistic and opportunistic manner to perceived funding opportunities, with little if any educational impact over the longer term (Lesniak, Le Billon 1996; Bates 1999). The question of how adult education might respond at local level to the Europeanisation process – which after all takes place in the context of powerful globalising tendencies, and the shift towards an informational economy – therefore remains an open one.

References

Bates, S. (1999). EU Fraud Squad Considers Charges. In: *Guardian*, 20 (November 1999), p. 2.

CEC (Commission of the European Communities) (1994). *Growth, Competitiveness, Employment. The Challenges and Ways forward into the 21st Century.* Luxembourg.

CEC (Commission of the European Communities) (1994). *Education and Training. Towards a Learning Society.* Luxembourg.

Dubelaar, J., Jarvis, P. (1995). *The Education of Adults in Europe 1995. The Interim English and Welsh Report.* Guildford.

Fairclough, N. (1999). Global Capitalism and Critical Awareness of Language. In: *Language Awareness*, 8 (2), pp. 71-83.

Field, J. (1998). *European Dimensions. Education, Training and the European Union.* London.

Jarvis, P. (ed.) (1992). *Adult Education in Europe.* Leicester.

Kozek, T. (1993). Wandlungen der internationalen Ausbildungshilfe für Polen. In: Ebmeyer, K.-U., Kossak, G., Schulz, H. (eds.). *Transformation durch Qualifikation: Weiterbildung im Übergang zur Marktwirtschaft.* Berlin, pp. 269-279.

Künzel, K. (1997). Ansätze und Irritationen europäischer Weiterbildungsforschung. Das EURODELPHI-Projekt 1993-1995. In: *Bildung und Erziehung,* 50 (3), pp. 331-353.

Lesniak, I., Le Billon, V. (1996). À quoi sont servi les milliards de l'Europe pour l'Est? In: *L'Expansion*, 535 (24 October 1996), pp. 122-124.

Liétard, B., Beaumelon, F. (1989). Vers un formateur européen? In: *Education Permanente*, 99, pp. 55-66.

Lloyd, C. (1993). European Community Policy and the Market. In: *Journal of Computer Assisted Learning*, 9 (2), pp. 86-91.

Marsden, D. (1994). Skills and the Integration of European Labour Markets. In: *Social Europe*, 94 (1), pp. 77-109.

Maxwell, R. (1996). Out of Kindness and into Difference. The Value of Global Market Research. In: *Media, Culture and Society*, 10 (1), pp. 105-126.

Plesser-Löper, C. (1994). Zur aktuellen Frauenförderung in der Europäischen Union. In: Hinzen, H. (eds.). *Erwachsenenbildung und Entwicklung*. Bonn, pp. 256-265.

Rees, T. (1995). *Women and the EC Training Programmes*. Bristol.

Ryba, R. (1992). Towards a European Dimension in Education. Intention and Reality in European Community Policy and Practice. In: *Comparative Education Review*, 36 (1) pp. 10-24.

Springer, B. (1993). *The Social Dimension of 1992*. New York.

BRON, A., SCHEMMANN, M. (eds.) (2000). LANGUAGE, MOBILITY, IDENTITY. CONTEMPORARY ISSUES FOR ADULT EDUCATION IN EUROPE. MÜNSTER, pp. 86-98.

Barbara Merrill / Christina Lönnheden

EXPERIENCING APEL AS A LANGUAGE FOR ACCESS

Post industrial societies are experiencing rapid economic and social changes fragmenting lives and societies. To compete on the globalised market governments need to constantly ensure that skills and knowledge are updated amongst its workforce. A front-end model of education is no longer sufficient to meet the changing needs of the new market economy. Working lives are becoming fragmented, as a job may no longer be for life. Instead employees are more likely to experience a series of jobs interspersed by periods of short-term contracts or unemployment. Lifelong learning has been adopted by national governments and the European Commission (EC) as a solution to the economic and social challenges currently facing societies. Great precedence is, therefore, placed on education as a key to economic success and the promotion of social inclusion and citizenship. Promoting the participation of learners in lifelong learning to acquire skills and knowledge is now high on the policy agenda of governments and the EC within Europe. The Commission's White Paper on *Education and Training* (1995) stressed the necessity for accepting new methods of skills and knowledge within education.

Widening access to education for adults has produced different models with different stages of implementation across Europe. The Accreditation of Prior Experiential Learning (APEL) is just one initiative within a lifelong learning strategy, but an important one, as it enables adults to return to learn at different levels, thus providing the potential to gain mobility in an individual's learning and work careers. APEL is, therefore, a significant factor in the move towards providing greater equality of opportunity and the social inclusion of groups marginal to the formal education system.

This article examines the role of APEL in facilitating not only the access and learning of adults but how the process and language of APEL enables adult learners to actively give 'voice' to their life and learning experiences, thus shaping a new self identity through learning. APEL encourages non-traditional learners to take their first steps back into learning and possible educational and career mobility both within and across European countries. To illustrate this we will draw on the findings of a three year project on APEL (1996-1999) funded by the European Commission through its SOCRATES adult education programme. The project partners were Belgium (University of Louvain), Finland (University of Turku), Germany (University of Bremen), Spain (University of Barcelona), Sweden (University of Stockholm) and the UK (University of Warwick). Other European countries were surveyed by the partner countries to include Austria, Ireland, Italy, France, and Portugal. Three main types of adult educational institutions were considered: further education, higher education and adult education. This was largely a developmental project with the aim of identifying and extending good APEL policy and practice through the exchange of knowledge across institutions and Europe. However, research tools such as a questionnaire survey and interview were used to establish what is happening in relation to APEL in different educational sectors across different European countries.

This article also attempts to reflect upon and discuss some of the issues associated with APEL in a speculative way by taking tentative steps to stretch the discourse to look at issues of language, identity and mobility. For example, to what extent does APEL use the language of learning in a different way to formal qualifications? Does the language of learning within APEL enable learners to access education more easily by drawing on "really useful knowledge" (Thompson, 1997) to the individual? Can APEL also be interpreted both as a biographical means of learning and a means for shaping a person's biography? Does APEL have the potential to offer the possibility of geographical mobility on the labour market within and across countries as well as individual social mobility?

Defining the Language of APEL

Understanding the concept of APEL is confusing as different acronyms are used for different learning environments. The letter 'A' in APEL is sometimes referred to in literature as accreditation and in other instances as assessment without differentiating between the two. Discussions in our project led to the rejection of both of these terms as we felt that neither adequately described the different applications of APEL as identified in our survey of European countries. Instead we used the broader term 'acknowledgement' as the form APEL takes in different countries is culturally determined by national education systems.

The UK Universities and Colleges Admissions Service (UCAS) suggests the following definitions:

> APL – the Accreditation of Prior Learning used as an umbrella term form to include both prior certificated learning and experiential learning
> APEL – the Accreditation of Prior Experiential Learning to refer to uncertificated learning gained from experience
> APCL – the Accreditation of Prior Certificated Learning for which certification has been awarded by an educational institution or another education/training provider (*Accreditation of ...* 1996, 7).

Further confusion arises as the term APL is commonly used, often interchangeably with APEL although in practice there is a distinction. APL refers to certificated prior learning "gained through organised courses, modules, workshops, seminars and similar activities" (Nyatanga, Forman, Fox 1998, 7). APEL, on the other hand, relates to experiences and learning gained informally in society. The current trend in the UK is to merge the two approaches in the following way: AP(E)L. In some countries, for example Spain, Sweden and Finland, the word is non-existent but the practice exists using a different term. What does APEL mean in practice? Definitions are not readily available. Much literature assumes that the reader is familiar with the term. However, one definition put forward by Evans is:

> The Assessment of Prior Experiential Learning (APEL) involves students or prospective students documenting their learning from life and work experience in such a way that they can use such documentation to gain access and advance standing in tertiary education institutions (Evans 1990, 122).

Another by Challis suggests that:

> The fundamental principle underpinning APEL is that learning is worthy and capable of gaining recognition and credit, regardless of time, place and context in which it has

been achieved. It thus represents a move to accept that learning is not dependent upon any particular formal setting, and to acknowledge it as being of value in its own right (Challis 1993, 1).

APEL challenges existing notions of what counts as useful knowledge by recognising that learning is not confined to formal educational institutions or the workplace.

> APEL is essentially about learning from experience. APEL also raises interesting questions about learning and assessment processes, what constitutes knowledge and the interaction and relationship between formal and informal learning (Merrill, Hill 1998, 21).

It assumes that skills and knowledge gained in both the personal and public domains are important and that everyone has life experiences of learning in different contexts. This may include the family such as caring roles, voluntary work, workplace, community, and earlier formal education or leisure activities. APEL, therefore, values informal learning as a knowledge base for further and more formal learning offering adults who do not have formal qualifications a means of access to adult, further and higher education. It also shifts the emphasis of the purpose of learning from outcomes to the process (Storan 1988).

The APEL process provides an important stepping stone in the path to returning to learn for those who may have been disaffected or failed by initial schooling. Informal learning is assessed and transferred into a commodity, a credit, which will then be recognised and acknowledged by an educational institution. However, such a process is not without contradictions in assessing and quantifying informal learning. Despite this APEL is a valuable tool for encouraging learners to reflect upon their experiences in their own language, identifying the learning processes and provide evidence to demonstrate that learning has taken place. Adult educators such as Freire have always stressed the centrality of experience in the process of adult learning while others such as Knowles (1990) and Brookfield (1983) point out that adults bring with them a wide range of skills and knowledge to the learning situation. APEL procedures are a valuable tool for understanding how adults learn and thus have a role to play in contributing to the development of adult education theory.

Purposes and Functions of APEL

APEL was initially used in the UK and other countries as an access or admission route into further and higher education to broaden and widen the student base needed as a result of economic and demographic changes. In this situation APEL offers an alternative route to traditional qualifications into education. Generally learners are asked to demonstrate, using a portfolio, that their informal learning experiences gained earlier in life have imbued them with the ability and capacity to study on a formal course (Fraser, 1995). APEL is now used in a variety of ways such as for assessment, accreditation, advanced standing or as a contribution to learning. In further and higher education APEL is being increasingly applied as a means to gain exemption from a particular course. Our European survey illustrated that

> APEL procedures are most commonly used to support applications for entry to educational institutions, whereas its use to support and contribute to learning is relatively limited, with the exception of Sweden (74.5%) and Germany (60.8%) and actual accreditation of prior learning is still less common (Hill 1999, 15).

In percentage terms the average use of APEL across Europe for admission was 61.8% compared to 23.9% for accreditation. Bailie and O'Hagan (1999) identify two other purposes: APEL for awards in work-based learning and APEL for progress to assist learners in community settings to progress into further and higher education studies.

Accessing the Language of APEL as a Learner

In theory APEL focuses on the language of the learner rather than the language of the institution or provider; the learner is, therefore, at the heart of the process. Language can also be a barrier to learning (Cross 1981, McGivney, 1990). The use of the acronym APEL, together with terms such as accreditation or assessment may well be off-putting to potential adult students considering returning to formal learning after having been out of the education system for a long time and/or may possess few or any formal qualifications. Taking the first step to enter a further education college or higher education institution can be daunting and some potential learners do not manage to do this. Institutions need to communicate about their programmes in the local community where people experience life which is, after all, the fundamental basis of APEL. This a dilemma facing institutions who implement APEL: how to break down and present the formal language constructed by educationalists into a language which is meaningful to those without, in Bourdieu's term, "cultural capital". The employment of communicative language becomes essential to encourage the access of marginalised adults in society:

> It is therefore incumbent on those wishing to attract new recruits to basic education and return-to-learn courses to develop communicative strategies which address the exclusion from social networks of many people who might otherwise take up learning opportunities (Bond, Merrill 1999, 210).

APEL is about facilitating widening access but potential learners will not be aware of this unless institutions tell them about it:

> What those institutions tell potential students about APEL will be driven by the extent to which APEL is credible within the institutions and also by the reality that different institutions see APEL merely as a means of opening doors to students who 'missed out' on previous educational opportunity, or, more radically, as a means of providing potential students with formal recognition of previous achievement which carries with it the possibility of exemption from parts of an academic programme or even academic credit (Merrill, Hill 1999).

Even in institutions where APEL is embedded, such as in the UK, potential adult learners may be told different things by different people in the organisation as well as different things across institutions when APEL is used for different purposes and in different ways. In France, the learner is not confronted by a variety of discourses as APEL is more uniform and standardised as it is managed by regional centres.

Initially most learners hear about APEL as being a means of entry into further or higher education for those without formal qualifications. Understanding what APEL is about is the first hurdle. An adviser then guides them into making an APEL claim, however miscommunication can easily occur:

> ... personal experience tells us that potential students, hope, even expect, that their experience will be enough on its own to secure admission. We are very used to the familiar story which runs something like "Well, I've worked in a hospital for years and years, so I don't need to know any more about that stuff. Why can't I miss out the introductory parts of the course?" The answer may well eventually be "yes you can, but the first task of anyone advising such incoming students is to convey the message that the experience is not enough on its own, and that what does matter is to demonstrate the learning which has occurred as a result of that experience" (Merrill, Hill, 1998).

This also involves the student demonstrating that the learning has occurred at the appropriate level for which they want to study. It is critical at this stage that APEL advisers do not use language that is off-putting and too academic.

In institutions which implement APEL successfully practitioners:

> ... will already have considered how to present a process which uses an academic language of accreditation through traditional structures of education... It may be argued that those individuals who have achieved access or credit through APEL processes are those for whom the language and structures are less daunting, either because of previous experience or because of other personal preparations prior to embarking on the process (Georgious 1999, 37).

Georgious (1999) is right to point out that there is an inherent danger that APEL, like other access initiatives, may still be failing to reach those adults who are the most excluded from education yet who could benefit from APEL procedures.

APEL as Biographical Identity

APEL individualises learning as the learner takes responsibility for their learning and progression. In this sense the APEL model fits in with wider social changes brought about by modernity. The move towards individualism during the 1980s and the breaking down of the welfare state, not only in the UK but also across Europe, heightened the need for self-reliance in all spheres of society, including education. While a learner may present experiences as individual life and work ones, these continue to be shaped by processes of class, gender and race. Prior experience and learning is part of and also shapes an individual's biography. In reflecting reflexively upon their learning experiences learners are reflecting upon their life experiences and biography. APEL has the potential to be an important element in a person's learning career. Learning, therefore, stems from experience and involves "a dynamic, ongoing interactive process between knowing and doing" (Hutchings, Wutzdorff 1988, 7). Alheit stresses that:

> Biography itself has become a field of learning, in which transitions have to be anticipated and coped with, and where personal identity is liable to be the result of long and protracted learning processes (Alheit 1995, 59).

APEL questions traditional assumptions and attitudes about knowledge and academic knowledge in particular by accepting life experiences as a form of knowledge. In this way the 'personal' becomes 'useful knowledge', a process which feminists recognise as being important in their research. The subjectivity and autonomy of the learner, therefore, lies at the heart of the APEL process. However, getting educational institutions, universities in particular, to acknowledge this can be a hard struggle.

APEL uses a person's past identity or biography to assist with shaping the learners' current identity and their future one. Giddens (1991) maintains that self-identity is a modern process whereby a person can reflexively construct a personal narrative through which they can understand themselves as being in control of their lives and future. APEL is assessing and accrediting personal learning for self-development and thus has the potential to empower the learner through changing identity. Empowerment is a nebulous concept but for Gore:

Empowerment carries with it an agent of empowerment (someone, or something, doing the empowering), a notion of power as property (to empower implies to give or confer power), and a vision or desired end state (some vision of what it is to be empowered and the possibility of a state of empowerment) (Gore 1993, 73-74).

In relation to adult education Antikainen et al. (1996) draw upon Mezirow's (1981) concept of "critical reflectivity" as their definition of empowerment refers "to an experience that changes an individual's understanding of him/herself and/or of the world" (Antikainen et al. 1996, 70-71). In the context of APEL Evans emphasises the following definition:

Empowerment, however, implies development, or at least the opportunity for development, so the learning which is experiential, being personal, is rooted in the idea of human growth and development, hence the interest in the connections between personal learning and public recognition in relation to empowerment (Evans 1992, 85).

For Challis (1993) the fact that APEL is completely student-centred makes it an empowering process for the learner which also increases their self-confidence:

The assessment and accreditation of what is revealed through this process takes place against criteria that are known to the learner, and against which suitable evidence of competence has been prepared and matched. The process is therefore one of empowerment, and makes the concept of 'failure' irrelevant. The process is non-competitive, because each learner's experience and learning is different from any other's (Challis 1993, 6).

Through empowerment individuals or groups acquire power to act upon and change their lives by viewing lives, experiences and learning from both a critical and reflexive perspective. APEL provides learners with such a forum. Lönnheden argues that in Sweden increasing the self-confidence of the learner "could lead to people getting more engaged and interested in democracy and civil movements" (Lönnheden 1999, 155) but warns that "if the methods are not applied to all students there is the risk that the outcome will be individualistic" (Lönnheden 1999, 155).

In our European study we were interested in who was accessing APEL as a form of learning in terms of age, gender, ethnicity and class but only a minority of the institutions we surveyed were able to provide this information. We suspect that the nature of the learning process, that is, making public personal experience, may be more appealing to women than men but we were unable to explore whether or not APEL is a gendered way of learning. However, we were able to ascertain which subject areas are most likely to offer APEL procedures. The picture is an imbalanced one. The social sciences and humanities offer the most opportunities for APEL procedures with less availability in the sciences and vocational areas which hints at a possible gender bias.

APEL as a Form of Mobility?

Mobility in relation to APEL could be looked at in two ways: individual social mobility and student or employee mobility across Europe. APEL offers a learner-friendly route back into education for those without formal qualifications, enabling those who wish to progress through further and higher education. For women in particular who have spent a period of time at home child-bearing APEL provides an opportunity to get back into learning and subsequently the labour market at a higher level than previously. APEL also offers an opportunity for career mobility for groups such as nurses who may choose to do a degree to purposefully move up the career structure. In Sweden, for example, it is possible to apply to university after four years of any type of work experience although an aptitude test is also required.

The practice and policy of APEL is not uniform across Europe. Countries are at different stages of development, employing different strategies and structures. APEL practices are bound by cultural contexts reflecting the diversity of post-compulsory education systems in Europe. The language spoken is not the same. A common language, but which also recognises cultural contexts, would enable adult learners to access, more easily, further and higher education in other countries. Although most adult learners are not geographically mobile because of family ties some groups such as refugees could benefit from a common policy and practice framework across Europe.

Looking forward

This article has attempted to briefly raise some issues and questions relating to the role of APEL in connection with language, mobility and a learner's biography. We recognise that this is very much a preliminary exploration, a starting point for looking at the conceptual and theoretical issues which surround APEL as a process of both access and learning for adults without traditional qualifications. These issues require further thinking and development. Literature on APEL is largely practice based, often including guidelines and models of good practice for practitioners and institutions. While this material is useful it is time to examine APEL in a more theoretical and critical way. APEL in recognising the importance of informal learning as a learning tool has challenged traditional notions of what counts as knowledge and learning experience. Getting this voice heard has been easier in some institutions (further education, vocational education) than others (traditional universities) and in some European countries (UK, France) than others (Spain, Belgium). Adult educators have argued for a long time that learning and experience are linked and, therefore, for the need for learning to begin with the language and experience of the learner. APEL also reverses the normal practice in formal learning situations in which learning is institutional and provision led as APEL places the learner at the centre of the learning process.

There is a need both within and across European countries for a more common language to ensure that those adult learners who could benefit the most from APEL are not deterred by the use of institutional and academic language. APEL is expensive in terms of staff time: It does not sit easily alongside the move towards marketisation in education. However, widening participation for non-traditional adult learners is important for ensuring social inclusion as widening participation is about providing greater social justice and equality in educational opportunities, not about putting on profitable courses. The survey in our European study indicated that there is a lot of enthusiasm amongst tutors for APEL and it is from this group of practitioners, who by sharing examples of good practices, are maintaining and encouraging the growth in APEL policy and practice. These practitioners recognise the value of informal learning in the learning process of adults.

References

Accreditation of Prior Learning. Briefing for Higher Education (1996). Cheltenham.

Alheit, P. (1995). Biographical Learning. Theoretical Outline, Challenges and Contradictions of a New Approach in Adult Education. In: Alheit, P. et al.: *The Biographical Approach In European Adult Education.* Wien.

Antikainen, A. et al. (1996). *Living in a Learning Society.* London.

Bailie, S., O'Hagan, C. (1999). Accrediting Prior Experiential Learning in Higher Education. Bridging the Gap between Formal and Informal Learning. In: *Assessment of Prior Experiential Learning as a Key to Lifelong Learning.* Conference Proceedings. Bremen.

Bond, M., Merrill, B. (1999). Advertising, Information and Recruitment to Return-to-Learning in Six European Countries. In: *Journal of Access and Credit Studies,* 1 (2).

Brookfield, S. (1983). *Adult Learners, Adult Education and the Community.* Milton Keynes.

Castells, M. (1996). *The Rise of the Network Society.* Oxford.

Challis, M. (1993). *Introducing APEL.* London.

Cross, K. P. (1981). *Adults as Learners.* San Francisco.

Evans, N. (1990). Pragmatism at Work in Britain. Some Reflections on Attempting to Introduce the Assessment of Prior Experiential Learning. In: *Studies in Continuing Education,* 12 (2), pp. 122-130.

Evans, N. (1994). *Experiential Learning for All.* London.

Fraser, W. (1995). *Learning from Experience. Empowerment or Incorporation?* Leicester.

Georgious, S. (1999). APEL in Europe - New Challenges. In: *Assessment of Prior Experiential Learning as a Key to Lifelong Learning.* Conference Proceedings. Bremen.

Giddens, A. (1991). *Modernity and Self-Identity. Self and Society in the Late Modern Age.* Cambridge.

Gore, J. (1993). *The Struggle for Pedagogies.* London.

Hill, S. (1999). Preliminary Indications from the Quantitative Evidence in the APEL Database. In: *Assessment of Prior Experiential Learning as a Key to Lifelong Learning.* Conference Proceedings. Bremen.

Hutchings, P., Wutzdorff, A. (1988). *Knowing and Doing. Learning through Experience.* San Francisco.

Knowles, M. (1990). *The Adult Learner. The Neglected Species.* Chicago.

Lönnheden, Ch. (1999). The Assessment of Prior Experiential Learning in Sweden. In: *Assessment of Prior Experiential Learning as a Key to Lifelong Learning.* Conference Proceedings. Bremen.

McGivney, V. (1990). *Education's for other people. Access to Education for Non-Participant Adults.* Leicester.

Merrill, B., Hill, S. (1998). APEL, Access and Learning. A UK Perspective. In: *DIE Zeitschrift für Erwachsenenbildung,* 5 (4), pp. 21-23.

Merrill, B., Hill, S. (1999). *Lifelong Learning through APEL. A UK Perspective.* 2nd Bremen Lifelong Learning Conference, February 1999 (not published conference proceedings).

Mezirow, J. (1981). A Critical Theory of Adult Learning and Education. In: *Adult Education,* 32, pp. 3-24.

Nyatanga, L., Forman, D., Fox, J. (1998). *Good Practice in the Accreditation of Prior Learning.* London.

Storan, J. (1988). *Making Experience Count.* London.

Thompson, J. (1997). *Words in Edgeways. Radical Learning for Social Change.* Leicester.

BRON, A., SCHEMMANN, M. (eds.) (2000). LANGUAGE, MOBILITY, IDENTITY. CONTEMPORARY ISSUES FOR ADULT EDUCATION IN EUROPE. MÜNSTER, pp. 99-110.

Tanja Možina / Branka Petek

ADULT EDUCATION AND SOCIO-POLITICAL CHANGES
THE CASE OF SLOVENIA

Introduction

We live in a period of intensive changes which affect us in every area of social life. They manifest themselves in the opening of the national borders, which further on launch various integration processes and mobility flows. All this brings changes to every individual's life and work. Simultaneously, establishing new relations is being required in the social community, as it triggers various confrontations imposing co-habitation of various cultures, nations and identities.

We will present the case of Slovenia, taking into consideration a broader socio-political context, challenges and issues which the young Slovenian country has been facing and will analyse the influence of those changes in the field of adult education. We are interested in the ways adult education responds to the new socio-political happenings in Slovenia and in what role adult education plays.

After the short presentation of the changes which have been experienced in the last decade in Slovenia, we will pay special attention to the contents and curriculum in the field of adult education and the positioning of it in broader socio-political and socio-cultural manifestations in Slovenia and the Europe. In spite of the rather general and broad topic, we will present the manifestations in the field of adult education in an illustrative way on a limited segment of adult education which has been consolidated in Slovenia during the last ten years. This is the education of adults in the field of foreign languages.

Integration Processes *versus* Preservation of National Sovereignty

Slovenia is a small country with a little less than two million inhabitants on the approximately 20.000 square kilometres of surface. It is one of the youngest states as it gained its independence only in 1991, when more than 90% of the citizens opted for the separation from Yugoslavia.

Within the last ten years Slovenia witnessed an intensive process of getting independent and establishing an independent state, moving gradually from a merely economic association towards a broader cultural and political space (Kek 1999).

The phenomenon of globalisation has probably been the most important among the changes undergone by many societies throughout the world. Globalisation surpasses merely the economic domain and captures an important part of our everyday life. That is why there is the fear of gradually loosing one's identity and sinking into the big formless sea of unified and simplified samples in every possible field. National cultures can as well as national economics and frontiers melt under the inevitable influences of the globalisation flows (Bajuk 1997, 14).

This kind of apprehension is even more present in a small country like Slovenia. This is one of the reasons why in the last years we have been witnessing more and more often the debates and the questioning of two parallels issues. On the one hand we have the issue of national identity, preservation of a nation's distinct characteristics and its uniqueness and on the other hand we have the issue of surviving as a small country when becoming part of international integration in general and the European Union in particular. The endeavours which we lately noticed in view to establish the conditions, necessary for us to be accepted in the European Union, have split up Slovenian political circles, Slovenian intellectuals and also Slovenian broader public to a certain extent.

On the political side the greatest fear is undoubtedly the possibility of loosing our sovereignty. This fact is very important for small countries, even more so for Slovenia which has only recently gained her independence. A fully entitled membership means transferring a part of sovereignty to the agencies of the European Union.

At the same time a suitable competence is being required from those who are going to work in various international agencies. This means in particular the skills of democratic dialogue, social participation, defending one's interests and needs, taking into consideration the rights of others, taking over the responsibilities for one's work etc. Thus, there is an opportunity for learning by joining the EU.

The apprehension here is being justified, considering the fact that Slovenia has only recently freed itself from the authoritarian communist government. Setting up the democratic grounds of the new country does not automatically mean that the citizens are able, skilled and motivated for participating in building up both a national and global social community. There is one characteristic in particular which was spotted for several years in all the countries in transition which is quite the opposite; the residents of the countries in transition have not really been taking part as they could in making political decision, in spite of formal and legal democratisation of society and new possibilities of cooperation. They do not make use of the new opportunities; instead they take a very passive and distrustful attitude to political structures and policy making at the national level. It became more and more evident that merely the change of the political system and the introduction of democratic relations in society do not automatically establish the democratisation of society and form civil society (Kontiainen, Manninen 1997; Jelenc 1997).

For the particular case of Slovenia this trend of changing between two poles can be observed as well particularly in the last two years.

- On the one hand we observe a need for strengthening the national identity which can be described as looking for and preserving the distinctive nation properties and place them along the authentic properties of other nations (regardless their size or impact);
- On the other hand it becomes more and more obvious that for the survival's sake the need to open the borders of a small country is imperative in the contemporary society of the capital and sophisticated information technologies. It cannot survive if it is not integrated in a broader community.

Changes in Education – Global and Regional Dimension

The aimed at membership in the European Union and the necessary integration process urge us to the regional division in education because this is how other countries within the European Union operate. This regional division and thus transferring the responsibility to them, will make us compatible with others and able to cope within European capital exchange, labour force and educational services at the regional level. However, we still have not resolved several basic issues about regional division and about the transfer of competence and responsibility from the national structures to the regional ones. In the area of education the Cupertino started at the regional level, within some international projects, such as Phare and Mocca, in particular in the area of vocational and professional training.

In the past Slovenian education was rather centralised. The educational reform and new educational legislation introduced new dimensions to the relation between the state and educational institutions. The processes of de-centralisation have been closely related to the processes of regional division, transferring the responsibility for planning of the education and organising various educational forms to every particular region. It also offers more autonomy and professional responsibility to the educators.

One of the basic principles of the educational reform is, that the newly developed curriculum should be comparable to at least three curricula from other countries. On the other hand, however, curricula should also pay attention to regional and local characteristics of the country and take them into consideration.

Generally, non-formal and cultural education at the regional level and the level of local communities has successfully developed for these last years, among others also with the introduction of study circles, as non-formal and democratic form of adult education.

Education is one of the areas in Slovenian political and social life which has been undergoing the biggest changes for the last five years. At the national level an intensive curriculum reform is going on, embracing all the areas of education including adult education.

The discussion about the need to reform the educational system started with Slovenia gaining independence and lasted until 1996, when several basic laws in the field of education have been ratified: *The Act of Higher Education* (1993), *The Act of Financing and Administration of Education, The Act of Nursery Schools, The Act of Elementary School, The Act of Secondary Schools, The Act of Vocational and Professional Training, The Act of Adult Education* (all in 1996). The goal of the reform was to establish a system of education, being adjusted to the national economy needs, compatible to educational systems in the European Union and at the same time preserving a high quality level.

The New Role and Tasks of Adult Education

Slovenia excels in a long adult education tradition. Since the second half of the nineteenth century up to World War II there was a strong emphasis on general and cultural educational activities and on the popular movements. The socialist society after World War II brought in another emphasis – the development of workers' education (workers' universities), vocational and professional training in the working organisations (educational centres), as well as literacy.

Adult educators were advocating a sufficient state support for adult education and its equal status in relation to the education of children. Already during the time of rigid and non-democratic social structures adult educators tried to achieve more open forms of education with the aim of stimulating the preservation of cultural identity and raising the level of general instructions.

Socio-political changes which Slovenia went through for the last decade, had an influence on the area of adult education as well. In 1991 the government of the Republic of Slovenia established the Slovenian Institute of Adult Education. Its basic mission is to develop the culture of lifelong learning and adult education in Slovenia. The other important turning point is certainly the ratification of the first National Programme for Adult Education which is being expected in the Parliament by the end of 1999. It will acknowledge the growing role and importance of adult education in the rapidly changing world.

In the part that follows we will present a concrete case of learning and teaching adults in Slovenia. What is more, we will also examine the way in which broader socio-political and socio-cultural factors are reflecting the contents and forms of the curriculum and how the forms and contents themselves can influence the social community and its democratisation.

Teaching Foreign Languages

In the introduction we pointed out the intensive changes which the opening of the national borders caused, implying economic but more and more cultural aspects. Cultures of various nations are being confronted. Language is one of the essential constituent elements of a nation's identity and its culture. Only in the special perspective of the mother tongue all the cultural, geographical, symbolic and social constituents of the historical national experience become obvious (Trim 1997, Debeljak 1997).

Teaching and learning of foreign languages have been promoted in an efficient and useful way due to the following reasons:

- the need, that as many people as possible should speak a foreign language in their profession (information role of foreign languages in education),
- the necessity to use a foreign language in everyday life (the usefulness of foreign languages for everyday life),
- the desire and need to know nearby and faraway cultures (cultural aspect of learning foreign languages),
- the part of the awareness of foreign languages and acquaintance with different cultures, embracing the personal growth of every individual (formative aspect),
- concluding and developing international connections with the help of the language and cultural contacts (economic and political aspect),
- ensuring the conditions for a peaceful coexistence of people (social aspect of development) (Čok 1999).

Not knowing the languages is the biggest communication impediment of all. Knowing languages of the member countries of the European Union, give power to communication and the defence of one's own interests in decision making bodies.

The European Union has been supporting the learning of foreign languages with various programmes of its own. One of them is LINGUA, meant for the encouragement and motivation for the study of the foreign languages. LINGUA includes all the official languages of the European Union and the official language of Ireland, Liechtenstein, Island and Norway which exceed the frame of the Union. Special attention is being paid to the least spread and taught languages.

In the last years a common set of foreign language assessment instruments has been launched – the Language Portfolio which has been, together with the Common European Framework of References, the result of previous projects of the Council of Europe in the field of language teaching and learning. One of the essential objectives among others strongly emphasised both self-instruction of languages and self-assessment of learning achievements (Razdevšek-Pučko 1999, Trim 1997). In Europe there have been growing tendencies for encouraging language learning, with a special purpose: dismissing the language barriers, promoting the mobility of people in the field of study and work, encouraging the multicultural learning and learning about distinctive European cultures.

While accepting the language as one of the essential elements of building cultural identity there are new issues arising in Slovenia, about what will happen to the Slovenian language once we enter the European Union. The worst 'scenarios' preview a complete disappearing of the Slovenian language and the adoption of both the languages and cultures of other stronger and bigger nations and thus finally loosing the own identity. Those with the optimistic view try to find positive ways in order to make the population aware of the importance of the mother tongue preservation and with it the preservation of the nation's culture. These scenarios thus emphasise the importance of the opening process to the world but also the preserving of the distinctive properties of a nation.

It is important to take into consideration, while developing the language courses, that teaching and learning should always include the social and cultural dimensions as well. We can therefore consider this kind of language teaching as a part of education for civil society and as a form of multicultural lifelong learning, which is one of the basic claims the current society imposes on us (Starkley 1997).

Objectives for Language Learning of Adults

For many years language learning has been one of the liveliest activities in Slovenia in the field of adult education. In the past this kind of education has been highly developed within the so called Workers' Universities. Many private institutions which have emerged lately, have noticeably enriched the provision in the field of language learning.

It is hard to assess the exact number of the current courses, as the statistical data have not been properly dealt with at the national level for the last couple of years. Explicit data about the situation in this field is provided by the analysis of the courses offered in 1992-1995, published in the review of adult education provision (SAEC 1995/96). It shows, that language learning prevails among all the other general, non-formal and out of school courses (nearly 90%).

Among changes brought into language teaching courses by recent curriculum reform, we would like to present those which influenced the socio-political changes in particular. The essential objectives of the renewed English language curriculum are as follows:

- The course participants should be trained for mutual and cross-cultural language communication while using the English language,
- The participants should be better trained for better knowledge of the social and cultural background of language use and learn about various cultures, connected to the English language,
- The participants should extend their language skills and pragmatic rules of the English language and at the same time they develop a positive attitude to the mother-tongue,
- Dealing with a wide range of texts, also literary, the participants should try to understand both the similarities and the distinctions of their own and other cultures. Thus, they develop the capacity for cross-cultural communication and critical attitude to some foreign texts and cultural phenomena, enriching their own (*Angleščina za odrasle* 1999).

Based on the pre-set curriculum objectives for English, and taking into consideration a broader socio-cultural context, in which and for which such a curriculum is being implemented, we can consider the learning of foreign languages for adults as **multicultural learning**.

The institutional side of the language teaching before 1991 was almost exclusively organised by Workers' Universities. As there was one in each large town and two in Ljubljana we could hardly speak about competition. After 1991 a lot of new private language schools were founded and the competition began. The two most visible effects of the competition were the rise of quality and the confusion caused among potential learners. As people had to communicate in foreign languages there was an increasing number of courses available on the market. Promises given by some schools about learning languages in a very short time with little effort were opposed by the traditional system bringing students from beginners to the examinations in five or six terms. Some people had to try several language schools before they found a suitable system.

The quality of language courses is, naturally, subject to great variations. With keen competition on the market, the demand for quality is bigger than ever. New methods are introduced (like direct methods, suggestopedia, communicative method etc.) in order to meet the needs of an average adult student. The freshly introduced methods enriched the old grammar-translation method which was still present in the 1980s. Nowadays the most successful schools base their work on a blend of old and modern methods which provide liveliness and variation.

Changes in the Slovenian political system made Slovenia an attractive place for the so called native speakers. They were mostly young people (native speakers of English or any other language) who travelled to foreign countries and wanted to earn some money by teaching their native language. The majority of them had no education and very little or no experience in the field of foreign language teaching. At the beginning of the 1990s they were widely employed by some schools in order to make them more attractive for potential clients. Nowadays the position has changed. Native speakers are employed often by almost all language schools provided they have a suitable education and at least some experience. However the decisions of students seem to confirm the opinion of some experts who think that only a teacher who speaks the student's mother tongue can be an effective teacher of a foreign language – especially at lower stages (Phillipson 1992).

The Practical Side of Language Teaching

The choice of languages which people preferably learn has been constantly changing since World War II. After the War Russian and English were popular and French was considered as the language of the political and social elite. The historical events caused that German and Italian were less asked for. In the 1970s and 1980s the situation began to change. Slovenia established a lot of political and economic relations with Italy, Austria and Germany. Consequently more and more people learned Italian and German. German used to be the most frequently learned foreign language by adult students around 1990, but nowadays half of the adult students are learning English. The Russian market has been recently opened to foreign companies and a lot of Slovenian business people travel there to do business with the countries of the former Soviet Union. Other languages (like French,

Spanish, Portuguese, Dutch, Hungarian, Arab, Chinese, Japanese etc.) represent a very small part of the whole spectrum of foreign language teaching.

The choice of materials (textbooks, workbooks, video and audio materials etc.) used in a language course is a crucial problem for the efficiency of course. We can follow several trends concerning materials.

- First there were books using the grammar-translation method, made particular for the public, using cheap materials, i.e. texts written by non-native speakers for the classroom use only and grammatical exercises.

- Second there are textbooks made for the large international public and not aiming at any particular group. They use relatively expensive and more attractive materials (authentic texts, games, pictures, photographs, cartoons).

- Third there are a few textbooks published under the influence of the new trend promoted by the European Community (Van Ek 1991).

In Slovenian adult education we successfully moved on from the first stage of grammar-translation method textbooks, which were mostly printed in the former Yugoslavia. They were definitely stopped being used after 1991 and we started using the second type of books which are mostly prepared by native speakers. They avoid any parallels with other cultures for purely economic reasons as they are meant to be sold globally. They are still widely used as there are only few books of the third type that have been published in Slovenia. However the new programmes for adult language teaching are undoubtedly a step towards intercultural learning.

Conclusion

The intention of this contribution was to offer a general view of the changes which have been going on in the field of adult education in Slovenia for the last years. We wanted to expose what has been going on in the context of socio-political and socio-cultural changes in Slovenia since its emancipation. These changes have been strongly influencing all the fields of the social and the everyday life. In times of this delicate stretching between global (European and world-wide) and national (regional and local) flows which the young Slovenian country has to face the active role of adult education is particularly shown in the following:

Adult education offers methods and contents to prepare the population for entering the broader social community and to take an active part in a creative and competitive way. It facilitates the knowledge acquisition and develops the capacities which are needed for the Slovenian population for confronting the European and world-wide economic markets.

Socio-political changes resulted in a different vision of foreign language learning for adults in Slovenia. From a subject reserved for the political, scientific and economic elite it turned into a basic need of every European citizen who wants to participate in processes of global scientific, economic and cultural development and democratisation. The long tradition of language learning helped to change the traditional concept of language learning into a modern intercultural concept providing the basis for a better communicative ability and life-long individual learning.

References

Andragoški center Republike Slovenije; 5 let (1996). Ljubljana.

Angleščina za odrasle. Izobraževalni program (1999). Ljubljana.

Bajuk, A. (1997). Slovenija v evropskih integracijskih procesih. In: *Nova Revija*, let. XVI, oktober, pp. 256-272.

Bučar, F. (1997). Ogroženost nacionalne istovetnosti. In: *Nova Revija*, let. XVI, januar/februar, pp. 1-7.

Čok, L., Skela, J., Razdevšek-Pučko, C. (1999). *Učenje in poučevanje tujega jezika.* Koper.

Emeršič, B. (1996). *Poročilo o izvajanju programa izobraževanje za demokracijo od študijskega leta 1994/95 do 1997/98.* Ljubljana.

Izpiti iz tujih jezikov v Sloveniji (1998). Ljubljana.

Jelenc, Z. (1997). Civic Education of Adults in the Former Socialist Countries in the Period of Transition. In: *European Integration and Active Citizenship.* Tallinn, pp. 7-12.

Jelenc, Z. (1998). *Vloga in razvoj andragoškega društva Slovenije v obdobju 1969-1991.* Ljubljana.

Kek, M. (1999). *Slovenija v evropski uniji?* Ljubljana.

Klemenčič, S. (1995). *Učimo se v študijskih krožkih.* Ljubljana.

Kontiainen, S., Manninen, J. (1997). Contribution of Adult Education in Relation to Problem Experience, Goals and Investment (a Comparative Analysis of Eurodelphi Data in Three European Countries). In: *European Integration and Active Citizenship.* Tallin, pp. 37-51.

Kroflič, R. (1998). Učno-ciljno in procesno-razvojno načrtovanje kurikula. In: *Kurikularna prenova (Zbornik).* Nacionalni kurikularni svet, Ljubljana, pp. 199-217.

Phillipson, R. (1992). *Linguistic Imperialism.* Oxford.

Svetličič, M. (1998). Slovenija, Evropska unija in globalizacija. In: *Teorija in praksa,* let. 35 (1), pp. 6-16.

Van Ek, J. A. (1991). *Objectives for Foreign Language Learning.* Strasbourg.

BRON, A., SCHEMMANN, M. (eds.) (2000). LANGUAGE, MOBILITY, IDENTITY. CONTEMPORARY ISSUES FOR ADULT EDUCATION IN EUROPE. MÜNSTER, pp. 111-118.

Janos Sz. Tóth

TRANSFORMATION OF ADULT EDUCATION IN HUNGARY
ORIENTATION TOWARDS THE EUROPEAN DIMENSION

Introduction

One of the characteristic features of adult education in Hungary is that there is only little information available concerning analyses and descriptions. In the past ten years research and data collection, if there was any in the field of adult education, was very weak. This is also indicated by the fact that the first national conference on adult education research after the transformation was held in 1999. Another reason is the change of the adult education system that took place in the conditions of the market economy. Today it is no longer possible to review the entire situation from a single perspective. The state controlled and monopolised the system in the past, but new and comprehensive structures that would perform the functions of information provision and analyses have not been established or consolidated yet. Due to the changes and diversity of adult education, no coordination taking into account the plurality of political or ideological aspects has developed between the various sectors of adult education such as non-formal, vocational oriented, private, state supported, non-profit, etc., which is the precondition of systematic data collection and its systematisation. When key organisations were requested for information, very few and modest answers were received, not only because this kind of cooperation is still quite cumbersome but also because the individual organisations themselves were not in possession of systematised data or comprehensive analyses of activities related to a subject. Consequently an analysis of the European dimension of adult education has to be done mainly from the institutional point of view.

The European Dimension in Hungarian Adult Education

To start off, the European dimension in Hungarian adult education can be described by the international networks and organisations the Hungarian institutions are involved in. A number of Hungarian adult education organisations including the Society for the Dissemination of Scientific Knowledge (TIT) and the Hungarian Folk High School Society (HFHSS)[1] are members of the European Association for the Education of Adults (EAEA). HFHSS established also bi-lateral contacts with EAEA's national member organisations.

The European Symposium on Voluntary Action (ESVA) is an international network of scientific researchers and experts who are interested in the sociological, pedagogical and politological questions of civil society. Its aim is to provide an international scope for the exchange and discussion of new ideas and research findings and publications. The ESVA network was transformed into an international foundation in 1992. Its head office is in The Netherlands, while its secretariat is in Budapest, and the members of the board come from Denmark, Poland, Finland and the United Kingdom.

With its conferences mainly held in Central and Eastern European countries, ESVA was able to exert powerful influence informally. This was first experienced in Moscow in 1991, where the meeting was held just two weeks after the attempted *coup d'état*. Although the streets and squares still bore the traces of barricades, the lectures and workshop discussions held at the conference gave encouragement and strength to people who had just been relieved of the nightmare. Members of the network and the representatives of organisations interested in its activities held annual meetings. The topics of these conferences centred around different ideas that constitute the corner stones of democracy, i.e. human rights, civil society and last but not least the traditions of voluntary activity in Europe.

Another forum of cooperation deserves mentioning here. The HFHSS and its sister organisations from several Central European and Balkan countries organised a series of seminars.

---

[1] Please note that Folk High School does not refer to the residential institutions of adult education in Scandinavia. People's colleges are also included here (Editor's footnote).

On several occasions the HFHSS acted as the host organisation. These meetings provided an opportunity for countries that shared the same fate to meet and hold discussions which were different from the dialogues conducted with Scandinavian and Western European countries. The conferences aimed at placing adult and public education on new foundations and at achieving a 'Euro-conformity' after the social, economic and political changes that took place. One of the striking similarities between all countries was the fact that in the conditions of market economy, adult education lost its former ideological control and along with it, its proportionately significant state support. The discussions also promoted a sense of competitiveness in the cooperation with organisations of EU member states on the one hand, and strengthened solidarity on the other hand through the exchange and discussion of experiences gained in Eastern-Western cooperation.

It would be extremely difficult to give a detailed account of all the activities conducted in the framework of international cooperation that have contributed to the modernisation of Hungarian adult education and to the strengthening of the European dimension.

After the fall of the Berlin Wall, a general rush started in the exchange of adult education experts, and at the beginning a number of western countries and their organisations received their Eastern European compatriots with great enthusiasm but often without well-considered programmes. In the early 1990s, Hungarian adult education organisations sometimes complained that the EU programmes were not well-designed and frequently aimed at solving the employment problems of western organisations. A good part of the budget of these programmes were used in the supporting countries. The programmes gave the impression that anything would be good for the people from the East, if only they gained access to some support. Later on these relations lost some of their spontaneity, the programmes were better organised and more professionally prepared, but at the same time enthusiasm and illusions started to diminish on both sides.

Institutions that served to promote the European integration processes and developments had been established in the meantime. These institutions were the following: Phare Democracy Program, Phare Partnership Program, and then additional adult education programmes such as Socrates, and Phare-Lien. Whereas programmes such as Tempus were serving the needs of the economy and were accessible to higher education institutions only, some of the new programmes were closely related to adult education like the ones aiming at the development of secondary level education for socially disadvantaged youth. While programmes became more professional and more bureaucratic, Hungarian professional organisations slowly became more prepared, better informed and trained for project applications. Hungarian higher education institutes set up centres for European Studies, mainly in the faculties of public administration, law and political sciences. Special training courses also called European Studies were introduced at the adult education departments of the Universities of Debrecen and Pécs and at the teachers' training college of Jászberény.

Cooperation with Scandinavia

As to exchange of experience, Hungarian educators representing the entire spectrum of the profession were enabled to conduct a continuous exchange of their knowledge and experience with their foreign colleagues on a wide range of issues from quality requirements in adult education and training to functional literacy. These professional relations centred around folk high schools on a reciprocal basis: on the one hand the aim was to learn about the objectives, contents and methods of European, mainly Scandinavian folk high schools, and about their role in society today. On the other hand our Swedish, Danish, Finnish, Dutch and British colleagues were interested in learning about the forms the Hungarian folk high school movement revived after the political changes had taken place. Especially useful experience was gained from Scandinavian folk high schools concerning community education and the flexible adaptation of institutions to changing economic and social requirements.

The efficiency of national level cooperation initiated by the Hungarian Folk High School Society was significantly enhanced by the fact that the exchange of experience was organised centrally. It was continued by the development of a multi-level cooperation between Hungarian and Scandinavian folk high schools. Hungarian folk high schools of small regions (for instance, Mezőföld Folk High School Society in Hantos, Győrffy István Folk High School Foundation in Szolnok and the Folk High School Association of the Budapest Region) developed relations with Danish, Swedish and Finnish folk high school institutions independently. An example of the new level of professional cooperation is shown by the Danish-Slovenian-Hungarian collaboration which is aiming at functional literacy and labour market re-integration of Gypsy communities of three regions in Hungary.

Thanks to these relations, the quarterly publication of the Hungarian Folk High School became a forum for international information exchange. Its successful operation is not only due to the fact that with the collaboration of the Finnish colleagues the HFHSS became a member of the European network of public and adult education periodicals and publishers but also to bilateral relations which provide accessible materials, guidelines, proposals and programmes from Brussels or Strasbourg.

Hungarian-German Cooperation

The German Adult Education Association significantly contributed to the development in the past ten years by being the only organisation that established comprehensive cooperation in the development of adult education in Hungary.

However, the cooperation between Hungarian and German professionals within adult education is not of a new date. In the 1970s, and particularly in the 1980s, there had been recurrent contacts between adult educators from Hungary and Germany, especially between representatives of the Society for the Dissemination of Scientific Knowledge (TIT) and the Hungarian Folk High School Society (HFHSS) and those of the German Adult Education Association (DVV). After the change of the political system in Hungary, this cooperation took an institutionalised form, leading to the opening of the Project Office of the Institut für Internationale Zusammenarbeit des Deutschen Volkshochschulverbandes (IIZ/DVV) in 1991. This made it possible to intensify the cooperation in times of great changes, when the partner organisations and adult education itself were undergoing a profound transformation and when there was a great demand for continuity in international contacts and exchanges of experience.

The agreement on cooperation and partnership in Europe signed in 1992 between the Federal Republic of Germany and the Republic of Hungary emphasised:

> The contracting parties recognise the particular importance of cooperation in the field of adult education. They particularly support the cooperation between the German Adult Education Association and Hungarian partner organisations (*Adult Education in ... 1997*).

Between 1991 and 1995 the cooperation began to focus on the themes of environmental and health education, vocational education and languages. The most important goals and types of work included counselling, initial and continuing training, publications and infrastructure support. The well proved system of partnership was carefully extended to the state, voluntary and university sectors of the adult education system.

The extension of the cooperation directly aimed at supporting state, university and voluntary sector partner organisations, their staff and programmes. It was focused on counselling, initial and in-service training of full-time and part-time staff, the development of teaching and learning materials, ongoing research and evaluation and hence on the overall direction to be taken in training. The project thus indirectly led all the participants in practical continuing education, in the partner organisations' local programmes and provision, especially in the fields of vocational education, agricultural, environmental and health education, foreign languages and cultural provision. It was also aimed at serving the particular needs of young people and women, the unemployed and disabled, in both urban and rural settings. The project therefore set out to work through multipliers.

It is difficult to sum up the various programmes conducted in the framework of German-Hungarian cooperation in the past ten years. Its significance lies in the fact that this was the only systematic project that was specifically aimed at the development of adult education, that broadened the possibilities of international cooperation. From a professional point of view it was a new element that promoted the development of the training of higher level adult education experts and gave inspiration for strengthening initiatives in adult education research and quality assurance. IZZ/DVV played an important role in producing professional adult education publications and in translating important international professional materials.

Future Prospects

The past ten years are unprecedented and irreproducible in history. National isolation was transformed into international openness in the course of processes characterised by the general strengthening of globalisation. Both the European Union and Hungary were initially unprepared for this change. The state of euphoria was followed by disillusionment and sobering. At the same time these processes were dictated by economic and political changes as a form of pressure coming from above and outside. Consequently, an imbalance was created in the healthy proportion between the local, national and international dimensions. The establishment of a general and complex system of requirements, which was the precondition of the changes in adult education could not have been achieved without the fundamental transformation of the macro-economic, political and legal frameworks. Hungarian adult education has overcome this critical point. The fashionable slogan of Europeanness was initially taken with submissive acceptance, which later changed into condemnation and intellectual resistance as a form of counter-reaction. However, cooperation pointing in the direction of real partnership and equality, the placement of national values in the foreground and their recognition as international values strengthened the partnership quality and professional feature of cooperation. The times of change and reform are an opportunity to intensify local and national features by enriching them with the European dimension directly. Hungarian adult education did not only follow and suffer from these changes, it could act as a partner being able to learn and take the initiative. Nevertheless, there is a lot to be done in Hungarian adult education in this new situation:

- the development and improvement of the skills of foreign language,
- the extension of knowledge, preservation and representation of local and national values,
- the development of capacities and techniques of international and European cooperation, the training and further training of adult education experts capable of international cooperation.

The development of an identity containing local, national and European features is the task of the decade to come. This process will have its negative and positive elements: the global society of our times is a "risk society"; however, it could also become a "rainbow society". Adult education has a role in influencing the outcome.

References

Adult Education in Hungary and Perspectives for Co-operation up to the Year 2000 (1997). Reports, Planning and Suggestions by IZZ/DVV, Budapest.

Assistance to Transition Survey (1995). New York.

Cox, A., Koning, A. (1997). *Understanding European Community Aid. Aid Policies, Management and Distribution Explained.* Brussels.

Harangi, L. (ed.) (1993). *Európai Látószögben. A HFHSS nemzetközi programjai 1989-1994* (In a European Perspective. International Programmes of HFHSS, 1989-1994). Budapest.

Jelentés a magyar közoktatásról 1997 (Report on Hungarian Public Education) (1998). Budapest.

Karácsony, A. (ed.) (1999). *A HFHSS nemzetközi kapcsolatai 1994-1999* (The International Relations of HFHSS). Manuscript, Budapest.

Training in the Market Economy. Challenges and Answers (1997). Budapest.

PART IV

LANGUAGE AND EUROPEAN DIMENSION

BRON, A., SCHEMMANN, M. (eds.) (2000). LANGUAGE, MOBILITY, IDENTITY. CONTEMPORARY ISSUES FOR ADULT EDUCATION IN EUROPE. MÜNSTER, pp. 121-140.

Michael Schemmann

LANGUAGE POLICY AND LANGUAGE LEARNING IN AND FOR EUROPE

Introduction

After more than 50 years of peace within Europe, efforts surrounding the European integration process are being discussed more controversially than ever. The advantages of European integration have been stressed in many research documents, and especially in literature produced by the European institutions themselves. The most striking advantages are generally noted to include the longevity of peace within the European Union member states, the establishment of an economic unit rivalling the U.S. and Japan, and the furthering of democratic culture through the integration of member states such as Spain and Portugal. However, despite such advantages, the integration process has increasingly received criticism by those people who perceive its overall development as lacking in democracy.

One area within the integration process which deserves further discussion and policy direction is that of language.

There are few other topics of more importance for both an improvement of the integration process and the future development of Europe than language. Not only do we read about the costs that are caused by the different languages spoken in the European Parliament or within commerce and economy, but also as European citizens we experience the difficulties of communication with other European citizens in everyday life, e.g. when travelling. For example, the European Union made it a strict rule that every Member Country's language is a working language, i.e. that all documents produced within the Union's institutions must be published in every Member Country's language. This rule, of course, necessitates an immense administrative body that consists mostly of interpreters. At the moment there are 11 languages within the Union. Considering bilateral communication and contacts that opens up 110 different combinations of languages. What is more, if the Union extends in the planned way, the number of official languages could increase to 30. This will mean 870 possible combinations (Schröder 1994, 151).

Obviously then, language is a key consideration for a Europe that is meant to grow together as one. Language is also key to the notion of a European citizenship and to European citizens' identification with the Europe in which they live. In this last sense, it is not possible to restrict this question to a single concept of Europe; i.e. it does not matter if we talk about the European Union, the Christian West, or the European continent.

The general question that needs to be asked is what language policy should be employed in Europe to support a process of integration instead of disintegration. The almost paradoxical situation that we are facing on the eve of the millennium is that even though the process of globalisation makes it possible, and in some situations even forces us, to communicate with everyone in the world and to know about everything happening in the world, people tend to refer back to their very localised surroundings – a process which Menzel describes in his study 'Globalisierung versus Fragmentarisierung' (Menzel 1998) and which Robertson sums up with the keyword 'Glocalisation' (Robertson 1998, Beck 1998).

This trend can be seen in language learning as well; even though there seems to be a language of globalisation, i.e. English, this language is not necessarily accepted as the leading foreign language in the world. Instead, in some countries certain regional and local languages have become increasingly more important and popular as a way of stressing local identity.

This article will discuss the issue of language learning and language policy for the European context in different steps.

First, an analysis of the state-of-the art in terms of language learning in Europe will attempt to identify a general trend regarding which languages are spoken by the largest number of people, and therefore, which languages can be expected to take a leading role in Europe or even become a *lingua franca*. Explicit references to current school statistics will also help develop an idea about future development. Secondly, this article will explore the necessities of a clear-cut language policy. By employing one example from academia, it will be made clear that the English language is predominant, with the possible consequence that those researchers who do not speak English might be excluded.

In a third step my analysis will examine the language policy of the European Union and will concentrate both on running programmes and on strategic papers and policy statements. Before concluding, the initiatives of the Council of Europe will be examined critically in a last step. The main goal of this last analysis is to question whether the language policy of the Council of Europe really supports the European integration process.

Language Learning Statistics

To start off it seems quite important to point out that this article is not concerned with the first language, or 'the mother tongue'. Within Europe, and especially in the European Union, there is a general consensus that national languages should be respected. Every citizen of Europe has and will always have a mother tongue. What is discussed in this context is the issue of the first foreign language. In order to make it possible for all Europeans to communicate with each other, a utopian vision would have all Europeans learning the same first foreign language so that there is a kind of *lingua franca*. Even though there are no regulations or agreements in that direction, a general trend can be seen within Europe; this trend currently points to English as the dominant foreign language.

The reasons for this can be traced back to the years after World War II. Hagège sees the foundations of the predominance of the English language in the period from 1945 to 1960. During these years, the English language closed the gap in Europe left by the German language as the language of war crime and horror, by the Russian language as a language of stagnation and political oppression, and by the French language as the language of the country that was busy dealing with the shock of the years of war and colonial wars still to come (Hagège 1996). Once established in this leading position, further aspects contributed to its outstanding position; one example is the fact that commerce and business are dominated by the English language. In recent years the World Wide Web has continued to strengthen the position of the English language and its global, and consequently, European influence. More and more, English has been acknowledged and accepted as the language of modern communication.

This trend is also confirmed when examining statistics about language learning in schools. In 1997 the European Commission presented a report giving key data about the educational systems within the European Union, and also including neighbouring countries which are members of the EURIDYCE network. The data from that report suggested that the fundaments for the predominance of English are certainly laid in schools, i.e. in lower secondary schooling, since that is the phase during which foreign language teaching generally starts, even though there are some examples of national policies already introducing the first foreign language at the primary school level. When taking a look at this data, one also gets an idea of what the dominating language will be at the beginning of the next millennium, since it is the students of today who will be the adults of the future.

In the years 1994 and 1995, about 89% of all pupils in secondary schools in the European Union were taught English. By comparison, 32% were taught French, 18% German and 8% Spanish (Europäische Kommission 1997, 74; see table 1). What is more, this trend is not just a European Union phenomenon, but also holds for the Central and Eastern European states as well as for Iceland and Norway. In many countries, more than 90% of the students are taught English as the first foreign language.

Table 1: Languages Studied by European Students by Percentage

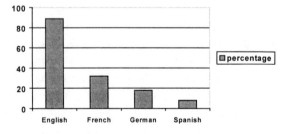

(Europäische Kommission 1997, 74)

Taking a closer and more differentiated look at the data gives us a more detailed picture of current language trends in Europe. For example, Belgium and Italy rank at the bottom of the scale as far as learning English is concerned, followed by Luxembourg and Portugal (between 60 and 76%).

The reasons for Belgium's low percentage are rather obvious, since Belgium is a bilingual country with one part of the population learning the language of the other part first, and vice versa. This is also reflected in the fact that among the Dutch-speaking Belgian pupils in secondary schools, about 98% learn French (Europäische Kommission 1997, 74).

However, to find explanations for the Italian results is very difficult, especially since Italians are neither outstanding in learning French, nor in any other foreign language given in the statistics. According to the statistics, Italy seems to have the least developed language learning and teaching policies in Europe.

Conversely, Luxembourg's performance in terms of language learning is certainly outstanding. Whereas Luxembourg's students fall below the European average as far as learning English is concerned, in terms of learning both French and German, they are at the top, with 98% for both languages (Europäische Kommission 1997, 74-75).

As far as the German language is concerned, according to the data used it is the third most popular language in Europe in terms of the number of foreign students studying it while French is second. It is mainly the neighbouring countries of Germany and the Scandinavian countries which exceed the European average of 18%. The explanation for this is partly an economic one. The most striking current example is tourism. Denmark and the Netherlands are both very popular holiday destinations for Germans, and in some regions tourism is the leading branch of the economic structure. The reasons for the popularity of German in the Eastern European countries, however, are to be found in the long history of German influence and dominance of the Eastern European countries.[1] An exception to this trend is Romania. Here German is of less importance, but French – with close to 80% – is even more popular than English. This certainly has to do with the fact that both French and Romanian belong to the Romance languages, and therefore are similar to each other and easier to learn once one has the basis upon which to learn the other. However, it must be stated that due to the dominance of the former Soviet Union in the Warsaw Pact states in these countries, the Russian language had the status of a *lingua franca* for quite a while.

---

[1] A detailed analysis reflecting on the relationships between the various Slavic languages and German is provided by Hagège (1996). For further prospects of the German language see Wolf (1999).

In Luxembourg a higher percentage than the European average results from the fact that it is obligatory for every pupil to learn German.

As far as Spanish is concerned, it is only in France that the Spanish language is of any significance; more than 30% of pupils learn Spanish in French secondary schools. This means that more French pupils are taught Spanish than German. This can be explained by the fact that both languages also belong to the same family, namely the Romance languages. Furthermore, it is again Luxembourg that lies above the European average in terms of learning the Spanish language (Europäische Kommission 1997, 75). This again supports the thesis that Luxembourg has one of Europe's most developed language learning policies.

To sum up the results of the analysis, the following points can be stated:

- It is obvious that the English language plays a predominant role as the first foreign language. What is more, it can be predicted that English will likely keep, or even extend, this position in Europe.

- The Member Countries of the European Union are split as far as the learning of French and German is concerned. The Central, Eastern and Northern European countries favour German, while the Southern countries favour French. Additionally, in some countries – for example, Romania – French is still of more importance than English.

- Spanish plays only a marginal role in the European language learning context; only in France it is of some significance.

All in all it seems that the various European countries have adopted language learning policies that put English in a prominent position. However, the presented results do not give any evidence of the quality of the English taught or spoken nor of the density. Besides that, there is also a lack of data concerning the language learning of adults. Additional research is necessary to provide more valid information about how the English language is spoken in Europe.

Foreign Languages in European Sciences and Academia

The predominance of English as the language of communication is also supported by employing an example from academia. However, it is a little more difficult to find clear trends which can be generalised; the whole issue has to be seen from a more differentiated perspective. That said, it can nevertheless be stated that English is the leading language in the sciences and social sciences.

Whereas German seemed to be the leading scientific language at the beginning of the twentieth century – especially in prestigious fields of research like medicine, physics, and chemistry, but also in fields like philosophy and psychology – German has been replaced by the English language. This is a consequence of the fact that it is mainly American universities and the scientists working there (who are not necessarily American) who dominate the scientific arena, who perform research successfully, and who publish their results in English.

From the perspective of a German researcher or student, the use of certain languages varies depending on the discipline. In psychology, for example, it seems that there is no way around the English language both for students of psychology who have to read articles and books written in English, as well as for researchers who must publish in order to be recognised by the scientific community. A similar trend can be stated for disciplines like medicine, geography, economics, and the social sciences.

However, looking at the study and research of adult education, the situation is less directed. As a German researcher in adult education, it is possible to have a university career in Germany without actually publishing in English. In fact, the German adult education scene seems to be quite self-referential. Additionally, most of the literature in the fields of sociology, political science, economics, and philosophy is translated into German. Since the market is quite large, it pays to make such an investment.

The actual consequences of not having to publish in a foreign language – and as such, not using the foreign language – can best be illustrated with an example from the European Society for Research on the Education of Adults. ESREA was founded in December 1991 and addresses all persons who are involved in adult education research (Hake 1992, Hake 1997). The particular situation of ESREA is that it initiates research projects involving researchers across Europe on European issues of adult education. Consequently, the language question is always at the centre of ESREA's work, in research, publications and conferences.

With more than 350 members from all regions of Europe, ESREA cannot help but struggle with the issue of language and equal access to its network (Hake 1993).[2] One major problem becomes obvious: It seems possible to include Central and Eastern European researchers next to those with a general bias for English as the leading international language, i.e. the Northern European and Scandinavian countries, the Netherlands, Germany (in part), and naturally, the UK and Ireland. But there is a striking lack of researchers from Southern and Western European countries. Italy seems not to be represented anywhere, and Spanish and Portuguese participants in networks such as ESREA are rare, as are French participants. In a publication by the network Adult Education and Citizenship, the editors hint that this is a problem that must be tackled in the future:

> It is clear that the ESREA network has been highly successful at mobilising scholars from eastern, central and northern Europe; we now need to extend the debate to encompass the differing societies of southern and far-western Europe, as well as those of its Mediterranean neighbours (Bron, Field, Kurantowicz 1998, 8).

In both their general meetings which take place every three years and the various network meetings different strategies in terms of interpretation have been applied. In some cases interpretation has been provided, in others not. Unfortunately, this often means that some European researchers are excluded from the meetings. In order to become a true European society that unites researchers from all European regions, it is clear that new strategies must be developed.

Language Policy in the European Union

Assuming that the issue of language is key to the integration process of Europe and possibly one main reason for disintegration, it becomes obvious that the organisations and institutions of Europe which work for an integration process to tackle the issue. In fact, the history of language policy within the European Union is as long as the history of the European Union itself. It therefore makes sense at this point to give a brief outline of the development of the EU in order to trace the development of its language policy.

---

[2] More information about ESREA can be found at (http://www.helsinki.fi/jarj/esrea/).

When the *Treaties of Rome* were signed in 1957 they did not concede an explicit competence to the European Community in terms of educational activities on a European level. However, in fields such as employment policy, the job market, and the establishment of a common market, the Community was given competencies, and these fields could not be separated from educational activities. As a consequence, the Community initiated some activities and programmes involving language learning during this time, always, of course, respecting the national sovereignty of the member states (Knoll 1996). For example, the LINGUA programme was initiated in 1990 when it was realised that with respect to the upcoming launch of the European market, the circulation of goods and ideas would be hindered by the fact that there were not enough people in Europe who were able to work in at least two of the Member Countries' languages (Gellert-Novak 1993). As a result, a particular effort for promoting the learning of foreign languages had to be made. From 1990 until 1994, the LINGUA programme concentrated on five different actions. Action 1 was concerned with continuing education for teachers, Action 2 involved enhancing mobility amongst students, Action 3 was intended for smaller companies, Action 4 for vocational education, and Action 5 for additional programmes (Raasch 1993). In 1995, LINGUA was united with other programmes like ERASMUS and COMENIUS in a new programme, SOCRATES.[3] This programme will run until 2000, when a SOCRATES II programme will be launched.

Articles 126, 127, and 128 of the *Treaty on the European Union* – signed in Maastricht, The Netherlands, in 1992 – gave the Union explicit educational competencies for the first time; but the principle of subsidiarity, which is the key principle of the Treaty, has to be respected (Läufer 1995, 204-206). As it is explicitly explained in Article 3b of the *Maastricht Treaty*, subsidiarity can best be described as "the desire that decisions should be taken at the lowest level of government at which the desired goals may best be achieved" (Field 1998, vii). With the *Treaty of Amsterdam*, the articles did not change; they just got a different enumeration and became 149, 150, and 151. Article 3b is now Article 5 (Läufer 1999).

---

[3] Further information about the current concept and outline of LINGUA, as well as about other projects, can be accessed under (http://www.europa.eu.int/en/comm/ dg22/socrates/lingua.html).

More recent documents tackle the language question within the Union in a more concrete way. The White Paper *Teaching and Learning. Towards the Learning Society* (European Commission 1995) defined as one general objective within the guidelines for the knowledge-based society a 'Proficiency in three Community languages' (European Commission 1995, 10). In the explanations the Commission stresses that it

> ... has become a precondition if citizens of the European Union are to benefit from the occupational and personal opportunities open to them in the border-free single market... In line with the resolution of the Council of Education Ministers of 31 March 1995, it is becoming necessary for everyone, irrespective of training and education routes chosen, to be able to acquire and keep up their ability to communicate in at least two Community languages in addition to their mother tongue (European Commission 1995, 67).

As for methods to achieve these goals, the White Paper suggests two points: first, to mobilise schools to provide language classes as early as primary school, and second, to define a 'European quality label' which has the following criteria:

- genuine use by all pupils of one Community foreign language in primary school and of two in secondary school
- involvement of teaching staff from other EU Member States
- use of methods promoting self-learning of languages
- creation of an organisation for contact between young people from different Member States (including communication methods involving information technologies) (European Commission 1995, 69).

It has been noted at several points that it makes sense to start learning languages as early as possible, so starting at the primary-school level or maybe even earlier is certainly a step in the right direction (Graf 1997a, Graf 1997b). Furthermore, motivating mobility among teachers and encouraging schools to employ foreign teachers will help foster a European identity through language learning amongst both teachers and pupils.

However, examining the demographic development of the European Union, it becomes apparent that relying only on investment in schools is not enough. In order to achieve an integration process and a European identity, all Europeans will have to engage in language learning by actively studying and speaking at least one foreign language; this explicitly includes adults. Adults form the majority of the European population and will increasingly dominate the European population within the next 40 years. Nevertheless the Commission ignores the language learning of adults and neither puts particular emphasis on it in its programmes, nor in its policy papers. This also supports the conclusion in Hake's analysis of the White Paper that there is little attention given to adult learners (Hake 1999).

The White Paper's idea of proficiency in three European languages must be discussed critically as well. In Knoll's comments about the White Paper, he asked where the effects of the development of a European consciousness could be found, if, for example, a young German learned Danish and Finnish (Knoll 1996). He pleads for a clear focus on certain languages with English in the first place, followed by German and then French. His positioning of French in third place is contrary to current tradition in international organisations such as UNESCO. Knoll argues for German as the second primary language due to the increasing importance of Central and Eastern European countries where English and German are currently the prominent languages for foreign communication.

However, Knoll's argument is quite convincing as far as a clear recommendation of one foreign language that is studied and eventually spoken by all Europeans is concerned. This thesis picks up on the discussion around English as a *lingua franca* which has been very controversial not only, but particularly in Germany for the last several years. The issue is discussed with a great deal of emotion, ideological convictions, commitment, and also polemic, so it is hard actually to sum up the arguments and give an outline of the different positions.

With regard to the further development of language policy in the EU, there are several factions. There are those who promote the idea of English as the *lingua franca*. Their definition of *lingua franca* is quite important in this context; it is understood as a language that is not meant to replace the native language, but instead serves as the first foreign language studied and spoken by all. A good command of the mother tongue is generally seen as an important basis for language learning. A *lingua franca* is neither meant to put an end to the variety of languages offered and learned in schools, nor meant to be the only working language of the EU (Schöndube 1996). The necessity of a *lingua franca* in times of globalisation seems to be obvious to them. Not only are people in almost every job confronted with the need to communicate in at least one language other than their mother tongue; it is also in private contexts that situations are increasingly arising in which a mutually shared foreign language is needed.

By contrast, a second faction opposes the idea of a *lingua franca* altogether. This faction argues that although English seems to be the most obvious choice as a *lingua franca* since it is – after Mandarin with 952 million speakers – the second most frequently spoken language with 470 million speakers (Schöndube 1996), the fact remains that those who speak it as their native language will always have an advantage.

What is more, there are also certain ideologies carried through this language. In Hagège's study on languages for Europe, he speculates that American English will more often be spoken in Europe in the long run (Hagège 1996). Without pointing to the differences in spelling and pronunciation, it can be stated that American and British English vary considerably. Critics see a particular kind of liberalistic and capitalistic ideal transported with American English. The catch phrases 'McWorld' and 'casino capitalism' (Menzel 1998) shall only be mentioned here, not discussed in a detailed way. There is also the fear that a *lingua franca* might have an impact on the mother tongue even though it is seen only as a first foreign language. As far as the publishing of youth literature or specialised scientific literature is concerned, there is the fear that they might only be published in English, and not in languages with only very few speakers, since it could be assumed that everybody will be able to read the book in English anyway. This, in particular, is the fear of the smaller countries in Europe (Schröder 1994).

There is no sufficient answer to this ongoing discussion since it is also a political issue. But considering that the Treaty on the European Union devoted Article 8 to the establishment of European citizenship, it makes sense to put more effort into language learning so that those people having European Citizenship are actually able to communicate with each other.

In conclusion, it seems that the best solution for an improved communication process is a *lingua franca*. One language spoken by all European citizens would help Europeans of different nationalities communicate with each other, understand each other's positions, and perhaps also interest them in European affairs and European policy.

Coulmas sees the question of languages as one of the central hindrances to a successful integration process within Europe:

> First, the ideological dead weight of the nineteenth century must be dropped, that is, linguistic nationalism. If there is to be more identification with the European idea and more of a European identity of its citizens, languages cannot continue to play the role of the most important catalysts of social community and thus appear to be an obstacle to creating a supra-national European unity (Coulmas 1991, 27).

Unfortunately, only recently there was one example which showed that we still have not yet reached the point of dropping this 'linguistic nationalism'. On the contrary, the trend is appearing to go in the opposite direction. One step in the wrong direction was certainly the recent move made by the German government to threaten to boycott all meetings of the European Council, under the Finnish Presidency, where German is not accepted as a working language. This might bring the German Chancellor a lot of sympathy amongst the German population, but in the long run it will be understood by the people as another sign not to have to make the effort to learn another language (Wernicke 1999).

Minority Language Policy in Europe

Whereas the European Union concentrates mostly on economic affairs within Europe, the Council of Europe has developed a distinct profile in terms of cultural and minority affairs. It has to be pointed out that the Council of Europe is fundamentally different from the European Union. Whereas the European Union is a supra-national institution, i.e. that the decisions made on the EU level have direct impact on the legislation of the member countries, the Council of Europe is an international organisation; i.e. the resolutions and decisions made on the Council of Europe level are only of a recommending character. When signing on as members of the

Council of Europe, the member countries commit themselves to following the decisions made, but there are no measures of importance to be taken against member countries that do not follow this commitment.[4]

Besides its other responsibilities, the Council of Europe deals with education and adult education in particular, as well as with minority questions. The processes of reconstruction of peoples in the context of the fall of the Berlin Wall has very much stimulated this interest. A particular focus has been put on the protection of minority languages and the support of languages that are being spoken only by a small number of people (Knoll 1996, Vulpius 1991). The most prominent document in this context has been the adaptation of the *European Charter for Regional or Minority Languages* by the member countries. The state of implementation into the national law is at different stages in the member countries. Whereas Germany passed a law on July 9, 1998 (*Bundesgesetzblatt* 1998, 1314), the French government is still discussing this matter. President Chirac has turned down a suggested change of the French Constitution which would have cleared the way for the implementation. He refers to a decision of the French Constitutional Court that sees the principle of the inseparability of the Republic, the equality in front of courts, and the unity of the French people endangered.

When analysing the Charter in a more detailed way, the significance that is attributed to education and media is striking. The Charter explicitly mentions the importance of education in this context in Article 8. The entire educational system is asked to provide support structures in order to study and use the minority languages; this also refers to the adult education sector (*Bundesgesetzblatt* 1998). Closely connected to this is Article 11, in which the media and their particular role are mentioned (*Bundesgesetzblatt* 1998).

The first item within the paragraph on objectives and principles of the Charter points out 'the recognition of the regional or minority languages as an expression of cultural wealth' (*Bundesgesetzblatt* 1998, 1318). The fact that there are different languages in Europe is seen in a positive light; consequently, it is concluded that these languages must be protected in order to maintain our collective cultural wealth. At the end of the document, it is

---

[4] For detailed information about activities and structure, visit the web-page of the Council of Europe (http://www.coe.fr/index.asp).

also explicitly defined which languages in Europe are minority languages in the sense of the European Charter and which are worth protecting.

In order to discuss the Charter, I will concentrate on the German situation in particular in the following paragraphs. Unfortunately, the Charter does not provide any information about the size of the concerned groups in each country. Therefore I have added estimated numbers of speakers in the following enumeration of the German minority languages from both Martina Boden's study (Boden 1993, 77-81) and a recent newspaper article (*Berliner Morgenpost*, 01.02.1998):

- Danish: the minority group lives close to the Danish border, in the Schleswig region of Schleswig-Holstein and consists of about 30,000 people,
- Upper Sorbian: the minority group lives in Saxony and consists of about 40,000 people,
- Lower Sorbian: the minority group lives in Brandenburg and consists of about 20,000 people,
- North Frisian: the minority group lives mostly on the west coast of Schleswig-Holstein and consists of about 60,000 people,
- Sater Frisian: the minority group lives in the southern part of Lower Saxony and consists of about 2,000 people,
- Roman: the minority group travels and lives all over Germany and consists of 70,000 people.

The Charter also recognises low German (*Plattdeutsch*) as a regional language; this is particularly relevant in Bremen, Hamburg, Mecklenburg-Western Pomerania, Lower Saxony, and Schleswig-Holstein, as well as in Brandenburg, North-Rhine Westfalia, and Saxony Anhalt (*Bundesgesetzblatt*, 1998, 1335).

Before entering into a detailed discussion of the language policy of the Council of Europe, I would like to make some remarks on the classification of minorities. For example, besides the above-mentioned minorities, there are also other groups of minorities in Germany whose languages are not given the same attention and the same status. The Charter explicitly excludes them: "... it does not include either dialects of the official language(s) of the State or the languages of migrants" (*Bundesgesetzblatt* 1998, 1316). Whereas the minorities mentioned above are considered autochthonous, the latter are allochthonous, or recently immigrated minorities. However, the 'top 5' minority groups in Germany as far as the population is concerned are as follows (see table 2):

Table 2[5]: Population of 'Top 5' Allochtonous Minorities in Germany

Turkish	2.107.400
Serbian/Montenegrinian	721.000
Italian	607.900
Greek	363.200
Bosnian/Herzegovinian	281.400

Considering this data, the following questions must be posed: why are these non-autochthonous minorities not considered as contributing to the 'cultural wealth' of Germany, and why are their languages not being proposed protection within the German system?

A first approach to answer these questions could be the respective sizes of the groups. There could be a pattern of being in favour of particularly small groups. But taking a look at the European context, it becomes obvious that the size of these groups cannot be a valuable criterion. It can best be illustrated by the fact that five million Danes are given a majority status with their language, whereas six million Catalans are considered a minority (Coulmas 1991, 27).

Secondly, both autochthonous as well as allochtonous groups of minorities are migrants differing in terms of recency. But as Haberland points out this is a very controversial issue: "'Recency' is of course a relative concept and the question whether English in Ireland (or even England) or French in France are autochthonous could lead to heated debate" (Haberland 1991, 185).

Finally, we could try to determine the minority status by looking at the idea of territory. There are minorities that are territorially compact, as opposed to territorially scattered (Haberland 1991). But this category does not really help either since the Turkish minority in Berlin or in the Ruhr area certainly can be considered as compact, whereas the minority group speaking the Roman language is definitely territorially scattered. The concept of space is not really helpful in this context either since it can be seen on various levels. Haberland even introduces the term of 'vertical minority'

---

[5] See the web site of the Federal Office for statistics (http://www.statistik-bund.de/basis/d/bevoe/bevoetab1.htm); for further information about European countries, see Dadzie (1997).

when analysing the population of a multi-storey apartment house. And finally, in times of globalisation and increased mobility, in times of free movement in the European Union, it seems almost anachronistic to apply such a category when defining a minority status.

All in all, it seems that the definition of which minority languages warrant official protection is highly controversial and the ambiguities outlined above certainly complicate any analysis of the language policies of the Council of Europe. Furthermore, considering the growth of linguistic nationalism as discussed earlier in this article, one must question whether the protection of minority languages as defined by the Council of Europe truly furthers the European integration process or whether it rather supports disintegration. There is no question that diverse languages are an important part of European cultural identity, but given the role played by the Council of Europe, one must question whether protecting some languages is more important than establishing a better communication system between the speakers of all European languages. The goal should not be to exclusively preserve languages which can only be used within small, limited communities, but to progress toward an integrated Europe without language barriers. One solution could be for the Council of Europe to create a language policy which furthers a *lingua franca* as the first foreign language, followed by minority languages as a second foreign language.

Conclusion

This analysis has made clear that there is neither a clear-cut policy for language learning within Europe, nor is there enough emphasis placed on this issue. Even though Coulmas has pleaded for a political decision as far as choosing a *lingua franca* is concerned "... rather than letting 'nature', that is, the economy run its course" (Coulmas 1991, 27), all indications indeed point to the economy as a decisive factor identifying English as the dominant contender. The question is whether European policy will follow suit with a decision agreeing on a single *lingua franca* to facilitate European communication. Central to this decision-making process is the immediate availability of language learning for adults. Relying solely on the language proficiency of future generations means waiting an additional 10 to 15 years for the significant contribution to European citizenship that such proficiency entails. Clearly language learning should occupy a central place in the current debates on lifelong learning within the European Union.

Finally, while the protection of minorities and minority languages is an important aspect of a democratic Europe, institutions such as the Council of Europe must develop policy that also contributes to the broader goal of peace and freedom within the European Union. As Robertson points out, the local is one aspect of the global issue, and both terms need not oppose each other (Robertson 1998). Facilitating dynamic, and sometimes even conflictual, exchanges between very different local cultures should be at the top of the agenda set by diverse institutions – from the schools, through to the providers of adult education, and including the Council of Europe. This is currently at least as important as the preservation of local identities. One key to moving in this direction is a mutually shared first foreign language, a *lingua franca* that would be recognised by all European institutions, and perhaps someday, by the majority of European citizens as well.

References

Beck, U. (1998). *Was ist Globalisierung? Irrtümer des Globalismus - Antworten auf Globalisierung.* Frankfurt/M.

Berliner Morgenpost, 01.12.1998.

Boden, M. (1993). *Nationalitäten, Minderheiten und ethnische Konflikte in Europa. Ursprünge, Entwicklungen, Krisenherde.* München.

Bron, A., Field, J., Kurantowicz, E. (eds.) (1998). *Adult Education and Democratic Citizenship II.* Kraków.

Bundesgesetzblatt Jahrgang 1998. Teil II Nr. 25, ausgegeben am 16. Juli 1998, pp. 1314-1337.

Coulmas, F. (ed.) (1991). European Integration and the Idea of the National Language. Ideological Roots and Economic Consquences. In: Coulmas, F. *A Language Policy for the European Community. Prospects and Quandaries.* Berlin/New York, pp. 1-44.

Dadzie, S. (ed.) (1997). *Adult Education in Multi-Ethnic Europe. A Handbook for Organizational Change.* Bonn.

Europäische Kommission (1997). *Schlüsselzahlen zum Bildungswesen in der Europäischen Union - 1997.* Luxemburg.

European Commission (1995). *Teaching and Learning. Towards the Learning Society.* Luxembourg.

Field, J. (1998). *European Dimensions. Education, Training and the European Union.* London.

Graf, P. (1997a). *Vom frühen Fremdsprachenlernen zum Lernen in zwei Sprachen. Schulen auf dem Weg nach Europa.* Frankfurt/M.

Graf, P. (1997b). Lernen in zwei Sprachen. Konzeptuelle Grundlagen. In: *Bildung und Erziehung,* 50 (1), pp. 23-29.

Haberland, H. (1991). Reflections about minority languages in the European Community. In: Coulmas, F. (ed.). *A Language Policy for the European Community. Prospects and Quandaries.* Berlin/New York, pp. 179-194.

Hagège, C. (1996). *Welche Sprache für Europa. Verständigung in der Vielfalt.* Frankfurt/M.

Hake, B. J. (1992). A Forum for Research on the Education of Adults in Europe? The European Society for Research on the Education of Adults (ESREA). In: *Internationales Jahrbuch der Erwachsenenbildung,* 21, pp. 191-205.

Hake, B. J. (1997). European Society for Research on the Education of Adults. In: *Bildung und Erziehung,* 50 (3), pp. 287-291.

Hake, B. J. (1999). Lifelong Learning Policies in the European Union. Developments and Issues. In: *Compare,* 29 (1), pp. 53-69.

Gellert-Novak, A. (1993). *Europäische Sprachenpolitik und Euroregionen. Ergebnisse einer Befragung zur Stellung der englischen und deutschen Sprache in Grenzgebieten.* Tübingen.

Knoll, J. H. (1996). Berufsbildung - Wege in die Zukunft. In: *Internationales Jahrbuch der Erwachsenenbildung,* 24, pp. 187-194.

Läufer, Th. (ed.) (1995). *Europäische Union, Europäische Gemeinschaft. Die Vertragstexte von Maastricht mit den deutschen Begleitgesetzen.* Bonn.

Läufer, Th. (ed.) (1999). *Vertrag von Amsterdam. Texte des EU-Vertrages und des EG-Vertrages mit den deutschen Begleitgesetzen.* Bonn.

Menzel, U. (1998). *Globalisierung versus Fragmentisierung.* Frankfurt/M.

Raasch, A. (1993). Das EG-Programm LINGUA und die kleineren/mittleren Unternehmen. In: *Grundlagen der Weiterbildung Zeitschrift,* 4 (6), pp. 345-348.

Robertson, R. (1998). Glokalisierung. Homogenität und Heterogenität in Raum und Zeit. In: Beck, U. (ed.). *Perspektiven der Weltgesellschaft.* Frankfurt/M. pp. 192-220.

Schöndube, C. (1996). Die Sprachenfrage bleibt heftig umstritten. In: *Zielsprache Französisch*, 28 (1), pp. 21-23.

Schröder, K. (1994). Zwischen sprachlichem Zentralismus und Kantönligeist. Thesen zur europäischen Fremdsprachenpolitik. In: *Zielsprache Französisch*, 26 (3), pp. 151-153.

Vulpius, A. (1991). Europarat. In: *Grundlagen der Weiterbildung. Praxishilfen.* Loseblattsammlung 1.20.60. Neuwied.

Wernicke, Ch. (1999). Feindbild Europa. In: *Die Zeit*, 28, p.1.

Wolf, N. R. (1999). Die deutsche Sprache in Europa. In: *AVH Mitteilungen*, 74, pp. 27-32.

BRON, A., SCHEMMANN, M. (eds.) (2000). LANGUAGE, MOBILITY, IDENTITY. CONTEMPORARY ISSUES FOR ADULT EDUCATION IN EUROPE. MÜNSTER, pp. 141-161.

Wolfgang Jütte

LINGUISTIC POLICY AND ADULT EDUCATION IN MULTILINGUAL STATES AS A DIFFICULT LIAISON
THE CASE OF SPAIN

The fact that languages and nationalities are connected has again gained relevance in Europe in the last years. A historical review would reveal that adult education has always been an advocate of the autochthonous language and culture and that there is a strong connection between adult education and the struggle for national culture and autonomy. This constantly stretches from the middle of the nineteenth century, from the Scandinavian folk high schools and the Flemish people's movement in Belgium to national movements today. Adult education raises awareness in society for threats to cultural and national identity, and this can even lead to the foundation of special institutions as the examples of Denmark and Finland illustrate.

Over the past years Europe has experienced radical changes and the dangers of radical ethnicism and aggressive nationalism could be followed. Here adult education is challenged to confront these new nationalisms. But adult education itself is also affected by a re-ethnicisation of politics and culture. It would therefore seem advisable for adult education to keep its distance to linguistic policy and the concepts of linguistic cultural identity.

The concept of a homogenous national state can be regarded as a myth (Hobsbawm 1992). Since the beginning of the nineteenth century nations have always been heterogeneous and the ethnic linguistic criterion for a nation is a relatively recent one. At the end of the twentieth century the simple equation of nation, state and language is common and leads to the founding of new states. In many cases this is problematic as linguistic conflicts cannot be separated from other political and social conflicts.

Linguistic Policy

The term linguistic policy is used to denote all political initiatives and decisions (rules, regulations, guidelines, etc.) which are aimed at promoting a language or languages. The efforts are usually concentrating on the public prestige and domain of the language and on the rights of the speakers. Linguistic policy can be passive and tolerant or active and supportive. In the latter case public resources (money, personnel, rooms) are provided for the promotion of the languages and their use is regulated in public (in education, administration, courts etc.).

The discussion about the implications which linguistic policy has for education generally focuses on the school system, but changes in the language situation usually lead to increased efforts to enhance adults' competence in the new official languages.

In the context of languages, adult education is usually associated with the teaching of foreign languages. Linguistic and foreign language policy play a central role in an extended Europe. Discussions on linguistic policy within the EU usually focus on the area in which a language is spoken, for example the role of German or French in Central or Eastern European countries. In contrast to this the following deals with 'national' linguistic policy.

The issue of 'national' linguistic policy is extremely relevant at the end of the twentieth century, a fact which is highlighted by recent political developments in Central and Eastern Europe where a number of new language laws have come into effect in the last years. For example, between 1989 and 1991 new language laws were passed in 11 successor states of the USSR[1] (Guboglo 1994), and it was the Baltic States in particular which took the lead. New concepts of state and language have usually led to extensive language promotion measures.

At the same time these are socio-linguistic areas of conflict which can also be termed language conflict. There is usually a hierarchical relationship between the languages. Former minority languages are raised to new

---

[1] Estonia (18.01.1989), Lithuania (25.01.1989), Latvia (05.05.1989), Tadzikistan (02.08.1989), Moldova (31.08.1989/01.09.1989), Kazachstan (22.09.1989), Kirghizia (23.09.1989), Uzbekistan (21.10.1989), Ukraine (28.10.1989), Belarus (26.01.1990), Turkmenistan (24.05.1990), Russia (25.10.1991).

official languages and former majority languages are threatened with becoming minority languages.

The Language Situation in Multilingual States

The language situation in multilingual states differs greatly, as becomes apparent from a cursory glance at the situations in Belgium, Latvia, Switzerland (Grin 1999) and Spain, and it is therefore difficult to make comparisons. Here Spain will serve as an instructive example to show the relationship between linguistic policy and adult education. From a structural point of view the language issue in Spain is similar to that in Canada, i.e. Catalonia and the Basque Country can be compared to the French-speaking province of Quebec as far as their language situation is concerned.

Instruction for adults in Basque and Catalan is part of a larger phenomenon: the aim is to develop linguistic and cultural autonomy against the backdrop of the problems of Spanish regionalism and nationalism.

The starting point taken here is the extensive effort undertaken in Catalonia and the Basque Country since the re-democratisation of Spain to promote their respective regional languages and cultures, for example the introduction of the regional languages as official languages in local public administration and education, the publication of print media in the autochthonous languages, the setting up of radio stations and television channels and the regional support for film and publishing and other active measures to promote the language.

At first an outline of the hispanicisation policy of the Franco regime with its cultural and linguistic repression of minorities and their consequences is given. Against this historical backdrop it becomes apparent how far-reaching and decisive a turning point the democratic Constitution of 1978 was in the history of Spain. It introduced two significant principles: the pluri-national and pluri-lingual character of Spain. Constitutional recognition of the great national, regional, linguistic and cultural variety represented a radical change compared to the immediate past. It is one of Spain's original achievements in the process of change in the political system. At the same time the question is investigated which changes the linguistic policy of normalisation and the measures to encourage adults to learn their regional language experience in the context of change in society as a whole.

The Language Situation in Spain

Spain as a nation-state has some unusual features: it is an organisation of states which is shaped by pluri-nationality and great linguistic and cultural diversity. The special construction of *España plurilinguie* (Siguan 1992) is reflected in the fact that over 40% of the Spanish population live in a region in which an additional co-official language is spoken alongside Castilian. The three 'historic' regions, in particular, the Autonomous Communities of Galicia, the Basque Country and Catalonia, uphold their own language and culture.

The language situation in Spain is characterised by its variety (Bochmann 1989, Koppelberg 1991, Siguan 1992). Apart from the Castilian language (*castellano*), which is commonly known as Spanish (*español*) – a development which was encouraged by the centralist Franco regime and its ideology of a nation-state – there are three other languages which have the status of official languages: Galician (*gallego*), Basque (*euskera*) and Catalan (*català*). Apart from these four officially recognised regional languages there are further minority languages and varieties of languages (e.g. Aranés, etc.). The language borders are not completely identical with the political and administrative borders. In addition it is necessary to mention the language of the non-territorial minority of the *Gitanos*, the Spanish gypsies.

Hispanicisation Policy and the Repression of the Regional Languages

The issue of the regions and their autonomy is a political one. The strained relations between central government and regional home rule have their origin in Spanish history and have often lead to political conflicts in more recent times. The Basque Country and Catalonia have experienced periods of autonomy, generally achieving more self-determination in democratic times and being repressed by authoritarian systems. The centralist tradition was at its height during the Franco regime, which propagated the ideology of a centralised Spanish national state (*Una-Grande-Libre*) and repressed all nationalist endeavours of these regions, vehemently denying their cultural independence. The repression was in particular directed against their languages and cultural independence (Kremnitz 1990) which were considered to undermine national unity. Basque and Catalan culture and languages were banished from public life: in local authorities, schools and mass media only Spanish was spoken. Furthermore the minority languages were also threatened by the intense process of industrialisation and urbanisation, the latter in the Basque Country in particular. At the end of the 1950s huge numbers of Castilian-speaking migrants from the rural areas of the south began to settle in the industrial centres in the Basque Country and Catalonia looking for work, and this led to changes in language structures. The 'Spanish' language also became more widespread due to the expansion of mass media.

However, at the same time a comprehensive movement to restore and retain the autochthonous language and culture, embedded in the anti-Franquist struggle, began in the affected areas. Conscious Catalan and Basque nationalism was anti-Franquist and thus the regions played an important role in the opposition movement in Spain.

Resistance, Nationalisms, Symbolism and Identity

There were various strategies for change and various forms in which the resistance to the Franco regime was organised. Whereas direct resistance was only offered in the first years of the regime, the opposition, made up of Marxist, left-wing Catholic and regional nationalistic groups, increasingly endeavoured to change the system from within (Bernecker 1990). The regional nationalistic groups were an important opposition force and will therefore be dealt with in more detail.

The repression and policy of cultural levelling carried out by the Franco regime in these areas led to various survival strategies and forms of resistance which went as far as armed struggle. One strategy was to retreat into civil society (Waldmann 1990, Pérez-Agote 1987). Since the end of the nineteenth century a tight network of cultural and social clubs had been formed in the Basque Country and Catalonia and a developed "... civil society which was to a large extent uncoupled from the political superstructure" (Waldmann 1990, 20). There were, for example, choirs, folk dancing groups, scouts, sports clubs and, especially in the Basque Country, mountaineering clubs and gastronomic societies. A popular way

of asserting one's cultural and national identity was to retreat into these societies, which thus had a political function, and the socio-cultural activities
of these societies came close to being political activities.

One of the consequences of the Franquist policy of repressing the regional cultures and languages was that a strong correlation between the
fight for democracy and the defence of the autochthonous languages and
cultures developed (Siguan 1992). Every conscious manifestation in
Catalan or Basque represented a political action and especially in the first
decade after the civil war, those using these languages were persecuted.

The "boomerang effect" of this persecution was that the symbolic content of these minority languages increased and they became "symbolic
crystallisation points" (Kremnitz 1992, 41) of resistance. Having one's
'own' language became an important symbol of collective identity. Defending it was a form of political struggle.

In this context the Basque separatist Organisation ETA (*Euskadi Ta
Askatasuna*) must be seen as being far more than a single political phenomenon. Its history of origin reveals that it was also a complex socio-
cultural phenomenon. It originated from a group which initially (1952-
1956) devoted itself mainly to studying Basque language and culture
(Waldmann 1989). As a social movement ETA provided an "answer to the
political inactivity of nationalism and in particular to inactivity concerning
the language" (Pérez-Agote 1984, 112). Endeavours to restore the Basque
language and culture were the foundations on which it developed (Ben-
Ami 1991).

This connection between nationalism and symbolism can also be seen
in the songwriter culture which developed in the 1960s in Catalonia.
Known as *Nova Canço* (new song), this culture can be seen as being a culturally influenced regionalist protest movement against the regime
(Lahusen 1991). Due to its poetic language it was often able to escape cen-
sorship and pass on social and political messages and thus transport
criticism of the regime to the public. Simply the fact that the songs were
often sung in Catalan led to them becoming a symbol for political resistance to the Franco regime. They also contributed a great deal to the popu-
larisation of the Catalan language.

New Concept of State and Language

Solving the problem of nationalities constituted a central task in the process of re-democratisation in Spain. The intention to respect the characteristic cultural and linguistic features of the country was expressed in the preamble to the Constitution of 1978:

> The Spanish nation inspired by the desire to establish justice, liberty and security and to promote the good of all its citizens, declares ... its intention ... to protect all Spaniards and peoples of Spain when exercising their human rights and cultivating their culture and traditions, languages and institutions (*Constitución Espanõla 1978*).

Although a policy of national unity is pursued in the Constitution, it guarantees "nationalities and regions the right to autonomy":

> Article 2: The Constitution is based on the indivisible unity of the Spanish nation, the common and indivisible homeland of all Spaniards, and recognises and guarantees the right to autonomy for the nationalities and regions, which are constituent parts of the nation and to solidarity between these (*Constitución Espanõla 1978*).

Here Spain became a pluri-national association of states or a "nation of nationalities and regions" (Liebert 1987). Viewed against the backdrop of strong centralism, this state structure was an important turning point in relations between the centre and periphery.

Not only the conception of state was now fundamentally changed but also that of language. In article 3 of the Constitution the autochthonous languages were recognised:

> Castilian is the official Spanish language of the state. It is the duty of all Spaniards to know this language and it is their right to use it.
> The remaining Spanish languages are also official in the Autonomous Communities and according to the respective statute.

The wealth of linguistic diversity in Spain is a cultural asset which is to be especially respected and protected (*Constitución Espanõla 1978*).

Between 1979 and 1983 seventeen Autonomous Communities (*Comunidades Autónomas*) were created which form today's Spain. More than 40% of the population of Spain live in an Autonomous Community with its 'own' language which exists as a co-official language alongside Castilian (see table 1).

Table 1: Autonomous Communities with Their Own Language

Region	Own Language	Population	%
Spain		38.473.418	100
Catalonia	Catalan	5.978.628	16.39
Balearic Islands	Catalan	680.933	1.76
Valencia	Valencian (Catalan)	3.730.628	9.70
Galicia	Galician	2.844.472	7.39
Basque Countries	Basque	2.136.100	5.55
Navarra	Biscayan, Basque, Castilian	515.900	1.34

(Siguan 1992, 80)

In their statutes these Autonomous Communities usually refer to their language as their 'own' language. In paragraph 3 of the Catalan Statute of Autonomy from 1979, for example, the following is written:

1. Catalonia's own language is Catalan.
2. Catalan is the official language of Catalonia together with Castilian, which is official in the whole of Spain.

The Socio-Linguistic Situation in Catalonia and the Basque Country

Before we turn to activities to promote language in Catalonia and the Basque Country, it is at first necessary to take a look of the current socio-linguistic situation, in order to illustrate the important differences in the language situations in these regions. Here the emphasis is on showing fundamental structures and dynamics rather than giving detailed data. The data given in the following section is based on the 1986 census and quoted from Siguan 1992.

Catalonia

A general survey of the knowledge of Catalan in Catalonia (see table 2) reveals that Catalan is understood by 89% of the population, spoken by 60% and written by 30%. Conspicuous here is the high proportion of passive knowledge and the low degree of active use of the language.

Table 2: Knowledge of Catalan in Catalonia 1986

Catalonia	Understood	Spoken	Written
100%	89.10%	59.81%	30.14%

Approximately half of the population of Catalonia was born outside Catalonia and they therefore did not learn Catalan as their mother tongue. The inhabitants who are not of Catalan origin can only speak and write Catalan to a small degree.

The degree of knowledge of Catalan varies considerably from one district to another. It is particularly low in areas where there has been a massive influx of Castilian speaking migrants since the end of the 1950s. The parts of the suburbs which are mainly inhabited by immigrants are therefore Castilian language ghettos, this is particularly true for the outer belt around Barcelona. The speakers of Catalan and the speakers of Castilian constitute two different groups from a sociological point of view: whilst the latter are mainly immigrants who are members of the working class and live in the industrial belts around Barcelona and Tarragona, the former are mainly middle-class and live in smaller towns or in rural areas (Siguan 1992).

Furthermore there is a correlation between the level of knowledge of Catalan and the level of education. The higher the level of education the more comprehensive the knowledge of Catalan. This is particularly true for the ability to write Catalan.

Basque Country

On account of its particular political administrative structure it is necessary to define the term "Basque Country" more precisely. The Basque Country was first formed as the "Autonomous Community of the Basque Country" with its three provinces (Biscay, Guipúzcoa, Alava). Because of its language, culture and history it is closely linked to areas in which the Basque language is or was spoken. These are – besides the three provinces of the Basque Country – the Province of Navarra and the three Basque-speaking regions in France in the western part of the Départements Pyréneées-Atlantiques, the historical provinces of Labourd, Basse Navarre and Soule. This area which includes the Spanish and French Basque Country is named *Euskadi* and *Euskalerria*[2]. Whilst *Euskalerria* describes the area of Basque-speakers, *Euskadi* is the political expression for the Basque nation. In the following the "Basque Country" is used to refer to the Autonomous Community of the Basque Country and *Euskalerria* is used for the whole region in which Basque is spoken, i.e. the seven historical provinces.

The data on the language situation in the Basque Country cited here is based on the 1986 census which was based on three central categories:

- *Euskaldunes*: people who can understand and speak Basque,
- *Cuasi-Euskaldunes*: people with a mainly passive knowledge of Basque,
- *Erdaldunes*: with no knowledge of Basque.

In spite of the strong nationalistic background in the Basque Country the number of speakers of Basque is small (see table 3); however, there are important regional differences. Basque is most widespread in the province of Guipúzcoa.

Table 3: Knowledge of Basque in the Basque Country

Region	Erdaldunes	Cuasi-Euskaldunes	Euskaldunes
Basque Country (total)	57.15%	18.18%	24.65%
Alava	75.68%	12.96%	6.72%
Biscay	63.67%	18.62%	17.63%
Guipúzcoa	38.84%	17.71%	43.44%

In the Basque country, as in Catalonia, there was a huge influx of migrants which means that over a quarter of the Basque population (approx. 30%) was born outside the Basque Country. A correlation between the place of birth and the level of language ability can be stated as well. Whilst 34% of the inhabitants of Basque origin and 26% of those born in Navarra

---

[2] Euskadi is often also used only for the Autonomous Community of the Basque Country.

speak Basque, only 2.5% of the inhabitants who come from other regions of Spain know the Basque language.

Linguistic Normalisation and Language Promotion Measures Aimed at Adults

The governments of the Autonomous Communities which have their 'own language' make great efforts to defend and foster their languages. They all have enacted laws on linguistic normalisation: in the Basque Country (November 1982), in Catalonia (June 1983), in Galicia (June 1983), in Valencia (November 1983), on the Balearic Islands (June 1986) and in Navarra (December 1986). Apart from representing the legal basis, these laws offer guidelines for linguistic policy and regulate the public use of the language. These Autonomous Communities have also created special authorities which are responsible for linguistic normalisation.

An important point in the laws on normalisation is the official linguistic ruling, especially in education, in the mass media and in the administrative authorities. It guarantees, amongst other things, that laws and decrees are published in both languages and that the citizen can address the administration in the language of his/her choice. As both languages are official, no-one may be discriminated on account of his/her language.

When considering the promotion of regional languages two target groups have to be distinguished: the autochthonous and the non-autochthonous population. On the one hand there are both literacy programmes and the general promotion of reading and writing skills for autochthonous groups of the population. They can speak their mother tongue but are not literate in it. Adults often have to learn the orthography of their mother tongue because it was usually only used orally in informal areas (e.g. with family and friends), whilst only Castilian was taught at school, and therefore was the language they wrote in. On the other hand there are programmes to teach the regional language to large groups of the population of immigrants, usually Castilian-speakers from other regions of Spain, who want to learn this language for the first time.

Catalanisation

Soon after the Franco dictatorship was established (1939) the first activities to promote the Catalan language began illegally. In the phase after the World War II new Catalan initiatives originated which developed into a new cultural movement. In the 1960s various private initiatives were founded in order to revitalise Catalan culture and language. One of the most important was *Òmnium Cultural*. This private institution was founded in 1961 with the support of Catalan industrialists. It organised Catalan courses for both children and adults and also trained teachers of Catalan.

After the Catalan regional government, the *Generalitat de Catalunya*, was reinstated in 1976 and the Catalan Statute of Autonomy was passed in 1979, a new dynamism was brought to public linguistic policy. In 1980 the head office for linguistic policy (*Direcció General de Política Lingüística*) was set up within the Department for Education and the Arts in the Catalan regional government One of its central tasks was the promotion of Catalan courses for adults. They include socio-cultural activities in order to encourage the active use of Catalan.

The re-introduction of the Catalan language in schools required special efforts in teacher training. As only half of the teachers spoke Catalan in 1978, an ambitious training plan was drawn up which gave tens of thousands of teachers the opportunity to improve their language competence in Catalan.[3] Since 1988 teachers have had to prove that they have sufficient knowledge of Catalan in order to qualify for a job in a state school.

Particular training efforts also had to be made in the public service sector as only Castilian was spoken in municipal authorities during the Franco regime. In 1985 a law was enacted which made knowledge of Catalan an entry requirement for positions in municipal authorities. In co-operation with local authorities and other interested parties, the head office for linguistic policy also organises "Campaigns for the shaping of political ideas", in order to drive forward the "Catalanisation" of areas of society.

---

[3] At their height in the school year 1981/82 18150 teachers took part in these courses, 7074 of whom were speakers of Castilian (Arenas i Sampera 1989, 64).

Basquisation

During Franquism the view that learning the regional language was an important prerequisite for regaining the national identity became accepted in the Basque national movement (Siguan 1992). Numerous initiatives for children and adults devoted to regaining Basque language and culture came into being, some of the most important of which were the Basque schools, the *ikastolas*. This was an illegal school movement initiated and supported by parents in which Basque was the only language of instruction. Three different periods in its development can be distinguished, and these are characteristic for the social and political changes in the Basque Country regarding Basque lessons (Dàvila Balsera, Eizagirre Sagardia 1992). They originated illegally (1943-1960), as they expanded and received strong support from the population, they were tolerated (1960-1976) and in the end they were legalised. This network of *ikastolas* which developed under the protection and with the support of the church, played a very important role in the process of restoring the Basque language.

Parallel to this Basque school movement a movement developed in adult education with the aim of teaching the Basque language. From 1964 onwards evening schools (*gau-eskolas*) were founded where adults could learn Basque. As early as 1967 various collectives joined together to teach reading and writing to Basque-speakers. One of the decisive founders of this movement against illiteracy was the AEK (*Alfabetatze Euskalduntze Koordinakundea*) which became an independent organisation in 1981. In the academic year 1990/91 approximately 28000 participants were enrolled in the 178 centres in the whole *Euskalerria*.

As the AEK's aim is to restore the Basque language it is the only institute of adult education to disregard the existing political and administrative borders and work in the whole region in which Basque is spoken, i.e. also in the French Basque Country. A further characteristic of the AEK's work is its basis-democratic approach.

Although the AEK's main focus of attention is on language courses it has also developed a number of socio-cultural activities in order to promote Basque culture and language. Publicity and consciousness raising campaigns are carried out in order to sensitise the population for the language situation in the Basque Country. Here the bi-annual relay race *Korrika* is of particular importance and not to be confused with a mere sporting event.

This is a relay race for maintaining the Basque language which takes place for nine days and nights covering 1200 km in the whole *Euskalerria* in which everyone is invited to take an active part.[4] In a simple form this signalises the willingness to restore the Basque language and represents the symbolic attempt to overcome the division of the Basque territory.

Above and beyond this the AEK also carries out publicity campaigns for the promotion of the *Euskera* in order to promote the willingness to learn and speak Basque in general. In 1989 for example the message was: "Being a Basque is not enough. Become a Basque speaker! The Basque language is the difference" ("*Ser vasco no es suficiente. Izan euskaldun! El euskara es la diferencia.*"). The aim of this campaign was to sensitise the public for the fact that the Basque language is the decisive distinguishing feature between a Basque (*vasco*) and a Basque-speaking Basque (*euskaldun*).

In 1983 the regional government of the Basque Country founded HABE (*Helduen Alfabetatze Berreuskaluntzerako Erakundea*), a public institute to promote literacy and the re-Basquisation of adults. Its work includes language courses for adults, teacher training, developing teaching materials, new methods of teaching and technical terms, translations services etc. HABE also both runs its own language schools and grants subsidies to public and private institutions which promote the language.

Unlike Catalan, Basque is not the internal administrative language of the region because it is not sufficiently widespread. As an illustration of this: only a quarter of all members of the Basque parliament are able to speak Basque and so translation is always required. The reason for this is that learning the Basque language is extremely difficult and requires considerable effort. In order to gain basic knowledge of Basque it is necessary to study full-time for one year. Nevertheless the government is making considerable efforts to increase civil servants' competence in Basque.

Linguistic Integration of Immigrants

Learning the autochthonous language plays an important role in the socio-cultural integration of immigrants in Basque and Catalan society and there are considerable differences in the adoption of language and culture

---

[4] For the detailled anthropological examination of this phenomenon see T. del Valle (1988).

between the Basque Country and Catalonia. The linguistic integration of immigrants takes place considerably faster in Catalonia than in the Basque Country (Martínez Espinosa 1991). To a large extent second and third generation immigrants learn Catalan – if not at school then in adult education classes. One reason for this difference lies in the languages themselves: Catalan, a Romance language, is considerably easier to learn than Basque, a pre-Indo-European language. A further difference lies in the social prestige of the two languages. A socio-linguistic examination reveals that in Catalonia Catalan has a higher social standing than Castilian – its use is therefore conducive to social advancement. This increases the willingness of immigrants to learn Catalan.

Linguistic Policy and Interest Groups within Society

Conscious re-Catalanisation and re-Basquisation is a more recent phenomenon which only became possible in a democracy. With the regained autonomy of the Basque Country and Catalonia and the presence of stronger middle-class nationalist government parties the situation of their languages improved because extensive measures to foster them were taken.

However, the normalisation of the languages does not only depend on the measures taken by governments but also to a large extent on the attitude of important groups in society. Private initiatives, *Obra Cultural Balear* on the Balearic Islands, *Acció Cultural* in Valencia, *Òmnium Cultural* in Catalonia and AEK in the Basque Country as linguistic policy pressure groups played a decisive role in regaining the regions' own languages.

Under Franco Catalan and Basque nationalists tried hard to restore their own language as a sign of their national identity. Many initiatives to promote the languages originated from the more radical circles. With the statute of autonomy the newly elected regional government incorporated many of these private projects into its linguistic policy. Whilst its linguistic policy is accepted by the majority of those who voted for the nationalist party, more radical groups consider it to be insufficient and continue to support their own initiatives (Siguan 1992). These initiatives criticise the official linguistic policy for being too moderate and accuse the political administrative machinery of doing nothing to stop the impending loss of the language. This is for example the case for AEK in the Basque Country, but in Catalonia too there are groups such as *Crida a la Solidaritat* (Appeal for Solidarity) who call for a more radical linguistic policy. The aim of these groups is the Basquisation and Catalanisation of all areas of society and they see themselves as part of a more extensive movement whose demands are not only restricted to the normalisation of the language but who view this as a step on the way to national home rule. Here teaching the language is a means of political mobilisation for nationalist goals and the 'radicalness' of their approaches has its roots here.

Re-functionalisation of Cultural Activities

During the Franco dictatorship both social and private life were highly politicised especially in the Basque Country and Catalonia. One result of the "social state of emergency" was that the symbolic content of cultural activities greatly increased and they thus gained a political dimension.

With the beginning of re-democratisation and social normalisation the areas of politics and private life increasingly became two separate areas. This privatisation of social life led to a shift in meaning of cultural activities. A 'depoliticisation' of cultural activities began; they lost their potential to mobilise the population for political ends. Parallel to this trend they were also re-functionalised in democracy, i.e. cultural activities took on their explicit functions again. Many socio-cultural associations, e.g. dancing groups, reported a drop in members due to this development.

Decreased Importance of the Symbolic Function of the Regional Languages

With the process of normalisation of society driven on by democratisation, symbols tend to become less important. This is illustrated by the Basque programme of language promotion (Larrauri 1989). The Basque language, which was viewed as an integrative element of the Basque nation, was learnt mainly for ideological and emotional reasons well into the 1980s. Immediately after the end of the dictatorship participation in language course rose up to 300%. New language schools were founded and the quality of the courses improved. There was, however, a shift in the motivation of the participants: receiving a certificate, which was helpful for gaining certain jobs particularly in municipal authorities, came to the fore. Instead of housewives and blue-collar workers, students were now almost

the only participants and their main aim was to gain a recognised certificate. Later it became difficult to get a job even with the language certificate
and participation in language courses dropped by 40% between 1986 and
1989. At present participants' reasons for learning the language are not so
much to find their political and personal identity, but rather to improve
their social and professional standing. This transformation in the motivation to learn a language can also be seen in Catalonia. Where emotional and
ideological reasons dominated in the past (e.g. "I'm learning Catalan
because it's my language"), practical and functional reasons are now increasingly mentioned (e.g. "I'm learning Catalan so that I can find a job
more easily or so that I can help my children with their homework")
(Martínez Espinosa 1991, 59).

This shift in motivation has its roots in the changed valuation of the
languages. The state's policy of repression towards the regional languages
led at the same time to them being over-rated politically, which in turn
generated a high motivation to learn the language. The link between learning the language and the political projection disappears. The political
connotations of the language decrease and its pragmatic value increases.
Thus the symbolic function of the language is lost whilst the communicative function gains significance.

Language Promotion as a Contribution to Cultural Identity

Language promotion is usually regarded as making a central contribution to
cultural identity. Here cultural identity is understood as a generic term under which a number of expressions are subsumed which are often not
clearly delimited, e.g. collective, ethnic, autochthonous, regional and national identity. Cultural identity is regarded, as in the case of Catalonia and
the Basque Country, as a fundamental part of national identity.

The individual's cultural identity, i.e. his/her consciousness of belonging to a certain linguistic and cultural community, is to a great degree
formed by language. The example of Basque and Catalan national movements illustrates that in spite of the important differences there is a close
relationship between the regional and national movements. This close relationship between language and nation is revealed for example in the
etymological examination of the Basque word "*euskaldun*" which means
both "Basque" and "person who speaks Basque" (Koppelberg 1991, 401).

Adult education is devoted to promoting and maintaining cultural and linguistic autonomies. However, because ethnic and cultural identity are not fixed characteristics, they are always in danger of being politicised and instrumentalised. In this respect adult education is also in danger of being functionalised in the argument about language.

The policy of normalisation endeavours to change the existing diglossic situation, i.e. Basquisation and Catalanisation are directed against the supremacy of Castilian and at trying to regain the social dominance of the regions' own languages. Changing this hierarchical relationship between the languages depends not least on political measures and the extent to which society is mobilised. In the case of linguistic policy it is an open-ended process and the question how far normalisation should proceed, whether to bilingualism or monolingualism, has not yet been answered. There is no doubt that politically controlled normalisation puts pressure on immigrants, for example by requiring them to make increased efforts as far as language learning is concerned.

In the last years Spain has increasingly become a destination for non-European immigrants. Even in regions where national cultural identity was repressed in the past it is not possible to merely take for granted an understanding for the linguistic and cultural independence of the immigrants: here there tends to be the danger that new ethnic minorities will be subject to pressure of assimilating culturally.

The emphasis which Grundtvig placed on the promotion of the Danish language and culture is well-known. Especially at a time where minorities in Europe are increasingly calling for the preservation of their collective identity it would certainly be informative to investigate what Grundtvig's term *Folkelighed* comprises. How can adult education promote the cultural identity of all members of society without producing new minorities?

In Catalan adult education sensitivity in issues of promoting and maintaining language and culture not only of the autochthonous but also of the allochthonal population, the new immigrants, is to be seen. Here the aim is not to mobilise immigrants for nationalist purposes or force them to be Catalanised but rather to offer them help in integrating into society, in order to respond to their exclusion, economic discrimination or loss of identity. Tolerance and respect towards the new minorities and the culture of their home country is revealed for example in the question whether they should learn to read and write only in Catalan or in their respective mother tongue (González Agápito 1992).

Against the backdrop of economic globalisation, immigration and tourism, heterogeneity will also return to countries which have been "linguistically cleansed" (Hobsbawm 1999). Adult education must therefore think about the appropriate way to deal with heterogeneity and difference.

References

Arenas i Sampera, J. (1989). *Absència i recuperació de la llengua catalana a l'ensenyament a Catalunya (1970-1983).* Barcelona.

Ben-Ami, S. (1991). Basque Nationalism between Archaism and Modernity. In: *Journal of Contemporary History*, 26 (3-4), pp. 493-521.

Bernecker, W. L. (1990). Oposición antifranquista. In: Bernecker, W.L., Fuchs, H.J., Hofmann, B. et al. *Spanien-Lexikon. Wirtschaft, Politik, Kultur, Gesellschaft.* München, pp. 305-311.

Bochmann, K. (1989). *Regional- und Nationalitätensprachen in Frankreich, Italien und Spanien.* Leipzig.

Constitutión Espanõla. In: Boletín Oficial de las Cortes, Nr. 170, 28.12.1978.

Dávila Balsera, P., Eizagirre Sagardia, A. (1992). Alfabetización y euskaldunización en Euskal Herria. In: Escolano, A. (ed.). *Leer y escribir en España. Doscientos años de alfabetización.* Madrid, Salamanca, pp. 187-211.

González Agàpito, J. (1992). Catalán o castellano: la alfabetización y el modelo de Estado. In: Escolano, A. (ed.). *Leer y escribir en España. Doscientos años de alfabetización.* Madrid, Salamanca, pp. 141-163.

Grin, F. (1999). *Language Policy in Multilingual Switzerland. Overview and Recent Developments.* Flensburg.

Guboglo, M. (1994). *Sprachengesetzgebung und Sprachenpolitik in der UdSSR und in den Nachfolgestaaten der UdSSR seit 1989.* Köln.

Hobsbawm, E. J. (1992). *Nations and Nationalism since 1780. Programme, Myth, Reality.* Cambridge.

Hobsbawm, E. J. (1999). Die neuen Nationalismen. In: *Die Zeit*, 6.5.1999, p. 38.

Jütte, W. (1994). *Erwachsenenbildung in Spanien. Ihre Entwicklung im Kontext gesamtgesellschaftlicher Modernisierung.* New York, Münster.

Koppelberg, St. (1991). Galegisch, Euskara und Katalanisch – Sprachen und Sprachpolitik im Spanischen Staat. In: Bernecker, W. L., Oehrlein, J. (eds.). *Spanien heute. Politik, Wirtschaft, Kultur*. Frankfurt/M., pp. 387-426.

Kremnitz, G. (1990). Wirkungsweisen repressiver Sprachpolitik. Dargestellt am Beispiel des Katalanischen in der Franco-Zeit. In: *Zeitschrift für Katalanistik*, 3, pp. 90-102.

Lahusen, Ch. (1991). *"Unsere Stimme erwacht ..."*. *Populäre Musikkultur und nationale Frage im heutigen Spanien*. Saarbrücken, Fort Lauderdale.

Larrauri, E. (1989). La fiebre del título. In: *El País*, 16.10.1989, p. 18.

Liebert, U. (1987). Spanien. Das Experiment einer spanischen Nation der Nationalitäten und Regionen. In: *Der Bürger im Staat*, 37 (2), pp. 115-123.

Martínez Espinosa, C. (1991). La lengua de los emigrantes en Cataluña. In: *Hispanorama*, 57, pp. 56-60.

Pérez-Agote, A. (1984). *La reproducción del nacionalismo. El caso vasco*. Madrid.

Pérez-Agote, A. (1987). *El nacionalismo vasco a la salida del franquismo*. Madrid.

Siguan, M. (1992). *España plurilingüe*. Madrid.

Waldmann, P. (1989). *Ethnischer Radikalismus. Ursachen und Folgen gewaltsamer Minderheitenkonflikte am Beispiel des Baskenlandes, Nordirlands und Quebecs*. Opladen.

Waldmann, P. (1990). *Militanter Nationalismus im Baskenland*. Frankfurt/M.

Valle, T. del (1988). *Korrika. Rituales de la lengua en el espacio*. Barcelona.

PART V
_____

LANGUAGE AS A MEANS OF CONSTRUCTING IDENTITIES

Bron, A., Schemmann, M. (eds.) (2000). Language, Mobility, Identity. Contemporary Issues For Adult Education in Europe. Münster, pp. 163-184.

Etienne Bourgeois

Sociocultural Mobility
Language Learning and Identity

Introduction: Learning from Sociocognitive Perspective

From a socioconstructivist perspective, learning can be viewed as a process through which the learner's prior knowledge is transformed into new knowledge through the learner's interactions with the environment. At the risk of oversimplification, this transformation process can be described as follows.[1] In a given situation and context, the learner is confronted with new information (whatever the source). To process this information the learner selects and activates the relevant prior knowledge structures from those available in his or her cognitive repertoire (this is what Piaget calls the "assimilation process"). In some cases, this information treatment process may result in a cognitive conflict, when the information being process does not 'fit' the prior knowledge structure. The emergence of such a conflict creates a cognitive perturbation, or disequilibrium, which the learner will then try to solve in one way or another. Piaget distinguished two basic types of cognitive conflict solving strategies. One consists of trying to overcome the conflict in a way that keeps the prior structure unchanged. For example, the discrepant information can be simply discarded or it can be reinterpreted so as to finally fit the initial structure. In this way, the conflict is solved by some kind of adaptation of the information to the prior knowledge structure. This is what Piaget called the "homeostatic regulation" of cognitive conflict. In that case, no learning occurs since the prior knowledge structure is left unchanged. In other words, the learner has

---

[1] For a presentation and discussion of the following model in the context of adult education, see Bourgeois and Nizet (1997). It draws upon Piaget's "equilibration theory" (Piaget 1964, 1967, 1968, 1975).

resisted to change. Research on social categorisation has widely evidenced the variety of mechanisms of this type. The other type of strategy consists of transforming the activated structure to accommodate the discrepant information. This is what Piaget called the "homeorhesic regulation" of the cognitive conflict or, in other words, the accommodation process. It is only in this case that learning occurs since the interaction of the learner with the environment eventually leads to some form of transformation of his or her prior knowledge structures.

But this is only one part of the story. Learning is not only a cognitive process, it has also a social dimension. Learning is a social process in two ways. First, most learning situations involve direct social interactions between the learner and other persons (e.g. peers or a teacher). As a typical instance, in a conversation the learner is exposed not only to an alternative cognitive input, such as a given point of view on reality, but also to another person who carries this point of view (and defends it more or less strongly) and with whom the learner is interacting. In other words, the interaction is both cognitive and social. Extensive research has been conducted for the last two decades on this type of situation and the effects of social interactions on individual learning (Bourgeois 1999, Cohen 1994). For example, the sociocognitive conflict theory (e.g. Perret-Clermont 1979, Doise, Mugny 1981, Mugny 1991, Perret-Clermont, Nicolet 1988, Doise 1993) proposes that under certain conditions, the cognitive conflict is more likely to result in accommodation of prior knowledge structure (i.e. in learning) when it takes place within the framework of a social interaction than in situations which do not involve such an interaction, to the extent that the conflict needs to be regulated at both the cognitive and the social level. Research on collaborative learning (e.g. Hertz-Lazarowitz, Miller 1992, Cohen 1994) reaches a similar conclusion. In this sense, learning is a sociocognitive process to the extent that it involves not only interactions between the learner's prior knowledge (ways of looking at things or doing things) and alternative knowledge, but also interaction between the learner as a person and other persons. However, learning can also be viewed as a social process in another sense. The sociohistorical (Vygotsky 1996) and sociocultural (Bruner 1996) theories of learning emphasise the sociocultural roots of knowledge (Greeno, Collins, Resnick 1996). In this perspective, knowledge is viewed as a sociocultural production. It is produced by a society, a social community with its own culture and practices. In other words, it is 'situated' in a given culture and society. Therefore, in the learning process the learner is confronted not only with a given body of knowledge, but also, beyond it, with other people (whether directly present as envisaged by the sociocognitive conflict theory or indirectly, through a book, a TV programme, a CD-ROM, or a web page) and with the underpinning culture and social practices of the social community which has produced and is using this knowledge. The learner's relationship to knowledge is also essentially a relationship to other people, society and culture.

Identity and Learning

'Identity Sensitivity' of the Learning Objects

This very schematic theoretical introduction is necessary to understand the crucial role of identity in learning as we see it. As a first approach to the notion – which will be further elaborated below – we can define identity as the way an individual sees himself or herself in relation to others, in terms of similarities or difference. It consists of a set of cognitions, behaviours and affects through which the individual defines himself or herself as both different and similar to others in a given context (Lipiansky 1992, Lipiansky, Taboada-Leonetti, Vasquez 1990). For example, the professional identity of an adult educator may be based on specific conceptions (implicit or explicit concepts and theories) of adult development and learning and the function of adult education in society, on his or her own understanding of the subjects he or she teaches, on certain teaching practices, behaviours and skills, as well as certain values and affects (positive and/or negative) concerning the profession, him or herself as a professional, as a person, and so on. Those specific cognitions, behaviours and affects can be partly idiosyncratic, to the extent that they are used to define his or her individuality as a person (personal identity), and partly shared by a group to which he or she belongs (e.g. the adult educator profession) and used by the individual to mark his or her membership to that group (social identity) as opposed to others. In other words, from the individual's point of view, some cognitions, behaviour and values are more or less salient than others in the individual's identity, depending on the extent to which they participate in, or contribute to, the individual's identity construction.

Now, in learning situations, the learner may be confronted with learning objects which relate to cognitions, behaviours and values that may be more or less salient in his or her identity. For example, in a professional development seminar, the adult educator can be confronted with an alternative theory of adult learning that directly questions his or her prior conceptions of adult learning in which his or her professional identity is grounded. In this case, the learning objects will be said to be 'identity sensitive' for that particular person at that particular point in his life history and in that particular context. Conversely, the same educator can be involved in another learning situation which mobilises learner's cognitions or behaviours that are less 'identity sensitive', that is, more peripheral to his or her professional identity (say, for example, car driving, cooking or medieval history). From the socioconstructivist perspective of learning outlined above, the learning process can therefore imply identity and culture conflicts beyond the strictly cognitive (or even sociocognitive) conflicts. To take a few extreme examples, when someone from a working class family is learning Medicine or Law at the university, he or she is confronted with new knowledge and skills, but by the same token, with a new social world, a new culture, a new language, new "habitus" (in Bourdieu's sense), a new set of social relationships, which may question more or less deeply, both his or her current personal and social identity. The same argument could apply to other typical instances, such as an adult illiterate person learning to read and write, or an immigrant learning the language of the host country. In all these instances, the stake of the learning process is not only the transformation of the learner's cognitive and behavioural repertoire but also the transformation of his or her relationship to his or herself, to others and to the world, and therefore, his or her identity as defined above.

'Identity Sensitiveness' and Responsiveness to Learning

The key question that arises at this point is whether the fact that the learning object is highly identity sensitive (i.e. strongly connected to the subject's identity) is likely to facilitate the learning process or, on the contrary, to obstruct it. The answer to this question can be quite contrasted.

On the one hand, in reference to research on social categorisation (e.g. Tajfel 1972), it can be argued that the more a given cognition (a concept or a theory) is grounded in the subject's social identity, the less it is likely to change. Indeed, challenging this cognitive structure would imply the challenge of the subject identity in which it is grounded, which in turn, would imply high costs for the subject, at both the cognitive and affective levels. Therefore, in this case, learning is perceived by the learner as a threat to his or her identity. To come back to the example above, the adult educator is less likely to modify his or her current conceptions about adult learning as far as those conceptions are central to his or her identity as a professional. If involved in a cognitive conflict – for example when confronted with an alternative conception of adult learning – the learner will strive to avoid the conflict or to solve it in a way that leaves his or her initial conceptions intact ("homeostatic regulation") in order to preserve his or her identity. From this point of view, identity can be viewed primarily as an obstacle to learning to the extent that the learning experience is perceived as a threat to the learner's identity.

On the other hand, on the basis of a few case studies (Bourgeois 1996, Bourgeois 1998, Bourgeois, Nizet 1999), we have shown that under certain conditions, identity can function as a powerful facilitating factor of learning. This is likely to happen in particular when the learning experience takes place while the learner is engaged in a mobility process at that point of his or her life history, and therefore is experiencing some transformation of his or her identity in the first place. In that case, the learning experience can be viewed not as a threat to an identity that the subject strives to preserve but, on the contrary, as a crucial resource to support and facilitate the ongoing identity transformation process. To give an example, this was the case of an adult learner, a farmer with a very low level of prior formal instruction, who entered a university-level programme in economic and political science through a special APEL access scheme. At the time he entered the programme, that learner was engaged in a social mobility process, striving hard to quit his occupation as a farmer and to get a leading position in the local section of a political party. This mobility process was extremely painful for him as it involves major changes in his identity as a person, as a worker, as a member of the farmer community, etc. At that point in his life history, he was in the middle of an internal identity conflict; he was literally torn between the pain to leave his older identity and social network as a farmer, the comfort and security of a world in which he had been raised since infancy and which was so familiar to him, the difficulty to cope with the feeling of guilty betrayal to his prior ingroup, and, on the other hand, the attractiveness of a new status and occupation, a new identity, a new social affiliation, which would fulfil his new personal and social aspirations, but at the same time were quite new and insecure and give him the feeling of 'not belonging there'. In this process, the learning experience was perceived by him primarily as a means to achieve his mobility objectives successfully and to overcome some of the obstacles he was meeting on the way. It meant to him the opportunity to acquire the language, the knowledge and the skills that would help him negotiate this major turn in his life history. In this case, identity functions as a powerful facilitator of the learning process.

In conclusion, it can be hypothesised that the fact that the cognitions at stake in the learning process closely relates to the learner's identity does not *per se* predict the learning outcomes. As we saw, in some cases it can result in a strong resistance to change whereas in others it can lead to the opposite outcome. At best, it can predict the intensity with which the learner will either resist the learning process or engage into it. Rather what makes the difference is the meaning the learning experience takes to the learner in relation to his or her identity dynamics (Bourgeois 1999). The hypothesis here is twofold. To put it roughly, if the learner is engaged in a 'defensive' identity dynamics, he or she is likely to resist any change in his or her (identity sensitive) prior knowledge to the extent that the learning experience is perceived as a threat to his or her identity, which he or she is striving to preserve. However, in the instance of 'defensive' identity dynamics, if the learning experience is perceived as a way to reinforce the threatened identity, then the learner is likely to be open to learning. If, on the contrary, the learner is being engaged in a 'transformative' identity dynamics, he or she is likely to be more open to learning as far as the learning experience is perceived as an effective way to support the identity transformation process. The meaning of learning, in particular in terms of identity strategy, can therefore deeply affect the learning process and outcomes at both a motivational level (in terms of attitude toward learning, persistence, direction and intensity of the learning process) and a cognitive level (plasticity of the activated prior knowledge structures). Before going on with a discussion of this general hypothesis in the particular case of language learning for immigrants, let us focus for a while on the notion we have introduced, namely the notion of identity dynamics.

The Notion of Identity Dynamics (or Strategies)

The notion of "identity dynamics" (Bourgeois 1996, Barbier 1996, Barbier, Galatanu 1998), which is close to that of "identity strategies" (Camilleri et al. 1990, Tap 1979, Tap 1988), implies rather a dynamic than static conception of identity. Such a conception can be summarised in five points (Lipiansky, Taboada-Leonetti, Vasquez 1990).

- It assumes that the subject's identity is not formed once for all in the first years of life. Rather, it undergoes ongoing transformations throughout the lifespan.

- Identity is constructed and transformed through the multiple interactions of the learner with his or her environment. In this sense, identity as a relationship to oneself is inherently dependent on one's interactions with others, not only at the interpersonal level but also at the sociostructural level (culture, institution, history, ideology, etc.). Self-image is constructed in relation to the others' image of oneself.

- Identity is multiple and structured. One has as many identities as social roles to be fulfilled in the different areas of one's life (as a spouse, parent, child, citizen, worker, etc.). Those identities are not merely juxtaposed; rather, they tend to be organised and structured into a more or less coherent whole.

- One continuously tends to achieve both a coherent and positive self-image beyond the tensions he or she may experience, e.g. tensions between one's self-image and the others' image of oneself, between one's 'acknowledged' self-image (what I am) and the desired self-image that is aimed at (what I would like to be), between the past and new identities, between one's multiple identities inherent in one's different social roles at a given point in time, etc. The emergence of such tensions inherent in the subject's life history creates a desequilibrium, which the subject will seek to overcome in a way or another in order to restore one's sense of unity and positive self-image.

- This implies a view of the subject as not totally determined by either internal or external constraints and contradictions. Rather, the subject is thought to have some capacity for free action and choice, to be able to act upon his or her self-image, hence the notion of identity strategies.[2] This notion implies that the subject is able to set up goals concerning his or her identity and to undertake specific actions, including learning, to achieve these goals. We now turn to a discussion of the relationship between identity strategy and learning in the particular case of immigrants learning the language of their host country.

Language Learning and Immigration

Ethnic Identity Language Learning

A priori, there are no reasons to believe that some learning objects are more or less 'identity sensitive' *per se* than others. It all depends on the person and the context (Bourgeois 1996). Nonetheless, it can be easily argued that in certain circumstances, some learning experiences are particularly likely to activate identity conflicts. This is certainly the case in the three examples of learning experiences we gave above, as they fulfil a central function in the transcultural mobility process of an individual. In the rest of this article, we will focus on the last of those instances, that is, the case of an immigrant learning the language of the host country. Extensive research has been conducted on this topic (Pao, Wong, Teuben-Rowe 1997). One major conclusion that can be drawn from it is the close relationship that exists between language and social identity, in particular, ethnic identity (e.g. Heller 1987, Heller 1988, Gumperz 1982a, Gumperz 1982b, Giles, Johnson 1981, Gilles, Johnson 1987). As Clachar puts it:

> Language ... creates an ethnic boundary, a cue for interethnic categorisation and distinctiveness... [L]anguage is a distinctive characteristic of membership in ... ethnic groups, a significant dimension for interethnic categorisation, and the medium for facilitating intergroup cohesion (Clachar 1997, 109).

Likewise, referring to Khleif (1975), Pao et al. argue that:

---

[2] Some authors prefer the notion of identity dynamics to that of identity strategies as the former leaves more room to the role of unconscious factors in the identity formation process. However, both notions underscore the idea of subject's intentionality in this process.

> ... human groups, when not suppressed, usually take great
> pride in the uniqueness of their language and use it to mark
> lines between ingroups and out-groups. Language creates
> consciousness and breeds definable loyalties. This solidarity
> of language is perhaps the key to how language influences
> ethnic identity (Pao, Wong, Teuben-Rowe 1997, 623).

If language plays such a key role in the formation and maintenance of ethnic identity, it can be expected that the identity issue will be at the core of the learning process when it comes to learning the language of another ethnic group. According to our general hypothesis as stated above, it could be expected that in those situations, the meaning of the learning experience for the learner will be strongly determined by his or her identity dynamics or strategies at that moment in terms of relationship to his or her ingroup and outgroup. As suggested earlier, if the learner is in an identity dynamics such that he or she is strongly identified with the ingroup and seeks to preserve this identity and his or her distinctiveness as a member of the ingroup, he or she is likely to resist the learning process. If, on the contrary, the learner is in a 'transformative' identity dynamics, seeking primarily access and assimilation into the outgroup, or to reconciliate his or her membership to both groups into a new original identity structure, it is likely that his or her "investment" in learning, to take Peirce's word, will be higher (Peirce 1995). In order to refine this hypothesis a little further, let us now turn to a discussion of the possible identity strategies that can possibly be used by the members of a given minority ethnic group in the position of immigrants in a given dominant group and culture.

Identity Strategies of Minority Ethnic Groups

For Camilleri, members of minority ethnic groups are typically exposed to two kinds of threats to their social identity. One is the threat to their positive self-image, as they are most of the time stigmatised and stereotyped by the dominant group. They are attributed characteristics which are most of all associated with negative and depreciatory judgements. The second threat concerns the integrity of their identity, as they are confronted with a culture (system of values, beliefs, behaviours, codes, language, etc.) which may conflict more or less with that of the ingroup (Camilleri 1990). In other words, encounters with the outgroup culture upset in the coherence of the system of representations and values by which they can make sense of themselves and their relationships to others. The ways they can cope with these threats and conflicts can be very diverse and the research literature on the topic provides various typologies to account for that variety. Reviewing all those typologies would be out of scope. However, we can roughly distinguish four basic types of strategies (Camilleri et al. 1990). The first two imply to choose to identify primarily with either the outgroup or the ingroup at the expense of the other.

The assimilation strategies. One possible type of response to the identity conflicts is to maximise identification to the (dominant) outgroup and minimise (if not reject) identification to the ingroup. In this case, the minority group members strive to adopt – both internally and externally – the culture and norms of the dominant group, they will try enhance their membership to the latter and be accepted by the dominant group.

The differentiation strategies. This type of strategies is opposite to the first one. It consists basically of maximising one's identification with the ingroup and minimising identification with the (dominant) outgroup. Several variants of this strategies have been identified. One consists of not only acknowledging, but also internalising and accepting the dominants' stigmatising perceptions and judgements on the minority group (internalisation) as legitimate. By doing so, the minority group accepts the dominants' definition of the status inequality. In another variant of the differentiation strategy, the identity attributed by the dominant group to the minority group is fully accepted but its negativity is turned into positivness (semantic reversal). In that case, the 'difference' is not only accepted, it is also openly claimed, sometimes aggressively. The fundamentalist strategy is very close to this strategy, as it consists of strongly asserting one's distinctiveness while rejecting any form of adaptation or concession to the dominants' code. They are proud and openly claim the traits for which they are negatively discriminated by the dominants. In the instrumentalisation strategy, members of the minority group accept the identity assigned to them by the dominant group, even though negative, to the extent that they can draw some benefits from it and use it to serve specific individual or collective interests. In the social visibility strategy, the minority group members accept the identity attributed by the dominant group but not the negative evaluation associated with it. In other words, they will strive to assert their distinctiveness and difference and to be accepted, recognised, legitimated by the dominant group. In that case, they will (most of the time collectively) try to impact on the evaluation criteria that are used by the dominant group so as to enhance a more positive evaluation of the minority group by the dominant group.

In the two types of strategies we have outlined above the identity conflict is solved primarily in favour of one of the two conflicting cultures, by identification primarily with either the dominant group in the first case, or the minority group in the second. The next type of strategies consists of avoiding the conflict and the choice to identify with one or the other group.

The conflict avoidance strategies. The dissociation or 'ad hoc' strategy is observed when the minority group members internalise the dominant group culture without giving up their attachment to the ingroup. The two alternative code systems are completely dissociated and coexist within the person, who is able to shift from one to the other depending on the circumstances and the demands of the environment. In another variant (the distance strategy), the ingroup members are able to stand with the identity conflict. They 'merely' acknowledge the difference and the lower status of their ingroup; they do not internalise the negative identity assigned by the dominant group but they relinquish the struggle either to change it or to quit the ingroup identity. Another way to avoid the conflict (anonymity strategy) is to 'dilute' one's identity in anonymity. In this instance, the subject will adopt a low profile, trying by several means to avoid social comparison, that is, any situation that requires to unveil and define one's social membership. The denial strategy consists of rejecting (or denying) the very assignment of a difference between the minority and the dominant group.

The conflict negotiation strategies. In those strategies, the minority group members strive to reconstruct a new identity that combines elements of both the ingroup and outgroup cultures and redefines their dual membership accordingly. For instance, in the combination strategy, the minority group members will reconstruct their identity in selecting and incorporating the most favourable items from the ingroup and outgroup cultures, either synchronically or diachronically. In some case, those items from both cultures will coexist internally without any articulation in the new identity structure (juxtaposition strategy) or they may be rationally articulated into a new complex and coherent internal structure. In some other cases, external adaptive behaviour in keeping norms with the outgroup that may coexist with internal identification primarily with the ingroup. In the reinterpretation strategy, the minority group members will try to reinterpret the ingroup culture so as to make it more compatible with the outgroup's culture. Another strategy of this type consists of focusing on the 'spirit' of ingroup's cultural codes, as opposed to its 'letter', in order to make it compatible with the dominant group codes.

Social Conditions which Determine the Choice of Identity Strategies

Research on social identity has also highlighted some conditions which can predict the type of strategy that is likely to be used by the members of low status social groups confronted with identity conflicts. In particular, Tajfel and Turner (1979), Tajfel (1982) and Hogg and Abrams (1988) suggested that if comparisons with the outgroup result in a negative social identity for the ingroup members, the latter will strive to achieve or restore a positive identity through various strategies. If the boundaries between the (low status) ingroup and the (dominant) outgroup are perceived as soft (little distinctive), individual upward mobility (assimilation) strategies will tend to prevail in order to restore a positive social identity. Conversely, if the ingroup/outgroup boundaries are perceived as clear-cut and hard, low status group members will tend to prefer social change strategies, i.e. collective strategies aiming at improving the minority group status relative to the dominant groups. In this latter case, two types of social change strategies can be used, depending on the perception of the social structure by the low status group. On the one hand, if there exist 'cognitive alternatives', that is, if the status inequality is perceived by the low status group as illegitimate and/or unstable, and then the low status group is likely to prefer 'social competition' strategies by which it attempts either to modify its objective characteristics or the dominant group's perception of those characteristics in order to enhance a more favourable evaluation and 'beat' the dominant group. If, on the contrary, the social structure is perceived as legitimate and/or stable, that is, if no cognitive alternatives are available, then the low status group will tend to modify the very evaluation criteria upon which social comparisons between the lower and the higher status groups are based in order to bring about more favourable comparisons and evaluation of the lower status group.

Although this approach does not completely account for the variety of possible responses to identity conflicts presented above, it nonetheless suggests that the individual choice of identity strategies in a given context is determined not only by individual dispositions but also by social conditions (such as the ingroup members' collective representation of the ingroup/outgroup boundaries or the legitimacy and stability of the social structure).

As we can grasp from the very schematic presentation, the minority group members' response to identity conflicts may vary to a large extent. Therefore we can expect that the meaning of learning the dominant group's language will vary accordingly, along with the feelings and affects associated with it. As a result their motivational and cognitive investment in learning will also vary to great extent. It is likely that for those people engaged into 'differentiation' identity strategies such as learning experience will be perceived primarily as a potential threat, whereas, on the contrary, it could be perceived as a more or less crucial resource for those engaged in an 'assimilation' or 'conflict negotiation' strategy and therefore investment in learning will be higher. The following study recently provided interesting empirical evidence with regard to this general hypothesis.

Ethnolinguistic Identity and Language Learning: Some Empirical Evidence

Clachar's study (1997) focuses on the peculiar experience of learning a language, which in one interethnic situation represents the ingroup language, while in another interethnic context it represents the outgroup language. This is the case of the Puerto Rican Return Migrants (PRRMs), who have been raised in the United States and return to Puerto Rico, facing the task of developing proficiency in Spanish, which in one interethnic situation (the US mainland) represented their ingroup language while in the new interethnic situation (Puerto Rico) it represents the outgroup language. In reference to the ethnolinguistic identity theory (Giles, Byrne 1982, Giles, Johnson 1987, Giles, Bourhis, Taylor 1977, Sachdev, Bourhis 1990) the author suggests that the PRRMs' development of Spanish proficiency in this paradoxical situation is influenced by five variables (Clachar 1997, 111-115).

Social Identity and Ethnic Identification. If ingroup members can draw a positive social identity from social comparisons with the outgroup, then ingroup members will identify with the ingroup and try to enhance their distinctiveness in their interactions with the outgroup. Conversely, if social comparisons with the outgroup result in a negative social identity for ingroup members, then the latter will adopt various strategies, such as those described above (individual mobility, social competition or creativity), in order to improve their social identity. Now, since language is a crucial dimension of social comparisons in interethnic situations, it is very likely that the ingroup members' attitude towards learning the outgroup's language will be strongly influenced by their social identity. In the case under study, Clachar therefore makes the hypothesis that if PRRMs strongly identify with their ingroup (the PRRM community), that is, if they draw a positive social identity from social comparisons with the outgroup (the island-raised Puerto Ricans), they are likely to cultivate the ingroup language (English), hence to evidence a low level of Spanish proficiency and a low level of investment in improving proficiency in that language.

Ethnolinguistic Vitality. The strength of ethnolinguistic identity may be enhanced by a variety of sociostructural factors, such as status (prestige of language, economic and political dominance, highly valued traditions and history), demography (both in terms of absolute size of the community and concentration of the group in a particular territory), and institutional support (institutional representation of the group mass media, education, government, industry and culture). The author makes the hypothesis that

> PRRMs who exhibit high perceived ethnolinguistic vitality from the point of view of their perceived status, demographic concentration, and institutional representativeness in the Puerto Rican society, are more likely to evidence a strong ethnolinguistic identity, an inclination to accentuate the ingroup language, English, and, thus, a low disposition to develop proficiency in Spanish, the outgroup language, even though functional mastery of it is a necessity in Puerto Rico (Clachar 1997, 112).

Awareness of Cognitive Alternatives. In keeping with the classical social identity theory (see above), the low-status group members' identity strategy are also influenced by their perception of the social structure, in terms of stability and legitimacy. If they perceive cognitive alternatives to the existing interethnic status quo (stigmatisation of the ingroup), that is, if they perceive that the interethnic social structure as unstable (it could be changed) and/or illegitimate (it is unfair), then motivation for socioethnic distinctiveness is aroused. As a result, ingroup members will tend to exhibit a strong sense of ethnolinguistic identity, emphasise their linguistic distinctiveness and therefore, will not be likely to improve their proficiency in the outgroup language.

Hardness versus Softness of Ethnic and Linguistic Boundaries. The importance of this variable is also emphasised in the classical social identity theory (see above). In reference to Giles (1979), Clachar argues that if observable characteristics are clearly associated with group membership, such as dress style, physiognomy, religion, language, etc., then "the intergroup distinctiveness is likely to be intense and linguistic and ethnic boundaries will be perceived as hard" (Clachar 1997, 113-114). She further argues that "the harder the linguistic and ethnic boundaries are perceived to be, the more strongly ingroup members will identify with ingroup norms and values and the more salient ethnolinguistic identity will be in interethnic situations". Therefore, "the more likely they will identify with the ingroup language, English, as a source of ethnolinguistic identity, and the less disposed they will be to developing proficiency in Spanish" (Clachar 1997, 114).

Multiple-Group Membership. In reference to Giles and Johnson (1987) and Hildebrandt and Giles (1983), Clachar points out the role of multi-group membership in the individual's identification with a particular group. She hypothesises that ethnic attachment to a given group is likely to be stronger for those individuals who identify with a few rather than many other social groups to the extent that they are exposed to more demands on their behaviour from the group. Therefore, it is expected that PRRMs who belong to fewer social groups are more likely to strongly identify with the PRRM community and hence be less motivated to develop their proficiency in Spanish (Clachar 1997, 114).

These hypotheses were tested on a population of one hundred and fifty-six PRRMs students from three university campuses in Puerto Rico. The five independent variables were measured by specific questionnaires and the dependent variable was measured by a Spanish proficiency test. A stepwise multiple regression analysis was performed to establish the correlation between each predictor and the dependent variable.

The findings demonstrated the expected effects of ethnolinguistic vitality, perceived hardness of linguistic boundaries and awareness of cognitive alternatives on Spanish proficiency. However, surprisingly, no significant correlation could be found between ethnic identification and Spanish proficiency nor between multiple group membership and Spanish proficiency. The lack of observed significant correlation between ethnic identification and Spanish proficiency is quite surprising, especially given the fact that the three predictors which correlate significantly with the dependent variable are known to have a strong relationship with ethnic identification. Clachar's interpretation of this discrepancy can be related to our prior discussion of the strategies that can be used to solve identity conflicts. She argues that the observed contradiction in the result may reflect an ambivalent and hindered sense of ethnic attachment due to the PRRMs specific history. In the US homeland, they were exposed to stigmatisation as a minority group and in response, they may have felt the need to assert their distinctiveness as Puerto Ricans and therefore, their allegiance to Spanish as an ethnic identity marker. When they returned to Puerto Rico, they were again stigmatised and discriminated as a minority group and may have responded to this situation by asserting their distinctive North American background and therefore their allegiance to English as a marker of this distinctiveness. As a result, their current relationship to Spanish proficiency may have been affected by ambivalent forces: the desire to become accepted and assimilated as members of the new society and at the same time the fear to lose their ethnolinguistic distinctiveness. The observed contradiction in the findings may therefore evidence such an ambivalence: the seemingly strong identification with the outgroup (island-raised Puerto Ricans) as manifested in their response to the ethnic identification scale and contradicted by the evidence of high perceived ethnolinguistic vitality, perceived hardness of interethnic boundaries and awareness of cognitive alternatives may reflect an attempt to publicly adapt to the outgroup's lifestyle and norms rather than a manifestation of a real internal identification and solidarity with the outgroup.

For Clachar, the peculiar history of PRRMs may also explain the surprising lack of correlation between multiple-group membership and Spanish proficiency. The data show that a large percentage (84%) of the respondents identified with a few social groups (only two) but, contrary to the predictions of the ethnolinguistic identity theory, the PRRMs' involvement in few groups could not predict their proficiency in Spanish. For the author, the explanation could lie in the nature of the group, rather than the number of groups to which the respondents report to belong. A closer look at the data shows that only 20% of the respondents were members of groups with a linguistic/cultural and political focus. The rest belonged to recreational or religious groups or did not report any affiliation. So, the PRRMs' involvement in few social groups could be seen primarily as an evidence of the PRRMs' tendency to avoid intergroup language conflicts with the outgroup rather than a factor that predicts identification with the ingroup and therefore a low level of Spanish proficiency. In other words, the nature of the social groups to which PRRMs belong would be a better predictor of Spanish proficiency than the number of those groups:

> One would expect PRRMs who are members of groups which are cultural and linguistic in focus to be more sensitive to such issues as ethnic categorisation and the salience of the ingroup language than PRRMs who are members of groups which are religious and recreational in focus. The former would not only be more concerned about maintaining their ethnolinguistic identity and linguistic distinctiveness, but may also be less disposed to developing proficiency in Spanish (Clachar 1997, 121).

So, the level of ingroup members' involvement in multiple groups did not predict the level of Spanish proficiency in this study because of the nature of those groups, which are mostly recreational and religious in focus. The predictions of the ethnolinguistic theory would probably have been verified (low level of Spanish proficiency) if the groups had been political and linguistic in focus.

Clachar's findings and interpretations could be related to the typology of identity strategies presented earlier. The PRRMs' attitude and behaviour towards learning the outgroup language (Spanish) reflects their response to a particularly complex and probably very painful identity conflict. On the one hand, due to their particular history as members of a subordinate group in two successive interethnic situations, they are currently experiencing ambivalent feelings about Spanish, which was the ingroup language in the former interethnic situation (in the US) and is now (in Puerto Rico) the outgroup language. In the current situation, improving one's proficiency in Spanish represents a way to enhance one's assimilation to the (dominant) outgroup and ultimately to recover a positive social identity. At the same time, it also means to relinquish a significant part of one's ethnolinguistic distinctiveness. As this study shows, one possible response to such a difficult identity conflict is to combine internal (or private) loyalty to the ingroup with external (public) loyalty to the outgroup. From this point of view, the willingness to learn the outgroup language reflects the adoption of an adaptive behaviour rather than the real, internal identification with the outgroup.

The subject can internalise the dominant group's norms completely or he or she can stand with some discrepancies between his or her external (public) behaviours and internal (private) beliefs and values. In the latter case, assimilation to the outgroup is only partial. Adaptive behaviours may then coexist with internal identification with the ingroup. This response was identified earlier as one of the typical identity conflict negotiation strategies. On the other hand, the finding that most PRRMs may tend to avoid intergroup conflict situations could be somewhat related to another strategy which was identified as the anonymity strategy.

Conclusion

As argued on a theoretical basis and illustrated by the study presented above the meaning of the learning experience and the affects associated with it may be grounded in the learner's identity and, if the case, the learner's response to identity conflicts. On the other hand, that meaning determines to learner's motivational and cognitive investment in the learning process. The role of identity may be more or less central, depending on the context, the object of learning and the time it takes place in the learner's history. It was argued that the identity issue is particularly salient in those situations where (a) people are experiencing some form of intergroup mobility and (b) the learning task they face is likely to affect their relationship to both the ingroup and the outgroup in this process. In particular, we focused on the situation of members of a minority ethnic group confronted with the task of learning the language of the dominant group. In such interethnic situations, members of the ethnic group are experiencing social identity conflicts, because they are often exposed not only to a stigmatisation from the dominant group but also to conflicting norms and values that threaten the coherence of their original identity. We examined various types of possible responses that can be used by the ethnic group members in order to solve these identity conflicts, that is, to restore a positive identity and identity coherence. It was then argued that the learner may attribute different meanings to the learning experience and consequently invest in the learning process to varying degrees, depending on the strategies adopted by the learner to solve his or her identity conflicts.

Of course, the discussion above does not imply that what is going on in the language learning process can be understood only in the light of identity factors. The meaning assigned by the learner to the learning experience alone could never entirely explain and predict the learner's actual performance in that process, nor could it be explained and predicted completely by the learner's identity dynamics alone. However, we hope to have highlighted the importance of the identity factors, in particular in certain learning situations. An awareness of the role of those factors in learning may help the adult educator to understand otherwise inexplicable motivational or cognitive problems can arise in the learning process and hopefully design and operate teaching strategies can take those factors into account successfully (Bourgeois, Nizet 1997).

References

Barbier, J. M. (1996). De l'usage de la notion d'identité en recherche, notamment dans le domaine de la formation. In: *Education Permanente*, 128, pp. 11-26.

Barbier, J. M., Galatanu, O. (1998). *Action, affects et transformation de soi*. Paris.

Bourgeois, E. (1996). Identité et apprentissage. In: *Education Permanente*, 128, pp. 27-44.

Bourgeois, E., Nizet, J. (1997). *Apprentissage et formation des adultes*. Paris.

Bourgeois, E. (1998). Apprentissage, motivation et engagement en formation. In: *Education Permanente*, 136, 101-109.

Bourgeois, E., Nizet, J. (1999). *Regards croisés sur l'expérience de formation*. Paris.

Bourgeois, E. (1999). Interactions sociales et performances cognitives. In: Carré, P., Caspar, P. (eds.). *Traité des Sciences et Techniques de la Formation*. Paris.

Bruner, J. S. (1996). *The Culture of Education*. Cambridge, MA.

Camilleri, C. (1990). Identité et gestion de la disparité culturelle: essai d'une typologie. In: Camilleri, C.et al. (eds.). *Strategies identitaires*. Paris, pp. 85-110.

Camilleri, C. et al. (eds.) (1990). *Strategies identitaires*. Paris.

Clachar, A. (1997). Ethnolinguistic Identity and Spanish Proficiency in a Paradoxical Situation. The Case of Puerto Rican Return Migrants. In: *Journal of Multilingual and Multicultural Development*, 18 (2), pp. 107-124.

Cohen, E. (1994). Restructuring the Classroom. Conditions for Productive Small Groups. In: *Review of Educational Research*, 64 (1), pp. 1-35.

Doise, W. (1993). *Logiques sociales dans le raisonnement*. Neuchâtel.

Doise, W., Mugny, G. (1981). *Le développement social de l'intelligence*. Paris.

Giles, H., Bourhis, R., Taylor, D. (1977). Towards a Theory of Language in Ethnic Group Relations. In: Giles, H. (ed.). *Language, Ethnicity and Intergroup Relations*. London, pp. 307-348.

Giles, H., Johnson, P. (1981). The Role of Language in Ethnic Group Formation. In: Turner, J.C., Giles, H. (eds.). *Intergroup Behavior*. Oxford, pp. 199-243.

Giles, H., Byrne, J. (1982). An Intergroup Approach to Second Language Acquisition. In: *Journal of Multilingual and Multicultural Development*, 3, pp. 17-40.

Giles, H., Johnson, P. (1987). Ethnolinguistic Identity Theory. A Social Psychological Approach to Language Maintenance. In: *International Journal of the Sociology of Language*, 68, pp. 69-99.

Greeno, J. G., Collins, A. M., Resnick, L. B. (1996). Cognition and Learning. In: Berliner, D. C., Calfee, R. C. (eds.). *Handbook of Educational Psychology*. New York, pp. 15-46.

Gumperz, J. J. (ed.) (1982a). *Language and Social Identity*. Cambridge.

Gumperz, J. J. (1982b). *Discourse Strategies*. Cambridge.

Heller, M. (1987). The Role of Language in the Formation of Ethnic Identity. In: Phinney, J., Rotheram, M. (eds.). *Children's Ethnic Socialization.* Newbury Park, CA, pp. 180-200.

Heller, M. (1988). *Codeswitching. Anthropological and Sociolinguistic Perspectives.* New York.

Hertz-Lazarowitz, R., Miller, N. (1992). *Interaction in Cooperative Groups. The Theoretical Anatomy of Group Learning.* Cambridge.

Hildebrandt, N., Giles, H. (1983). The Japanese as Subordinate Group: Ethnolinguistic Identity Theory in a Foreign Language Context. In: *Anthropological Linguistics,* 25, pp. 436-466.

Hogg, M. A., Abrams, D. (1988). *Social Identification. A Social Psychology of Intergroup Relations and Group Processes.* London.

Kastersztein, J. (1990). Les strategies identitaires des acteurs sociaux. Approche dynamique des finalités. In: Camilleri, C. et al. (eds.). *Strategies Identitaires.* Paris, pp. 27-41.

Khleif, B. (1975). *Ethnic Boundaries, Identity and Schooling. A Socio-cultural Study of Welsch-English Relations.* Washington, DC (ERIC Document Reproduction Service N° ED 108 517).

Lipiansky, E. M. (1992). *Identité et communication. L'expérience groupale.* Paris.

Lipiansky, E. M., Taboada-Leonetti, I., Vasquez, A. (1990). Introduction à la problématique de l'identité. In: Camilleri, C. et al. (eds.). *Strategies Identitaires.* Paris, pp. 7-26.

Mugny, G. (1991). *Psychologie sociale du développement cognitif.* Berne.

Pao, D. L., Wong, S. D., Teuben-Rowe, S. (1997). Identity Formation for Mixed-Heritage Adults and Implications for Educators. In: *TESOL Quarterly,* 3, pp. 622-631.

Peirce, B. N. (1995). Social Identity, Investment, and Language Learning. In: *TESOL Quarterly,* 29, pp. 9-31.

Perret-Clermont, A. N. (1979). *La construction de l'intelligence dans l'interaction sociale.* Berne.

Perret-Clermont, A. N., Nicolet, M. (eds.) (1988). *Interagir et connaître.* Cousset.

Piaget, J. (1964). *Six études de psychologie.* Paris.

Piaget, J. (1967). *Biologie et connaissance.* Paris.

Piaget, J. (1968). *La naissance de l'intelligence chez l'enfant.* Paris.

Piaget, J. (1975). *L'équilibration des structures cognitives.* Paris.

Sachdev, I., Bourhis, R. (1990). Language and Social Identification. In: Abrahams, D., Hogg, M. (eds.). *Social Identity Theory. Constructive and Critical Advances.* London, pp. 87-119.

Tajfel, H. (1972). La catégorisation sociale. In: Moscovici, S. (ed.). *Introduction à la psychologie sociale,* Vol. 1. Paris, pp. 272-302.

Tajfel, H., Turner, J. C. (1979). An Integrative Theory of Intergroup Relations. In: Worchel, S., Austin, W. G. (eds.). *Psychology of Intergroup Relations.* Montery, CA.

Tap, P. (1979). *Relations interpersonnelles et genèse de l'identité.* Toulouse.

Tap, P. (1988). *La société Pygmalion.* Paris.

Vygotsky, L. S. (1996). *Thought and Language.* Cambridge, MA.

BRON, A., SCHEMMANN, M. (eds.) (2000). LANGUAGE, MOBILITY, IDENTITY. CONTEMPORARY ISSUES FOR ADULT EDUCATION IN EUROPE. MÜNSTER, pp. 185-199.

Cecilia Almlöv

LANGUAGE AND THE CONSTRUCTION OF A GENDERED IDENTITY

Introduction

There has been an interest in female and male language over a long period. The Swedish linguist, Carl Gustaf Cederschiöld, devoted a whole chapter to this topic in his book published already in 1900. There he specifically described how women's language is characterised by a great amount of talk and with frequent interruptions. It might be assumed that he overheard the conversation between his wife and her friends and from his impressions he then generalised about all women's language. Furthermore he stated: "It is well known that women have difficulties in following the parliamentary rules of a real discussion". (Cederschiöld 1900, 23).

Cederschiöld, as noted above, was particularly interested in women's talkativeness and their lack of an argumentative style (Celderschiöld 1900). In Swedish vocabulary there are many derogatory words for talkative women, such as *babbelfia* (Babble Mary), or *skvallerkärring* (scandalmonger), but nothing corresponding to talkative men. From these cultural prescriptions about women's language one might expect women to talk a lot in all circumstances. But do they really talk more than men?

Within language and gender research one of the most well examined linguistic features is the amount of talk. If we take a closer look at existing research findings, men tend to talk more in formal settings, such as political debates (Adams 1992), research seminars (Almlöv 1995), classrooms (Einarsson, Hultman 1984) and faculty meetings (Eakins, Eakins 1979) to mention a few. In informal settings it seems that women are likely to talk more, for example in married couples' conversations (Nordenstam 1987), and among friends (Tannen 1984). Moreover there exists evidence which suggests that women talk more when they are involved in conversations with other women, in same-sex groups. However, it can be deducted from this that Cederschiöld might have been right about his wife, she was talkative (even though he did not have the modern techniques as researchers of today have), since she was both involved in informal talk and in talk with other women, in a same-sex group (Cederschiöld 1900).

A New Focus in Language and Gender Research

How is it possible, then, to relate these gender differences in talk to a gender identity? In language and gender research there have, until recently, been two alternative ways of interpreting the results (Cameron 1992). First, the dominant approach suggests that there might be an imbalance of power between the sexes and that this, then, would explain the differences in talk. The more powerful party tends to talk more, to interrupt more often and to be dominant in other ways. The second approach, a so called two-culture-viewpoint, suggests that the differences between female and male actor's linguistic styles, are due to their socialisation in peer groups in the childhood. From this perspective girls' and boys' play in same-sex groups give rise to two different cultures and two different linguistic styles. Girls are disadvantaged by their linguistic style since it teaches them to be quiet and nice. Clearly, then, these two perspectives focus on how the gender identity is reflected in our talk.

In language and gender research the interest has recently been moved from studies on how the gender identity is reflected on a linguistic level, to studies on how the identity is constructed in the process of talk (Eckert, McConnell-Ginet 1992). The new approach suggests that the gender identity is constructed constantly through the use of the language and in the interaction with other members of the society. Thus, the surrounding society is a cultural product with cultural prescriptions about what femininity and masculinity are. An unreflected subjectivity interacts with these cultural norms and a new gender identity is created. Language plays a central role in this process. "Subjects produce their own linguistic behaviour, and judge the behaviour of others, in the light of the gendered meanings attached by the culture to particular ways of talking" (Cameron 1997, 28).

Furthermore, the new theoretical perspective for example studies women's language as part of identity, not as before, but as two separate categories. "Being a woman (or a man) is a matter, among other things, of talking like one" (Cameron 1997, 28). But to analyse the gender construction in language gives rise to several analytical problems. However, one linguistic approach which might give answers to them is the so-called doing gender approach, which stresses the activity in talk (West, Zimmerman 1987).

> Doing gender regards membership of a gender not as a pool of attributes 'possessed' by a person, but as something a person 'does'. In this sense, membership of a gender constitutes a performative act and not a fact. Gender is continually realised in interactional form (Wodak 1997, 13).

This analysis of the gender identity in linguistics can be related to a poststructuralistic tradition and its focus on subject positions[1].

In this article I will first try to illustrate the doing gender approach within language and gender research, by referring to two interesting articles dealing with children's conflict talk. I will show that it is possible to reinterpret the gender construction in language from this new perspective. Furthermore, I will discuss the importance of interpreting the findings in a broader context. The doing gender approach is useful as a tool in the analyses, but I will suggest that in addition we need to consider whether a contextual frame is necessary or not.

Children's Conflict Talk

I have chosen two articles based on research to illustrate the examples of doing gender, and will present them as well as compare them with each other.

In children's play there are many episodes of conflicts or disputes. The conflicts deal with access to toys, but most conflicts develop to a negotiation about roles and a confrontation with wrongdoers in the group. The

---

[1] Here the term subject position refers to Fairclough's use of the term (Fairclough 1989). He uses it instead of 'social roles' in order to focus on the activity. "Occupying a subject position is an essentially matter of doing (or not doing) certain things, in line with the discoursal rights and obligations of teachers and pupils – what each is allowed and required to say, and not allowed or required to say, within that particular discourse type. So this is a case where social structure, in particular form of discourse conventions, determines discourse." (Fairclough 1989, 38).

conflicts can, as in the following example, start by a challenge. Here Tony and Chopper, two black boys from Philadelphia, argue[2] (Goodwin 1997, 113).

Example One: Boys Conflict. Gimme the Things

1. Tony: Gimme the things.

2. Chopper: You sh:ut up you big lips. (Y all been hangin around with thieves.)

3. Tony: (shut up)

4. Chopper: Don't gimme that. = I'm not talkin to you.

5. (pause 1.4)

6. Tony: I'm talkin to y:ou!

7. Chopper: Ah you better sh:ut up with your little – di:ngy sneaks.

8. (pause 1.4)

Further in this sequence Chopper is accused to be a wrongdoer, and he defend himself and argues directly. This directness in talk and a confrontational style in handling a conflict might be more common in boys' conversations than in girls'. Girls seem to be indirect in most of their confrontations with one another and prepare to confront an absent member in the future by creating a two-against-one situation.

Let us now turn to a number of articles. The first article, by the sociolinguist Amy Sheldon, shows how 3-5 year old boys and girls manage conflict in a day care centre (Sheldon 1997). A female and male gender identity is constructed through their conflict talk, where girls use a so called double-voice discourse, which is a conversational style that confronts without appearing confrontational. Girls are nice and powerful at the say time. The boys on the other hand are more direct and solve problems more aggressively.

The second article, by Marjorie Harness Goodwin, focuses on older black children, 9-14 year old, playing in the back yard in Philadelphia,

---

[2] This transcript is made in a conversation analytical tradition (Sachs, Schegloff, Jefferson 1974), which explains the detailed level of the transcript and its closeness to the real talk with all linguistic features. It can be difficult to read for a reader used to a another convention of transcribing data.

USA (Goodwin 1993). Here one way to manage conflicts is through story telling. Girls are likely to tell stories about absent group members. By doing this they start a conflict that will be solved in the future time when the absent party will return. Boys on the other hand are more direct and confront the members of the group when they are present (see the example above).

Before I comment on these articles I think it is necessary to explain the differences, in language and gender research, surrounding methodology.

Methodological Considerations

In language and gender research there are three common traditions, the sociolinguistic, conversational analytical and the discourse analytical. The sociolinguistic approach is normally quantitative. Sociolinguistic studies, often beforehand, decide what type of event that will be focused, and then document as many episodes of that event as possible. There are two ways of collecting data: to record new conversations or to use old ones. For example the researcher might be interested how the pronunciation of consonants among children changes when they talk to the elderly. A hypothesis could be that younger ones would be more likely to pronounce consonants clearly to avoid misunderstandings. The researcher will analyse the data and listen to the pronunciation of all consonants without listening to the content. It is then possible that important and typical events of the talk are hidden behind the consonants. I am of course not suggesting that an investigation of consonants is uninteresting, but what I suggest is that a focus on the identity construction makes a qualitative approach more attractive.

Another tradition that grows is analytical discourse. In this approach the qualitative way of collecting data, observing and analyse it is more common. In the analysis the data will be treated as a 'talking' data. The object of study will emerge out of the data after listening to the recordings several times. (The conversation analytical approach (CA) is qualitative as well, and well established in linguistics as well as in other fields, for example in sociology.)

We know a lot more about boys' conversational skills than we know about girls'. One reason might be that the quantitative studies have focused on boys' talk since it is more dramatic. There is research on boys' conflicts because we expect boys to be involved in conflicts. However, if we chose a qualitative analysis, there are episodes in girls' talk that might be of interest as well. If the researcher takes the actor's point of view new types of event will be analysed, such as in this case, girls' conflict talk.

Girls Manage Conflicts with a Double-Voice

Let us now turn to the first study of children's talk. In this study both girls' and boys' talks are in focus. The researcher, Amy Sheldon, visited a day care centre for 3-5 year old children and arranged 12 same-sex groups, with three children in each, and video recorded them playing (Sheldon 1997).

One way to illustrate children's way to manage conflicts is to take a closer look at one transcribed episode. In this sequence the girls in the study were playing with dolls and pretending that the dolls were sick children. One of the girls, Elaine, took the role of a nurse and kept the control over the medical equipment. Arlene was a mother and wanted to give her baby an injection. The conflict then starts with a struggle for the equipment. Let us take a closer look at the episode[3] (Sheldon 1997, 236).

Example two:

1. Arlene: I get to do some more things too. Now don't forget- now don't touch the baby until I get back, because it IS MY BABY! [said to both of the other girls] I'll check her ears okay? [puts down the syringe and picks up the ear scope]

2. Elaine: Now I'll- and I'll give her- I'll have to give her [the same doll] a shot. [picks up the syringe that Arlene has put down]

3. Arlene: There can only be ONE thing that you- that- NO, she- she only needs one SHOT.

4. Elaine: Well, let's pretend it's another day that we have to look in her ears together.

---

[3] From the transcription we learn that this is a less detailed on than the one quoted earlier, and it belongs to a more discourse analytical approach.

5. Arlene: No, no, yeah but I do the ear looking. Now don't
               SHOT.[lowering the voice but still insisting] DON'T SHOT
               HER! I'm the one who does all the shots, 'cause this is my
               baby!

6. Elaine: [whispers] Well- I'm the nurse and nurses get to do the
               shots.

7. Arlene: [spoken very intensely] An' me'- And men- well, then men
               get to do the shots too even 'cause men can be nurses. But
               you can't shot her.

Throughout their conflict, and while they struggle for control, these girls
manage to be engaged in the same theme with a conflict co-occurring. This
shot-sequence continues, and the girls negotiate and try to convince one
another to gain the control over the shots. They use several linguistic
strategies in order to succeed and soften the conflict: the use of the tag-
question okay? (turn 1), they try to introduce a new scenario by talking
about what will happen another day (turn 4), they can work together (turn
4). Nevertheless, after all Elaine's efforts to gain control, Arlene has still
the role of a 'nurse' and insists on doing the ear looking and shot all by
herself. Elaine has been trying to balance her own interests with Arlene's in
a nice manner, but with her goal in mind, to shoot her own baby. Another
feature that is more likely to show up in girls conversations is the use of a
muted voice. This strategy appears when the conflict reaches its peak of in-
sistence. By using the muted voice it is possible to confront the other more
direct with demands such as: DON'T YOU DARE (to shoot the baby).

However, the major strategy is the so called double-voice discourse.
This double-voice talk is a form of problem solving process. The girls try
to control the conversation and to be nice, and at the same time keep their
goal by the use of several other linguistic strategies. They negotiate about
their roles, and then comment that it is just a game, they justify their goal
and communicate clearly, in their way to try to soften the power conflict.

In the conflict talk girls operate with harmony as a frame. As soon as
there is an aggressive tone, girls try to construct a new direction in the conversation to make the interaction smooth again. This strategy can be found

in an academic setting as well, when graduate students present their research in seminars (Almlöv 1995). As soon as there are 'too' many critical comments on the students work, women in the seminar group raise their hands in order to give supportive comments. Also of interest is here that women are more likely to combine critique with support, while men can appear as only critical individuals. See examples below:

Supportive-Critical Comment

This theoretical approach seems relevant for your purposes, but you must explain your purpose more extensively.

Critical comment

Your data collection is not well documented.

For men the harmonious frame might not be as important in an academic setting as it might be to women. In an interview, a graduate man told me that the supportive women disturb the critical atmosphere which should characterise a seminar.

If we return to the children's conflict talk, than the conversations in the boys' group were also confrontational. In contrary to the long episode about the shot, it is possible to conclude that instead of solving the problems through talk they shift themes and play a new game. Even this strategy can be found in the academic seminar where the male professor changes topics very abruptly when a graduate student insists to stay with her own interpretation. Instead of a negotiating procedure the topic shift in what seems to be a more common strategy.

However, the verbal threats were not strong enough in boys' talk. Threats of physical force also played a major role in their talk, which could not be found in the girls talk. But, the girls, on the other hand, used comments like: Then you can't come to my birthday! And the response was of course: I don't want to come to your birthday. They hurt one another on another level – to be considered as a friend or not.

In our culture girls are expected to behave nice even in conflicts. If they are loud they are regarded as 'bossy'. In contrast, boys can be more aggressive and loud without appearing 'difficult', but instead be considered as strong. From this we can conclude that the cultural prescriptions about language behaviour differ for girls and boys. Sheldon's study provides evidence that girls find new ways to combine the expected niceness with power (Sheldon 1997).

- Girls do not avoid conflicts, but instead create a successful linguistic style to manage conflicts, a double-voice discourse.
- Girls keep their goals and negotiate at the same time and try to convince other members of the group that their opinion is the best. During the conflicts they can go on with the same theme of play.
- Girls are confrontational and competitive in play. Is it possible, than, to say that girls can be involved in conflicts, and manage them in a different way than boys?

In sum, girls challenge stereotypes about gender and negotiate their gender identity in conflict talk. They refuse to identify themselves with the positions offered to them in our culture, that is simply to be nice. Thus, a more realistic view is to see that girls create a conservative gender identity, niceness, beside a new one, power. They perform gender in their interaction and reconstruct gender identities.

Tell a Story and Start a Conflict

One further illustration of conflict talk among children is the study by Marjorie Harness Goodwin (1993). Interestingly, in her own neighbourhood, she recognised a group of children playing in the back yard. After observing them for one and a half year she was allowed to record them in their play. She observed the setting without any previous decisions about types of events that were theoretically interesting (games, rhymes). After listening to all recordings the conflict talk emerged out of the data as central episodes of the children's way of acting in every day conversations.

First, she found that girls and boys play in quite different groups. Evidence emerging from her observations is that boys seem to engage in games that are competitive. They are all ranked in relation to their capacities and abilities in play. From their play it also seems that their conflicts tend to start with verbal threats, but then continuing with threats of physical force, which can be compared to similar findings, noted earlier in Sheldon's study.

If we turn to the disputes among girls, there is another linguistic pattern of starting the conflicts. Girls seldom give one another commands. Instead of directly confronting one another, girls complain about someone who is absent and prepare themselves for a later conflict. This talk is initiated with a storytelling procedure called 'instigating', where a girl learns that the absent group member has been talking about her behind her back. A reporting activity starts like a trial, in which all that the absent girl, in this case Kerry, has been saying is reported.

Example three: Girls conflict. She said.

1. Julia: Isn't Kerry mad at me or s:omp'm.

    (pause 0.4)

2. Bea: I'on kn//ow.

3. Barbara: Kerry- always -mad- at somebody. I 'on' care-

4. Julia: ⌈ Cuz- cuz- cuz I wouldn't , cu:z she ain't put my name on that paper.

/---/

5. Barbara: Kerry always say somp'm.=When you=

6. Bea: ⌈ She-

7. Barbara: =jump in her face she gonna deny it.

8. Bea: Yah:p Yah:p.=An she said, h' An- and she said, hh that

9. Julia: ⌈ Right on.

10. Bea: you wouldn't be actin like that aroun- around people.

11. Julia: So: she wouldn' be actin like that wi' that other girl. = She the one   picked me to sit wi'them.

/---/

The instigating sequence, he-said-she-said, is followed by a long discussion about Kerry and what she had said about the other. Another activity co-occurs, an effort to create a two-against-one situation, in which Kerry will be the 'one party'. Then the absent party will be in trouble when she returns, she will be alone and she might be excluded from the group as well. So, girls' conflicts can be a way to exclude or include members of the group.

A Contextual Frame

We expect women to be socio-emotional experts and that they should be more engaged in talk with one other. Many studies have also found women to be more supportive and work harder to keep the conversation going. They indicate their interest in what other say by giving feedback responses like hmm, yes, that's right and by asking more questions (Nordenstam 1987). To refer the famous linguist Pamela Fishman, women do the 'interactional shit work' (Fishman 1983). They are sensitive to the context and act in the conversation to keep harmony.

The partner's sex might also influence linguistic styles. Existing findings show that girls and boys changes their linguistic styles when they change conversational partners. In an interesting study of school children (Ohlsson 1999), working in small groups, the boys and girls interacted differently when they changed from same-sex to mixed-sex groups. In the investigation, the experimental groups were told to suggest five things they would like to bring with them, if they had to stay in the forest for a week without any adults. What will you bring? The group had to decide five things altogether in a process of negotiating and developing their own suggestions. The end product, then, was a list from each group containing five suggestions of what they need in the forest.

First, in a study of the interaction, there was evidence that the group of girls was characterised by a democratic atmosphere and many jokes, but when they were mixed with boys they talked less and did not joke at all. Secondly, in a content analysis, their suggestions changed from relevant tools to matters of care taking. The girls suggested that an axe would be of importance, but in the group of boys they insisted instead on bringing medical equipment to be able to take care of the chain sawing boys. These results, then, appear to provide support for the notion that gender identities constantly change in the process of talk. In this case the doing gender perspective helps to reveal interesting patterns in the interaction between boys and girls. Girls construct a conservative gender identity when they interact in mixed-sex groups, but an intellectual gender identity in same-sex conversations.

It seems that language and gender research needs the performative gender approach to capture the language process and the construction of an identity in it. Thus, an adequate analysis of what girls and boys do, must take into account not simply the doing gender process in language use, but also the larger context in which language is used. Similar discussions can be found in other fields of research already in the 1980s. The historian Joan Scott discusses gender identity and how to analyse it in history. Historians need to "examine the ways in which gendered identities are substantively constructed and relate their findings to a range of activities, social organisations, and historically specific cultural representations" (Scott 1986, 44). We must, then, as the historians, concentrate on the process of construction, but also in addition relate the findings of linguistic patterns in talk, to a so called "social order" (social institutions, social space etc.), a term used by the linguist Norman Fairclough. One theory which might shed light on linguistic findings involves social activity and its relation to a discourse (text or talk). Fairclough offers a contextual frame that might be relevant for the doing gender approach.

An Order of Discourse

Fairclough constructs a theory in which he connects the order of discourse to the social order, theory to practice. He poses several important questions, and discusses the relationship between language, identity and society as a whole, a try to connect micro to macro. He concludes that our interaction is determined socially and has social effects (Fairclough 1989).

> Even when people are most conscious of their own individuality and think themselves to be most cut off from social influences – 'in the bosom of the family', for example – they still use language in ways which are subject to social convention (Fairclough 1989, 23).

It would appear, then, that our gender identity is related to the society and the linguistic context, order of discourse. Each level of the society, the practice, can be related to a similar level in discourse. Fairclough illustrates his theory as follows (Fairclough 1989, 29).

A.	B.
1. Social order	1. Order of discourse
2. Types of practise	2. Types of discourse
3. Actual practices	3. Actual discourses

The term social order (social institutions) refers to the structuring of our social space. This order can then be divided into types of practice, what we do in the social space (activities in that social order). In a social order (for example a police station) there are several types of practices (gathering data from a witness, interrogation). Actual practice at the micro level is focus for study. These orders and practices can be related to discourses (texts or communication). The order of discourse is the most general of the discourses (written police interviews, witnesses testifying through talk) can be related to many types of discourses (interviewing a thief by using for example both writings and talk). The actual discourse is used in our researched text.

In society as a whole there are many social orders (social institutions, or social spaces). Language and gender research have to connect the different levels of discourse and investigate different social orders to reveal patterns in the gendered discourses (text and talk). The two studies referred to above belong to two different actual practices and discourses. Both deal with talk, but one in a back yard in a city, and the other in a day care centre. The analysis of both articles reveal similarities and differences. But, what we need to consider is that they can be compared in a careful way, since they belong to different practices. By using this approach it is possible to bring some order to the growing field of research and a greater awareness of the implications of context.

Conclusion

In this article I have approached the doing gender concept by referring to two articles about conflict talk. What I have illustrated is that it seems possible to use the doing gender concept in the analysis of interaction in same-sex or mixed-sex groups. For example, Sheldon found that girls' talk which at first seemed to develop a conservative gender identity, 'niceness', turned out to give evidence for a more complex expression of identity, niceness and power co-occurring through a double-voice discourse. The girls 'did gender' and created a new identity in which the more conservative niceness co-occurred with the power (Sheldon 1997).

As we have seen, it is by developing detailed analysis of episodes of talk that we can capture both girls' and women's, boys' and men's interactional skills. However, children's talk represents a unique case, since it reveals the conversational patterns in early childhood and the construction of the gender identity in talk with friends, adults, at school and in leisure time. But, as said earlier, the identity is constantly constructed in talk, and it would be interesting to see how the gender identity develops and changes through lifelong discourses.

The use of the doing gender approach proved to be fruitful. But, I suggest that the context has to be taken into account. Further research is needed to understand the complexity of our gender identities and language, in different contexts, or so called social practices.

References

Adams, K. (1992). Accruing Power on Debate Floors. In: Hall, K. et al. (eds.). *Locating Power*. Proceedings of the Second Berkeley Women and Language Conference, Vol. 1. Berkeley, pp. 1-10.

Almlöv, C. (1995). *Kvinnor och män i forskarseminarier. En studie av interaktionen på tre institutioner vid Uppsala universitet*. Skriftserie från Centrum för kvinnoforskning vid Stockholms universitet, No. 11. Stockholm.

Cameron, D. (1992). *Feminism and Linguistic Theory*. London.

Cederschiöld, G. (1900). *Om kvinnospråk och andra ämnen. Anteckningar och reflexioner*. Lund.

Eakins, B., Eakins, G. (1979). Verbal Turn-Taking and Exchanges in Faculty Dialogue. In: Dubois, B.-L., Crouch, I. (eds.). *The Sociology of Languages of American Women*. San Antonio, pp. 53-62.

Eckert, P., McConnell-Ginet, S. (1992). Communities of Practice. Where Language, Gender and Power All Live. In: Hall, K. et al. (eds.). *Locating Power*. Proceedings of the Second Berkeley Women and Language Conference, Vol. 1. Berkeley, pp. 89-99.

Einarsson, J., Hultman, T. G. (1984). *Godmorgon pojkar och flickor. Om språk och kön i skolan*. Malmö.

Fairclough, N. (1989). *Language and Power*. New York.

Goodwin, M. H. 1993. In: Tannen, D. (ed.). *Gender and Conversational Interaction*. New York, pp. 110-143.

Maltz, D. M., Borker, R. A. (1982). A Cultural Approach to Male-Female Miscommunication. In: Gumperz, J. J. (ed.). *Language and Social Identity.* Cambridge, pp. 196-216.

Nordenstam, K. (1987). *Kvinnlig och manlig samtalsstil, Färsk forsk 11.* Göteborg.

Ohlsson, M. (1999). Att konstruera kön. En studie av skolelever i enkönad och blandad grupp. In: *Svenskans beskrivning 23. Förhandlingar vid Tjugotredje sammankomsten för svenskans beskrivning,* Göteborg den 15-16 maj 1998. Lund.

Scott, J. W. (1988). *Gender and the Politics of History.* New York.

Sheldon, A. (1997). Talking Power: Girls, Gender Enculturation and Discourse. In: Wodak, R. (ed.). *Gender and Discourse.* London, pp. 225-245.

Tannen, D. (1984). *Conversational Style. Analyzing Talk among Friends.* Ablex, NY.

West, C., Zimmerman, D. (1987). Doing Gender. In: *Gender and Society,* 1 (2), pp. 125-151.

Wodak, R. (1997). *Gender and Discourse.* London.

BRON, A., SCHEMMANN, M. (eds.) (2000). LANGUAGE, MOBILITY, IDENTITY. CONTEMPORARY ISSUES FOR ADULT EDUCATION IN EUROPE. MÜNSTER, pp. 200-213.

Tordis Dahllöf

EXCHANGING A WORD OR TWO...
MEETING BETWEEN PEOPLE AS CROSS-CULTURAL ENCOUNTERS

The title of this article "Exchanging a word or two..." is the same as the book recently written and published by me in Swedish, within the field of cultural science. Its focus is on certain phenomena which are relevant to the society we live in at the end of the twentieth century (Dahllöf 1998). The words of the title are taken from a well-known poem by the Swedish poet Hjalmar Gullberg (Gullberg 1945)[1]. It continues: "... made it easy to walk./ All meetings between people should be so." The subtitle of my book is: *Scientific Encounters are Cultural Encounters are Human Encounters*. Here I intended to emphasise the importance of cross-cultural and cross-disciplinary encounters. In other words, as one Finnish folklore expert puts it: "Knowledge does not have to be split up as science does" (Honko 1976, 27).

I am an ethnologist with a background in cultural history and I am at present interested in human cultural encounters and in questions of identity where I am a keen proponent of the cultural breadth which is evident when one is a bearer of two cultures and two languages, for instance Polish and Swedish (Dahllöf 1985a, 1985b, 1994, 1998). Apart from addressing my fellow-researchers in other disciplines, I am well acquainted with the philosophy of the Swede Hans Larsson who emphasises the links between intellect and feeling, and for whom intuition and convergent thinking are central concepts (Larsson 1944b, 1945).

---

[1] The lines of poetry are well known for a Swedish audience and are taken from the poem *Människors möte*. They can be found in the *Dagens dikt* anthology, a lyrical book of thoughts and aphorisms.

An empirical documentary material in my ethnological research I tend to take from fiction and poetry, where I can detect or rather meet the author and his/her work. I regard the author as almost a colleague or a partner in research.

This extension of the research tools, which is by no means generally accepted in the world of academia, have felt liberating in my case. This approach is important to me as to fulfil my wish that my own research results will have relevance for the society we live in.

The Writer as an Exposer of Cultures

The philosopher Hans Larsson has written the following in his book *Min filosofi* (My Philosophy, 1944). Since I so often use literature in my research, I do so not as a critic or literary historian but in order to get a better grip on some philosophical motivation or other, better than one gets by way of traditional philosophy (Larsson 1944, 91). For the same reason, I, as an ethnologist, have used literary texts these last few years. When I was younger, I would not have dared, it would not have been regarded as a legitimate scientific praxis. Nowadays, it is more acceptable to utilise "hybrid/literary texts" but the scientific world in general is afraid of crossing the boundaries between disciplines – all the more if literary material is employed – despite the trend of talking about inter-disciplinary studies.

As an ethnologist I have human beings in the sense of cultural beings as my object of study reality and I feel it is entirely legitimate to use literature as a source of documentation of reality. The responsibility for how this documentation is used is entirely my own, but the skill to render it visible is that of the writer. One good support in this choice of material is the South African writer and Nobel Prize winner Nadine Gordimer. She has said about herself, and about her many-sided writings that not one of her pieces of reportage can ever be as true to life as her fictional production (Gordimer 1995).

When I read about crises and wars in former Yugoslavia, and their background, I find that Slavenka Drakulic's books are a great help in the understanding of the array of cultures and religions that constitute that region of Europe (Draculic 1995). Over the years, I have also followed the novels of the Swedish Greek writer Theodor Kallifatides who has presented to a wide Swedish audience how it feels inside to be an individual in two cultures, a user of two languages (Kallifatides 1989). The richness of belonging to two cultures is something we ought to appreciate and accept. Being two people in one without denying anyone is very important.

But there are no simple answers to such big questions that concern changing countries and languages. The Swedish writer Vilhelm Moberg who has charted Swedish-American emigration in a multi-volume work has stated in *Din stund på jorden* (Your Moment on Earth; 1963) – a novel with an autobiographical background: "Native land is a singular concept. It can never become a plural." When he returns home on a visit, he no longer feels at home there and states: "You should accept the emigrant and learn to be reconciled with him. Forgive him for living under a delusion that moving his body would help him on this Earth" (Morberg 1963, 263).

Another issue connected with migration is that of bilingualism. As a field of research, it is frequent in today Sweden. But there are arguments both for and against it, and they still waken strong emotions. Seen histori-cally, we should have learned the lesson from the way we have treated the languages of minorities in our own country, i.e. Saami (Lappish) and Tornedal Finnish (in Northern Sweden). Language is culture and without a mother-tongue you are crippled. This, however, does not contradict the fact that we should always learn the language of the new country properly.

"Närpes language is a world language" says the Swedish writer, Anna-Lisa Bäckman (Dahllöf 1991) about her Finland-Swedish dialect. For her any mother-tongue includes everything that is important for a person. She refers to her meeting with her relatives in Canada, who where born there, but still are able to speak the old language. She could communicate with them just through the Närpes language.

In the anthology entitled *Världen i Sverige* (The World in Sweden) all the various foreign writers posit the same idea. In the perspective of a life-time we must gain the insight that our mother-tongue is both intellectual and emotional capital, as the language researcher Leena Huss (1991) points out.

Culture is Learned

In the time that passes between the first cry uttered by a child and the mute, wordless appeals of the old, we, as cultural beings, are exposed to constant impressions and influences. Between the basic construction of genetic material and the superstructure of the social environment we cruise towards the final port which we imagine to provide the key to the code of the consistent thread of life of the ego. We like to think of ourselves as constantly in control of the all decisions and the content of our life, while in fact we are constantly bounced between conflicting aims and guidelines actually set up by others.

A lifelong process, thus, where upbringing and the constant comment of older people and their actions guide the development of the child. This field of tension can best be analysed by way of the texts of authors such as the Canadian Margaret Laurence who depicts the relationship between the Scottish-Canadian girl Vanessa and the Indian half-blood Piquette in the collection of short-stories entitled *A Bird in the House* (1994). They live in the Canadian wilderness, not so much with each other as alongside each another, and their cultural home environments prevent them from really encountering.

Another example is the Danish author Dea Trier Mørch in her enchanting book *Kastanjeallén* (Chestnut Avenue; 1974) which describes how the author grew up in a Danish village. She is surrounded by adult women and a wonderful maternal grandmother who possesses, apart from a capacity of down-to-earth matters, a talent for art and painting, but is sadly lacking in recognition. Trier Mørch not only describes traditions around the festivals of the year and the grandeur of spring and summer, but also a cultural feeling for the expansion of existence in all directions, not least with regard to children. The children are taken seriously, as seriously as they deserve (Trier Mørch 1974).

On one occasion the heroine Maja is asked by her youngest maternal aunt if she wanted to have children when she grew up. Her answer is that she wants to have four children from four different men of different nations without getting married at all (Trier Mørch 1974).

What lies behind this remarkable answer needs to be analysed elsewhere. Maja's own father was in hospital, far away from the family. Her maternal grandfather was a concrete presence but it was her grandmother with her grown-up daughters who ruled the roost. The grandfather's importance lay outside of the family circle. Is this also an inheritance that Maja has internalised?

The Swedish ethnologist Börje Hanssen has emphasised the importance of taking into consideration the upbringing of a child and contacts between people in any specific culture (Hanssen 1973).

> Cultural givens do not float freely between generations and have to be inculcated in a child by way of upbringing. Even the way the patterns affect us is of significance. We are not influenced by society, nor do we influence our environment, but we are *integrated* in society by way of our consciousness and our environment is a part of ourselves. (Hanssen 1973, 43)

There is one further factor in the socialisation of children into adult life which is not considered here but which has a central effect on them and that is the children's books and descriptions of children of the respective country, not forgetting children's songs and rhymes (von Zweigerk 1965).

The conclusion is that by growing up and socialising in a specific cultural context: family, language, social class humans learn. It is through experiencing culture that their identity forms. This lifelong process is well described in fine literature.

Ethnicity or Ethnic Life

Learned culture is a part of a broader concept of ethnicity or ethnic life to which we socialised. How ethnicity is expressed by writers in fine literature is exemplified in this section.

Both ethnicity and ethnic life are loaded concepts and are, unfortunately, also controversial. Ethnicity is a highly complex concept and ethnicity *per se* does not exist, says the Swedish peace researcher Björn Hettne (1989). However, it is when language, religion, race, etc. collide with the social and economic institutions of a country that problems arise. Every country has a great deal of historical material which bears witness to the difficulties encountered by individuals and groups changing environment. "We" and "others" have always existed. They are in fact socio-psychological phenomena and fiction writers are the surest witnesses of such experiences.

It is not a new phenomenon, however.[2] What is new today is the fact that large ethnic groups move into, e.g. European environments, while in the past they were placed at the map's periphery. The most obvious examples are the indigenous peoples who are to this day discriminated against by the white population. We can understand that better by moving over to literature and read, for instance, a poem by aboriginal poet Kath Walker *The Past* (1970) or Mapucho Indian Georg Munroe's poem *Forever Yesterday* (1966) or *Vidderna inom mig* (Expanses Within Me, 1991) by the Saami Nils-Aslak Valkeapää. Here we can encounter the authenticity of the culture other than our own and its people, and as a consequence we are able to understand them better.

Another moving document is the novel *The Diviners* (1985) by the Canadian Margaret Laurence. Half-blood Jules, of Indian background, meets the Scottish woman, Morag. Both carry their cultural baggage with them. They have a daughter, then drift apart and Morag sees that her daughter is branded as a "filthy half-blood" and it becomes Morag's life's work to rehabilitate her daughter's red heritage. To be aware of own ethnicity and to deal with it in depth is exemplified by the above references to the authors writing about minorities.

The Uppsala migration researcher Harald Runblom has pointed out that cultural encounters are no quick rendezvous but are protracted processes lasting generations (Runblom 1988). This can be exemplified by the integration of Jews in international and Swedish environments. Especially cultural traditions but also religion and to some extent language, constitute a binding link among them throughout the world; and the state of Israel is their own national experiment. At the same time Jews are successfully integrated into many societies, e.g. Swedish society. Jewish families contributed to Swedish literature and artistic culture, while Yiddish culture of East European provenance for example has found other commercial outlets.

The example of successful integration we can find in Bertil Neuman's fine description of his East European Jewish heritage in the book *Något försvann på vägen* (Something Disappeared On the Way, 1989). Neuman, the Swedish businessman, begins to examine his own cultural background when his three-year-old son one day states that: "I don't want to be a

---

[2] For example the Saami (lapps), Gypsies and Jews in Sweden.

Jew!". On the other hand the example of awakened ethnic awareness in many Swedish Jews who were well assimilated in Swedish society can be noticed after the World War II and the Holocaust.

The contacts of Swedes with new ethnic groups in the late twentieth century has given rise to the question: What is Swedish ethnicity? Many thorough research reports have been written in which one can find several answers (e.g. Daun 1989). The Swedish cultural heritage is mostly rooted in the Lutheran Church. In modern times, both Christianity and its moral but also more secularised Swedish culture is represented by the concepts of people's education (*folkbildning*) and the ideology of "people's home" (*folkhemmet*). Both gave the ground and a flavour to the modern Swedish welfare state. As important elements of contribution to Swedish ethnicity one can mention population structure of the country; its successful policy of keeping itself put out of wars conducted on the continent; or – not the least – a strong awareness of the of natural environment, a feeling which Sweden shares with its Nordic neighbours. Swedes are also regarded as shy, anxious and almost always attempting at avoiding all conflicts. While I enumerate these characteristics, almost prejudices, it strikes me that the younger generation would, partially, have given different answers to questions like: Who is a Swede or how is it to be a Swede? Important conclusion comes of it: cultural heritage has historical roots, although it does change with time.

Writing about one's own cultural identity, about Swedish ethnicity, is a difficult task. I shall therefore quote an 'outsider', the French scholar, Jean François Battail, who has worked as a university lecturer in Sweden. He points out that Swedes are not at all more provincial than people in Paris or London. He makes reference to Swedish social movements, folk high schools, proletarian literature as well as the concept of "ståndscirkulation" (movement between classes) which is rarely found outside Sweden. Encounters across different ethnicities require a self-esteem of ourselves without arrogance and without complexes. I agree with Battail that we should be ourselves, but at the same time I advocate that we need to learn more about ourselves, about our own cultural heritage and how to deal with it. This enables us to understand others.

Regional Identity

Now in 1999 we are experiencing a cruel struggle between the supporters of the national state and the attempts by smaller regions to break away, in a determined attempt to express their local identity. The Balkans different nations are struggling for own nation-state against a federal 'construct' with the horrifying example of war and terrorism. In Ireland, on the other hand, the very same nation, has a long tradition of struggle, based on religious differences, one which is not yet over. England has recently given limited autonomy to Scotland and Wales, the Inuit in northern Canada have been given an independent space.

Local identity has been given spatial reality and in that environment live people who are linked by territory, of course, but also by language, traditions, work and social life. The fact that most people have a 'sense of locality' a feeling of belonging which they leave with greater or lesser reluctance, is proved by ethnological base material and fictional literature all over the world. Emigrant literature is one of the types which depicts this process of belonging, extending over time.

This deeply human sense of belonging somewhere often collides in modern times with social planning measures. An ethnologist can often detect conflicts between the various bodies set up by society and the values and interests of the local population. What is of more importance, the people themselves, or their environment in form of "*platskänsla*" (sense of place) (Asplund 1983).

What we do know today is that people living in sparsely populated areas are refusing to move, are arguing to stay in a politically cogent manner. This self-awareness could not be developed in older days. People knew what they wanted, but what did feelings matter when necessity forced them to move? Even today this human dimension is often neglected.

Relationships: Individual and Society – Education and Culture

A child grows up in an ethnic and local environment, becomes a young person who is accepted or rejected by adult society and is educated by it To become what? What is she/he becoming of? These questions are taken up by researchers in Sweden who deal with social aspects when different cultures (both Swedish and immigrant), or way of being, meet. But I find the human dimension is sadly neglected both in education and in working life.

The aim of my work, as I see it, is to make such aspects visible and fulfilled in all the work we do, not least in a research environment. The Norwegian anthropologist Marianne Gullestad stresses:

> One of the points I want to emphasise is that all scholarly contributions should be considered in relation to the economic, personal, social and personal contexts in which they are produced. Scientific projects are situated knowledge (Gullestad 1992, 13).

We do research not only for our research colleagues, but for other people as well, to contribute to other and broader aspects of society.

A Central European would presumably refer to Pierre Bourdieu's *Homo Academicus* to show the world view of academics.

Education begins, as is well known, in school. Ironically, a societal institution such as school receives posthumous fame in biographies of teachers and the way children experience the teachers. The teacher is the school. For that very reason teacher training is especially important. Two arguments can illuminate what I mean. First the Bourdieu disciple Françine Muel-Dreyfus argues that identification within the job means an integration of both – individuality and career. It will then be dependent on the social history of the career in question and on the individual if the career or the individual have to give way (Muel-Dreyfus 1985). Second the Swedish ethnologist Boel Westerberg stated: "To a much larger extent than we perhaps realise, we are not communicating with people of flesh and blood but with roles and status – and societal institutions" (Westerberg 1987, 95).

What is central is that we must regard school environments as meeting places for human culture, not simply as places where knowledge is imparted. That is why as an ethnologist I am interested in school and in education as a cross-cultural meeting place. Many memories of school bear witness to the fact that pupils were ignored in the daily struggle for learning the right things. In former times, there was also a cultural discrepancy between the way men and women viewed a career as a teacher. Many male teachers used teaching as a way of earning their daily bread in order to have some time left over for academic or political work. Female teachers, on the other hand, were fully committed to the educational and empathetic side of teaching. And what happens afterwards? How much of a school mentality is taken up as mental baggage into higher education? We shouldn't consider school world and higher education just as worlds for themselves, separated from outside world, but as a cross roads there individuals and education relate to each other and to the outside world. Thus, we should also take a macro perspective.

Nevertheless, or because of that, I felt free to go beyond the Swedish educational system, in order not to become bogged down in local instances, and to highlight the complexity of being both a teacher and a member of society. One example is the American anthropologist Margaret Mead, another the historian Geoffrey Blainey.

The female scientist Mead became successful and is often referred to as "anthropology's grandmother", despite internal criticism of her short time filed research and suspect scientific grounds, whilst the Australian, a well-known historian, Blainey takes a wrong turn in the immigration debate and is labelled as a racist. One Swedish example is the explorer Sven Hedin who crossed the Takla-Makan desert and the mountains of Tibet to seek the elusive Lake Lopnor. A blot on his escutcheon was the influence of Nazi ideology on his work (Berg, Holmquist 1993).

No longer can we separate the scientist or his/her reports from the environment in which he/she is doing his/her research, nor from the surrounding social and cultural society, let alone the role the mass media play in the dissemination of scientific research. Ethical and moral values come into the picture and no scientist can afford to ignore these, claiming them to be irrelevant.

It should not be regarded as a change of identity if a child grows up, equally if one changes cultural competence and language prowess. But it has been, and still is, a dilemma for academics to climb up into a 'higher' environment without denying their roots. Some cope with this climb with loyalties to their origins intact. One Swedish example is Ronny Ambjörnsson who described his life starting out from a working class home in Gothenburg and ending up a professor at Umeå University.

As is well known, science is meant to explain without adding an emotional dimension. Against that way of thinking, I would place the ideas of the philosopher Hans Larsson on intuition, and the will and feelings forming one whole. Nevertheless it is the intellect, according to him, that governs the intuition. In his research, he often introduces empirical evidence from fine literature (Larsson 1944a, Larsson 1944b). But here, I would like to quote again from Honko: "Nowadays, empirical research cannot for ever continue on the researcher's terms alone" (Honko 1976, 254). The same way of thinking can be found in the book *Etniskt liv och kulturell mångfald* (Ethnic life and Cultural Diversity; 1993) written by ethnologists Ingvar Svanberg and Mátyáz Szabó. They point out the following: "Producing knowledge about the terms under which people live simply from the promises of science is an out-of-date way of thinking and cannot be defended on ethical grounds" (Svanberg, Szabó 1993, 30). Lauri Honko states: "Giving causal explanations can be scientifically tempting, but it should also be allowed to become interested in people and their fates without causalities. If one understands something in depth, the need for explanation ceases" (Honko 1976, 254).

In this section I tried to show that the dilemma and problems one faces while being involved in education are also the dilemmas of researchers themselves. Being a researcher one cannot escape from moral responsibility regarding other individuals and society at large. Even here we can talk about cross-cultural meetings. But in the sense of being able to understand others, i.e those, who are subjects of our research.

Conclusion

"Our identity is not confirmed till we show it to others" the social psychologist Meyer Fortes states (Fortes 1983, 389). This observation is also valid for our identity as researcher or scientist. It has been difficult to summarise a book – albeit a small one – and be forced to remove all the textual quotes which I used to illustrate my ethnological text (Dahllöf 1998).

Both my book and this article are about meeting between people and the role such meetings play in our identity as bearers of culture, language and ethnicity. But they are also about researchers studying culture communication of human beings. The more subtle our methods of research are, the surer we become of our arguments. The more we examine disciplines bordering our own, the more help we receive in our own analyses. Our interdisciplinary stock of knowledge becomes ever larger and more useful for cultural and social researchers.

I would like, once again to emphasise the fact of the strength of both regional identity and international scope. Perhaps in the way the Australian historian Manning Clark says about Australian identity: "A gum tree is not a branch of an oak" (Clark 1980, 4). This implies a wry smile at the cultural hegemony of the English culture. My personal and careful approach to try to understand the culture of the Aborigines and their cultural bearers has allowed me to see clearly and to adopt Ruby Langford's autobiographical novel *Don't Take Your Love To Town* (1988): "I thought of the difference between white people saying: 'I own this land' and Blacks saying: 'We belong to this land.'"(Langford 1988, 262).

I will give the last fitting word to Stellan Arvidsson a Swedish writer, educationalist and politician (Arvidsson 1954).

The Word

I know only one word which is sacred to all:
an old word, borne on fire, soiled,
which is mocked on the common Earth of Aryan, Jew,
Chinese and Negro,
a word which interprets the noblest an Aryan,
Jew, Chinese and Negro knows,
the word, constantly betrayed:
humanity.

References

Arvidsson, St. (1945). The Word. In: Radiotjänst (ed.). *Dagens dikt.* Stockholm.

Asplund, J. (1983). *Tid, rum, kollektiv och individ.* Stockholm.

Battail, J. F. (1985). Svensk humanism sedd utifrån. In: *Tvärsnitt 3.* Stockholm.

Berg, L., Holmqvist, St. (1993). *I Sven Hedins spår.* Stockholm.

Clark, M. (1980). *The Quest of Australian Identity.* St. Lucia.

Clifford, J. (1997). *Routes. Travel and Translation in the Late Twentieth Century.* Cambridge, MA.

Dahllöf, T. (1985a). Det multikulturella Kanada. In: *Multiethnic, 2.* Uppsala.

Dahllöf, T. (1985b). Identitet och antipod. En studie i australiensisk identitetsdebatt. In: *Uppsala Multiethnic Papers 5.* Uppsala.

Dahllöf, T. (1991). Kultur finns som realitet mellan människor. In: Wijc-Andersson, E. (ed.). *Kultur - Text - Språk. Det finns mer i en text än en ord.* Uppsala.

Dahllöf, T. (1994). *Verkligheten i dikten. Författaren och forskaren i sin kulturmiljö.* Stockholm.

Dahllöf, T (1998). *Byta ett ord eller två... Kunskapsmöten är kulturmöten är människomöten.* Stockholm.

Daun, Å. (1989). *Svensk mentalitet. Ett jämförande perspektiv.* Stockholm.

Drakulic, S. (1995). *Balkan Express. Fragment från andra sidan kriget.* Stockholm.

Fortes, M. (1983). Problems of Identity and Person. In: Jacobsson-Widding, A. (ed.). *Identity. Personal and Sociocultural. A Symposium.* Uppsala.

Gordimer, N. (1995). *Writing and Being.* Cambridge, MA.

Gullberg, H. (1945). Människors möte. In: Radiotjänst (ed.). *Dagens dikt.* Stockholm.

Gullestad, M. (1992). *The Art of Social Relations. Essays on Culture, Social Action and Everyday Life in Modern Norway.* Chicago.

Hanssen, B. (1973). *Kulturens permanens och förändring.* Lyngby.

Hettne, B. (1989). Att studera internationella relationer. In: *Padrigu Papers 1989.* Gothenburg.

Honko, L. (1976a). *Forskarens ideologi.* Oslo, Bergen, Tromsö.

Honko, L. (1976b). Om fältarbetets roll i traditionsforskningen. In: *NIF Publication 5.* Turku.

Huss, L. (1991). *Simultan tvåspråkighet i svensk-finsk kontext.* Uppsala.

Kallifatides, Th. (1989). *En lång dag i Aten. Berättelse.* Stockholm.

Langford, R. (1988). *Don't Take Your Love to Town.* Victoria.

Larsson, H. (1944a). *Min filosofi.* Stockholm.

Larsson, H. (1944b): *Postscriptum.* Stockholm.

Larsson, H. (1945). *En bok om Hans Larsson.* Lund.

Moberg, V. (1963). *Din stund på jorden.* Stockholm.

Muel-Dreyfus, F. (1985). Utbildning, yrkesförändringar och grusade förhoppningar. In: Broady, D. (ed.). *Kultur och utbildning.* Stockholm.

Svanberg, I., Szabó, M. (1993). *Etniskt liv och kulturell mångfald. En handbok i invandrardokumentation.* Stockholm.

Trier Mørch, D. (1974). *Kastanjeallén.* København.

Valkeapää, N.-A. (1991). *Vidderna inom mig.* Copyright the author. DAT. Café Existens.

Walker, K. (1970). *My People. A Kath Walker Collection.* Brisbane.

Westerberg, B. (1987). *...det är ju vi som är negern.* Lund.

BRON, A., SCHEMMANN, M. (eds.) (2000). LANGUAGE, MOBILITY, IDENTITY. CONTEMPORARY ISSUES FOR ADULT EDUCATION IN EUROPE. MÜNSTER, pp. 214-227.

Elżbieta H. Oleksy

ACTIVE HEROINES IN POLISH FILM
CONSTRUCTION OF FEMININITY THROUGH THE LANGUAGE OF THE CINEMA

There has been an agreement among theorists that even though the cinema is technically speaking not a language, films generate meanings through the systems that operate like languages. Gerald Mast argues that the cinema, being the most "hybrid artistic process in human experience," is a mixture of other arts as music, dance, painting, photography, literary texts and literary "modes" (a synthesis of Aristotle's dramatic and narrative "modes"). He says:

> Given the analogies with these six other arts, and given their undeniable contributions to the effects of some or all kinds of films, it seems reasonable to claim that the cinema communicates not only by manipulating its own "language" (whatever it is), but by manipulating the "languages" of all of them. ... If one tried to eliminate all languages from cinema except the uniquely cinematic "language," one might well be left with a silent "scratch film" or one of Man Ray's collages (Mast 1997, 18-19).

In order to understand the notion of the cinema as a set of languages we need to look, if only briefly, at its signifying practices: the methods through which the cinema's meanings are produced.

Film narratives produce their own signifying systems: various codes through which we construct our view of a film or our view of the world (Turner 1994, 119). We do it by closely analysing a film as a 'text'. For instance (and I've selected only one example for the purpose of further analysis), we scrutinise the composition of images within the physical confines of the shot, i.e. the frame, and the function of the frame in either limiting or enlarging space around the image on the screen. In the cinema space is a symbolic medium of communication, and the amount of space that a character occupies often implies ideas dealing with power, class, race and gender. In films dominant characters are almost always given more space to occupy than others. When a film deals with the loss of power or the social impotence of a character, less space is given to that character. Power and powerlessness are defined contextually in the film. It goes without saying that the composition of images within the frame has much to do with the ideology that a film's language communicates.

In *Women's Pictures. Feminism and Cinema* Annette Kuhn explores the relationship between ideology and representation. We are, she argues, constructed by ideology to such an extent that our ways of representing the world to ourselves become "naturalised": "we take", she says, "our conception of that world for granted." This concept carries a resonance for social constructions of gender. If ideology, Kuhn adds, "effaces itself, the process by which this takes place could, for instance, explain ... the taken-for-granted nature of social constructs of femininity" (Kuhn 1992, 4-5). This is precisely what I want to explore in the Polish context: How are the changing ideologies affecting the visualisations of women. What is of primary importance is not only how the media responded to changing ideology, but also whether the change affected our ways of looking at these visualisations.

In the four decades following the World War II, two constructions of feminine identity dominated the Polish visual media: the superwoman and the so-called Polish Mother. The first label, usually identified as a post-feminist Western construct, was used for the first time in reference to the women of East Central Europe in the early 1990s (Corrin 1992). In the West the superwoman was a product of the 1990s consumer discourses. Asserting that the feminism's battles had been successful and its ideology could now be buried, advertisers propagated 'post-feminism' as a utopia where women could do whatever they wanted. It's very easy to decipher the ethos of success embedded in this ideology: women could achieve anything if only they had sufficient will and enthusiasm. Various critiques of this discourse have pointed out that the liberty of women heralded by post-feminism remains within male-defined parameters. I will not rehash this criticism, for it is generally well-known (Coppock et al. 1995).

Expectations and obligations of women remain contradictory in post-feminist discourse, but this was even more the case in Stalinist rhetoric that was enforced on the countries of East Central Europe after the World War II. Formally Polish women enjoyed rights that Western women might have envied. In agreement with Marxist doctrine that women's emancipation entails their integration into the labour market, the Polish Constitution of 1952 gave women full civil and political rights, as well as access to most trades and professions, many of them formerly in 'male' preserve. The state legalised abortion and divorce for a nominal fee and declared to provide free child care facilities.

Polish media of the period propagated the superwoman construction of feminine identity in a series of productions faithful to the doctrine of socialist realism (set up in the Soviet Union during the 1930s) which was enforced on Poland in the first decade after the war. Polish artists, whose œuvre was characterised by socialistic realism, portrayed the society in optimistic and socialistic terms. A propagandist production *Women of Our Times*, shown in 1951 as the so-called *Polish Film Chronicle* (short propagandist films shown in the theatres before feature films; they usually contained commentaries on current political, social and cultural events), was entirely devoted to women. Its aim was to draw attention to the achievements of communism in the professional advancement of women. It presented women in various professions traditionally classified as 'male': architects, managers of textile factories but also manual workers like bricklayers, locksmiths, etc. It also contained information on women's access to education and childcare, organised leisure for women, women as consumers. This image of the superwoman was propagated by the media for about a decade after the war and was subsequently discredited as one of the absurdities of the Stalinist period. Criticism of such productions has usually focused on attempted masculinisation of women.

No doubt, the mobilisation of women during this period resulted from ideological commitment. Very important is that it also addressed the specific needs of a country whose economy developed rapidly in this initial period and thus created a demand for women in the labour market. With the first economic crisis in the late 1950s, job opportunities were reduced particularly for women. They were thus enticed back to their homes, a policy that proved to be completely unrealistic, for one salary was not sufficient to maintain a whole family. As a consequence, women bore the double burden of full-time work, as well as the full responsibility for the well-being of the family. The media reacted accordingly. The laudation of maternity and the affirmation of women's traditional domestic duties became the focus of the media. This task seemed particularly attractive to the Polish media, since in the times of progressive social unrest the image of the Polish Mother carried ideological connotations: it was firmly rooted in the tradition of historical crises and Polish resistance movements.

In Polish cultural history, the ethos and moral identity of the nation was metaphorised as maternity. The Polish Mother was the personification of patience and altruism. While this symbol has its counterparts in the cultures of Poland's neighbouring countries ("Deutschlands bleiche Mutter" in German or the Russian "matreshka," a folk symbol of fertility), its significance in Poland has uniquely patriotic connotations. The idea of Polish womanhood is at once related to the religious cult of the Holy Virgin and to the heritage of the Polish resistance movement. Patriotic and heroic womanhood was a subject often pursued by Polish artists and writers of the nineteenth and early twentieth century. During the partition of Poland, the mission of the Polish woman was the service of the country; she was a preserver of national identity, a propagator of Polishness. Home and motherhood, in every culture a domestic and private space, carried in Poland, and especially during the partition of Poland, public connotations. According to Jan Prokop, "home, as the 'channel' through which Polish national identity was transferred took on the role of independent Poland" (Prokop 1999, 416) – in other words, home was the incubator of patriotism. A high position was accorded to Polish women who minded the heart and transmitted the culture, while men fought or were exiled.

In the post-war films the symbol of the Polish Mother is portrayed almost invariably as a tragic figure. Elżbieta Ostrowska has demonstrated how well the symbol suited the needs of films of the so-called moral unrest and, since her work on the topic is well known in Poland and elsewhere, I will not rehash it here (Ostrowska 1996, 1998). It seems enough to say that this patriotic stereotype appears in such films as Wanda Jakubowska's *Ostatni etap* (The Last Stage, 1948), Jerzy Zarzycki's *Zagubione uczucia* (Lost Feelings, 1957), Andrzej Wajda's *Człowiek z żelaza* (Man of Iron, 1981) and Janusz Zaorski's *Matka Królów* (Króls' Mother, 1987). Instead I would like to move on discussing several films that attempt to disrupt both post-war stereotypes of women.

Of all the films shot throughout the eighties, only one earned the unanimous approval of the Polish critics: Agnieszka Holland's *Kobieta samotna* (A Lonely Woman, 1981; the title in English is also referred to as A Woman on Her Own). It is based on both sources of stereotypes, the superwoman and the Polish Mother, but only to deconstruct them. The main character in this film, Irena, is a postwoman, a profession that is not often held by women in Poland. Her portrayal recalls visualisations of women from the *Polish Film Chronicle* of the 1950s. Unlike these women, however, there's nothing heroic or monumental about Irena. She's bland, and her blandness makes her exceptional.

The Lonely Woman is set in the early 1980s. Although the film occasionally alludes to the socio-political context, its message transcends the spacio-temporal dimension. It is a study of loneliness and the struggle for humanity against the dehumanising forces of reality. Irena lives in the slums near Warsaw, and her basic concern is the survival of her son and herself. When she finds a companion, someone to love and to break the vicious circle of loneliness, she actually only finds isolation again. Determinism that underlies the narrative reduces Irena to the status of a victim, by a concept of ideology that admits no contradictions and keeps no space for resistance. At the level of cultural production, this film does not offer any ground for resistance or agency.

Several other films attempt to escape the conventional stereotypes of women. For further discussion I have chosen two of them: Andrzej Wajda's *Człowiek z marmuru* (Man of Marble, 1977) and Barbara Sass' *Bez miłości* (Without Love, 1980). Both films portray the process of the empowerment of women; in each of them a woman attempts to claim the symbolic space which is culturally reserved for men.

Most criticism of *Man of Marble* concentrates on how the film narrates the tragic story of one oppressed individual – the bricklayer, Mateusz Birkut. The story, set in the 1970s, with flashbacks to the 1950s is briefly like this: Agnieszka, a graduate student of a Film School, sets out on a project that is as ambitious as politically risky. She wants to produce a diploma film about an exemplary worker and a union activist of the Stalinist period, Mateusz Birkut. She discovers her topic while she watches some old newsreels and spots a huge marble statue of a worker – Birkut, as she later discovers. Her interviews with the people who knew Birkut (he is already dead at that time) reveal that he was a national hero whose accomplishment was to lay one thousand bricks in a record time. Agnieszka's film shows how Birkut topples down from his high positions; a revered figure revered by the party functionaries and how he becomes a victim of the communist system. A rhythmical structure of this film has been noted, the structure linking the stories of the two leading characters that are interdependent and demonstrate similar traits (Falkowska 1996, 167). Just as Birkut once risked everything to defy the system, it is now Agnieszka who risks her newly-begun career by bringing the project to the end.

Wajda's film is just another example of the revisionist project – the critique of Stalinism. The uniqueness of this film, compared to others made roughly at the same time, lies in the fact that Wajda assigns the role of a romantic rebel against the system not to a member of the intelligentsia but to a 'plebeian' – a manual worker. A recent commentary, however, made by Ewelina Nurczyńska-Fidelska, strikes a new key. Birkut's rebellion, she says, "serves as a behavioural model for an intelligent woman and constitutes the reason of her rebellion" (Nurczyńska-Fidelska 1996, 239). This acknowledgement of the role the central female character plays in the film, if only briefly suggested, is the only positive comment made on the heroine in the existing criticism of *Man of Marble*. Other critics only reiterate the opinion expressed by Maria Kornatowska in *Film i eros* (Film and Eros, 1986). She says that Agnieszka "is in fact a young man in a girl's attire, and not even so, for the jeans suit she wears exposes masculinity, rather than femininity, of her movements and behaviour" (Kornatowska 1986, 178). She further notes that Agnieszka is wrongly placed in the role of the questing knight, because this role belongs to the 'classic repertoire of men's roles.' She identifies Krystyna Janda – Wajda's favorite actress – who plays Agnieszka as a cultural adrogyne, a "figurative male" (Hills 1999, 38). She makes similar commentaries on Dorota Stalińska, the actress set in the three parts of Barbara Sass' sequel *Bez miłości* (Without Love, 1980), *Debiutantka* (The Beginner, 1981) and *Historia niemoralna* (An Immoral Story, 1990) that I will address subsequently. Kornatowska finally stresses out:

> Krystyna Janda seems to be an ideal actress for Wajda's
> heroines, the women who do not accept their femininity and
> suppress it, whose aim is not so much to fully realize their
> personality but to play an important role, dominate, espe-
> cially in the sphere of public life (Kornatowska 1986, 179).

Not to mention here as to what, in the critic's view, constitutes 'femininity'. We can only infer that it is unacceptable for a woman to play an important role – 'especially in the sphere of public life.'

Borrowing from Yvonne Tasker the term "action heroine" (Tasker, 1993), Elizabeth Hills argues that one of the reasons why it has been prob-lematic to conceptualise active women in film as heroic female characters has to do with the "binaristic logic of dominant theoretical models on which a number of feminist theorists have relied" (Hills 1999, 39). Femi-nist film criticism, in particular, since the 1970s inspired by Laura Mulvey's theory of the gaze (Mulvey, 1975), positions women as passive according to binary oppositions of active male and passive female or in terms of lack (of a penis/phallus). Seen from this perspective, Hills argues, "active and aggressive women in the cinema can only be seen as phallic, unnatural or 'figuratively male'" (Hills 1999, 39).

Hills's analysis concerns the construction of female identity in the tra-ditionally 'masculine' genre of the Hollywood action cinema. Drawing a parallel between Polish cinema and Hollywood I do not want to suggest any generic analogies. Wajda's *Man of Marble* is a film of 'moral unrest' and Sass' trilogy can be seen as belonging to the genre of woman's cinema. Neither do I imply that Kornatowska's criticism has been inspired by femi-nism. On the contrary, I contend, it is steeped in the traditional manner of viewing femininity in Polish culture. I will argue that some new manners of understanding Polish womanhood have to be developed in order to explain the changing representations of women in Polish cinema. We need, as Hills says, "to think differently about active and aggressive heroines in order to create new ways of conceptualizing transgressive female characters" (Hills 1999, 40).

Wajda's *Man of Marble* – and this is my attempt to propose an alterna-tive understanding of this film – offers probably the first attempt in Polish post-war productions to address openly the issue of the social construction of gender. The questing heroine, who is the driving force of the narrative, possesses the attributes traditionally associated with men in the Polish culture. She is assertive, independent, dynamic and courageous. She derives her power from her ability to think and live independently. She is a competent manager of a film crew consisting of four men. Responding to the criticisms of the *Man of Marble* film crew that Janda's performance in the film was a "caricature", Wajda said this: "I did not agree with this [criticism] for a minute; I wanted this film to be contemporary, not only in the shots and narration but, above all else, in Agnieszka's way of behaviour" (*Wajda. Filmy* 1996, 71). And Janda confessed that Wajda made clear to her that she "must act in such a way as to make the viewers love or hate her. Which one doesn't matter, they just mustn't stay indifferent" (*Wajda. Filmy* 1996, 72).

It has been confirmed by a number of spectators that one of the reasons why Agnieszka seems unconvincing as a woman in Wajda's film is that we often see her in the scenes that have traditionally been in the male preserve. While, for instance, Irena in Holland's film is shot in tight frames, in closed, claustrophobic spaces that are traditionally designated to signify the feminine, Wajda's heroine is frequently not only shot in open spaces but also in full control of these spaces. Space, as has been noted, is a symbolic medium of communication which often conveys ideas dealing with power or powerlessness.

The issue of women's attempts to escape claustrophobic spaces in fact resonates in a number of post-war Polish films. In Krzysztof Zanussi's *Za ścianą* (Behind the Wall, 1974), the motif of a woman's loneliness and helplessness is conveyed through the closed space – the 'wall' metaphor. Readers of Charlotte Perkins Gilman's *The Yellow Wallpaper* might of course recognise this metaphor as one that suggests stifling confinement and insanity. Very much like Gilman's heroine, the woman in Zanussi's film becomes obsessed with the claustrophobic room she inhabits. She knocks furniture about, topples objects and complains constantly about her spaceless apartment. And this idea of being confined to a closed space is built into the scenario of helplessness that the woman's story carries. She is a biologist who failed to write a doctoral dissertation and is fired from university. While looking for a lab job she meets a professor of biology. Coincidentally they live in the same apartment house. Following the job interview, she waits for him in the corridor of the building and invites him to her apartment to show him her work. This is where all the subsequent scenes are shot. She is filmed in a way that emphasises her passiveness, vulnerability and powerlessness – always in a tight frame. All point of view shots within the frame are predominantly from the man's perspective and the woman here is filmed in a way that emphasises, to borrow Mulvey's phrase, her "to-be-looked-at-ness" (Mulvey 1975, 11). The only time we see her in a loose frame is at the end of the film after her attempted suicide. She goes to the balcony to water plants and we see her against the panorama of the city.

Wajda's *Man of Marble* and Sass' *Without Love* can be singled out as films which attempt to contradict the 'ultimate scenario of helplessness' that being a woman signifies in Polish film. Interestingly, the heroines of both films have professions associated with the media (Agnieszka is a beginning filmmaker and Ewa, the heroine of Sass' film, is a journalist). Both films begin with similar images shot in tight frames: the women are drowsing on back seats of cars after a day's work. There's a certain softness to both faces – softness and vulnerability. But this is only at the beginning for a very short time, for in subsequent scenes they are constantly on the run, struggling to escape the closed spaces of apartments, crowded offices, etc. The most significant scenes in *Without Love* occur in open spaces, such as, for instance, during Ewa's frequent trips to the Okęcie Airport in Warsaw, where she goes with her daughter to watch planes taking off. The metaphor of escape that these scenes convey can be seen in a larger perspective of the heroine's attempts to achieve freedom. Agnieszka, as has been noted, is not only presented in open spaces, but whenever she is actually shot in a closed space, her movements transgress the space she is afforded, she intrudes into other people's space, such as in the initial studio scene when she watches the first documentary with Birkut: she seems to outgrow the space she is afforded which is additionally emphasised by the placement of her body diagonally across the frame.

Sass' *Without Love* is the first film in the trilogy, I mentioned before, with characters carrying the same name, i.e. Ewa, played by the same actress, Dorota Stalińska. Set within a decade, all three films testify to the director's sensitivity to women's issues. In an interview Sass said the following about the first film in the series: "My film narrates a story of a woman, told by a woman; it represents the feminine sensitivity and value system. I wouldn't like my film to be undistinguishable. It has to be evident that a woman made it" (*Filmowy Serwis Prasowy* 1980, 17-18).

While it might be contentious to argue that *Without Love* is an explicitly feminist film (Sass herself consistently avoids the label 'feminist'), it is certainly a film that lends itself to feminist exegesis. The narrative is motivated by a retrospective event from Ewa Bracka's past. She was abandoned by a man, apparently an Italian journalist, "with a baby in [her] belly." Arguably, the issue of single motherhood was put on the 'agenda' by feminists, alongside other issues of responsibility in sexual relations. Ewa links the event from her past with the style of life she adopted subsequently: "The aim of life is quite simply to live," she asserts and adds, "[t]o live in the best possible way, at any cost." Living in the best possible way means to her the achievement of professional recognition and financial stability and, eventually, emigrating to Italy, where she spent two years to practice her profession. Set in the thaw of the early 1980s, this motif alludes to the Poles' dreams of emigration as tantamount to the achievement of material and also professional success. But, as she said there are bound to be costs involved in achieving her goal. She can only break through if she finds a hot-selling topic. Looking for one, she befriends a young woman from a workers' hotel. She sells the story the woman tells her together with her photo to the newspaper apparently without the woman's consent. The girl attempts to kill herself, and Ewa's unethical behaviour is condemned by her peers. The last scene of the film depicts Ewa as she is walking holding her daughter's hand and a shopping bag. This finale has led some critics to conclude that Ewa ultimately capitulates to patriarchy (Kornatowska 1986, 158, Korska 1998, 72). Arguments raised by these critics remind of the controversies surrounding the reception of such Hollywood films as *Thelma and Louise* (1991) and the *Alien trilogy* (1979, 1986, 1992). Sass' film, to synopsise the criticism, cannot be regarded as a 'woman's picture' because it does not present women's culture as intrinsically 'good', i.e. ethical and non-aggressive. Ewa, in Sass' film, with her aggressive behaviour and manipulating ways, earned the critics' disapproval as a "figurative male". This argument is also often repeated in reference to Agnieszka from Wajda's film. Both women are seen as female characters trespassing male territories, as the heroines of intrinsically male narratives.

In all fairness credit must be given to Kornatowska for having antici-
pated a later criticism of the heroines of the Hollywood action films in her
assessment of Wajda's and Sass' characters. Like Carol Clover in her analysis of what she calls 'the final girl' of the slasher film (she uses Ripley, the
female lead in the *Alien trilogy*, as an example), she does not allow active
heroines in Polish film to be defined as "normatively female" (Hills 1999,
43). Using a Freudian framework throughout her book, she claims that cas-
tration anxiety is resolved by gendering the heroine as masculine and
phallicising her image. She argues that in Agnieszka's case it is resolved by
placing a big (allegedly masculine) umbrella in the backpack she carries, as
well as by the masculine gestures that she adopts. In one of the early se-
quences in the film, Agnieszka bends her arm in the elbow and kisses her
hand – a common masculine gesture of defiance. Janda said in an interview
that when she made that gesture (she apparently suggested it herself to the
script) she "knew then who [she] was; [she] had to fight single-handedly
against everybody" (Janda 1992, 40-42).

The argument used by Hills in her criticism of Clover's analysis,
applies to Kornatowska as well:

> ... Clover can read Ripley and other "final girls" as a para-
> digm of figurative males only because she sees
> resourcefulness and aggression as "masculine" traits, and
> guns and technology [masculine accessory in Agnieszka's
> case] as compensating for some original lack... The use of
> phallocentric logic to position resourceful, intelligent and
> courageous female survivors as "figuratively male" seems
> to me to be a "particularly grotesque" form of selection and
> interpretation and one which has severe political conse-
> quences feminist film theory (Hills 1999, 44).

Kornatowska's assessment of active heroines in Polish film did have serious consequences for Polish film scholarship (including a handful of texts
that might be classified as feminist). In subsequent critiques of active
heroines, Polish critics reiterate her opinions in unison. Interestingly, some
of the same critics see the figure of the Polish Mother equally limiting and
debilitating. It is, however, important to understand that in the deeper
structures of the criticism of active heroines looms the dismissal of the
figure of the Polish superwoman as a compromised construction of the

Polish feminine identity of the post-war years. While it is understandable that this criticism is politically well-grounded, it does not stand the test of time. An age gap is evident in contemporary responses to the *Man of Marble*. While the majority of mature women find Agnieszka's characterisation offensive to womanhood, younger women (I interviewed 30 undergraduate students at the University of Warsaw and 18 graduate students at the University of Łódź) say that they think that she is convincing as a character of a "modern woman" (their attribute). It thus seems to be a matter of political urgency to reconceptualise our notions of active women in Polish film as well as Polish culture. Only by doing this we can open up new ways of thinking instead of confining ourselves to the "repetition of being" (Hills 1999, 49).

We can of course claim that both films discussed here are polysemic (Kuhn 1982), that they accommodate a range of readings, including feminist ones. We can read both female characters as symbolically masculine. The question, however, arises whether it would not be more productive to see them as "transformative, transgressive and alternative women" (Hills 1999, 49), as role models for new generations of Polish women. From this perspective *Man of Marble* and *Without Love* can be seen as dialogues with the patriarchal signifier that Jacques Lacan labeled "the Law of the Father". Both women try to claim the Symbolic realm which is culturally reserved for men. Their experience is offered as a hypothetical possibility of response to patriarchy. Ewa evolves away from dependency on men toward a psychic development. The Oedipal crisis first described by Freud and further elaborated by Lacan in terms of the paternal Symbolic has a direct relevance to Ewa's initiatory experience. Ewa's negative confrontation with the Symbolic – in being abandoned, pregnant by a man whose child she carried – is especially noteworthy, for this is precisely when she takes on directly the Symbolic realm. Like Agnieszka in *Man of Marble*, Ewa is determined to succeed in the male world and the film depicts the process of her empowerment.

Throughout Poland's distraught history women have played an important public role. They were active in all resistance movements during the two hundred years period of the partition of Poland, during its occupation by the Germans in the World War II and in the Solidarity underground movement in more recent years. When in the early nineties Shana Penn conducted interviews with former Solidarity women activists, she discovered what very few Poles knew at that time and what, even today, many still neither acknowledge nor appreciate.

When, on December 13, 1981, the communist regime imposed martial law in Poland and thousands of people, including most of the male leaders, were imprisoned, women created a clandestine network that endured, despite repression, for more than seven years keeping Solidarity alive. This role, which cannot be overestimated, has never been officially recognised following the change over in 1989, and these women's achievement has been erased from the collective memory. What Penn discovered was that the women activists she had talked to, with only one exception, fully accepted this status quo. "In their own eyes," she says, "their underground accomplishment had not been revolutionary but necessary" (Penn 1994, 66). Having struggled underground for independent Poland, these women relinquished activism after the transition was made to democracy. Being questioned about this unexpected change of attitude, one of Penn's respondents said: "... women can only wield power as long as we pretend not to have any power. We were invisible" (Penn 1994, 64).

To reiterate: these women perceived themselves and their roles in the Solidarity as second-rate to those of men. This is not only a question of politics but also of looking relations. No one has explored this relationship better than the African-American film scholar bell hooks. To travesty one of the crucial statements she makes in *Black Looks, Race and Representation*, critical female looking at relations emerge as a site of opposition. This happens only when individual women arduously resist the imposition of dominant ways of knowing (hooks 1992, 128). It is merely through resisting the traditional binary gender codes which identify activity with masculinity and passivity with femininity that we can appreciate active heroines in Polish film and establish new spaces and roles for women in Polish culture.

References

Coppock, V. et al. (1995). *The Illusions of 'Post-Feminism'. New Women, Old Myths.* London.

Corrin, Ch. (1992). *Superwomen and the Double Burden. Women's Experience of Change in Central and Eastern Europe and the Former Soviet Union.* London.

Falkowska, J. (1996). *The Political Films of Andrzej Wajda. Dialogism in Man of Marble, Man of Iron, and Danton.* Providence.

Filmowy Serwis Prasowy (1980).

Hills, E. (1999). From 'Figurative Males' to Action Heroines. Further Thoughts on Active Women in the Cinema. In: *Screen,* 40 (1), pp. 38-50.

hooks, b. (1992). *Black Looks. Race and Representation.* Boston.

Janda, K. (1992). *Tylko się nie pchaj.* Warszawa.

Kornatowska, M. (1986). *Eros i film.* Łódź.

Korska, J. (1998). Barbara Sass-Zdort "1936" - kobiety pod presją w Polsce lat osiemdziesiątych. In: Stachówna, G. (ed.). *Kobieta z kamerą,* Kraków, pp. 71-85.

Kuhn, A. (1982). *Women's Pictures. Feminism and Cinema.* London.

Mast, G. (1977). *Film/Cinema/Movie. A Theory of Experience.* New York.

Mulvey, L. (1975). Visual Pleasure and Narrative Cinema. In: *Screen,* 16 (3), pp. 6-18.

Nurczyńska-Fidelska, E. (1996). W kręgu romantycznej tradycji. O twórczości Andrzeja Wajdy. In: Sobotka, K. (ed.). *Mistrzowie kina europejskie.* Łódź, pp. 229-250.

Ostrowska, E. (1996). Obraz Matki Polki w kinie polskim – mit czy stereotyp? In: Nurczyńska-Fidelska, E., Batko, Z. (eds). *W stulecie kina. Sztuka filmowa w Polsce.* Łódź, pp.80-93.

Ostrowska, E. (1998). Filmic Representations of the 'Polish Mother' in Post-Second World War Polish Cinema. In: *The European Journal of Women's Studies,* 5, pp. 419-435.

Penn, Sh. (1994). The National Secret. In: *Journal of Women's History,* 5 (3), pp. 55-69.

Prokop, J. (1991). Kobieta Polka. In: Bachórz, J., Kowalczykowa, A. (eds.). *Słownik literatury polskiej XIX wieku.* Wrocław.

Tasker, Y. (1993). *Spectacular Bodies. Gender, Genre and the Action Cinema.* London.

Turner, G. (1994). Film Languages. In: Graddol, D., Boyd-Barrett, O. (eds.). *Media Texts: Authors and Readers.* Clevedon.

Wajda. Filmy (1996). Warszawa.

SELECTED BIBLIOGRAPHY

Compiled by Marcus Reinecke

This bibliography presents a selection of books and articles from scientific journals published on the subject "Language – Mobility – Identity". The publication selection is based on the following criteria:

First, the titles represent a limited period of time. All books on this list were published between 1995 and 1999, and all articles from 1997 to 1999. By no means an exhaustive list, this choice was made to ensure, on the one hand, relevance and on the other hand to compile a manageable selection.

Second, all titles are written in English which does not mean that they were all written by native English speakers.

Third, this selection does not only consider publications in the field of adult education but also includes interdisciplinary works.

And finally, besides searching in the different OPAC of German and European university libraries', this bibliography was also compiled using the following databases, EBSCO Information Service, ERIC Bibliographic Database, ISI Citation Database, JADE Journal Article Database, NCBE's Bibliographic Database and SCAD.

Books (1995-1999)

Abromeit, H. (1998). *Democracy in Europe. Legitimising Politics in a Non-State Policy*. New York.

Ager, D. E. (1997). *Language, Community and the State. Linguistic Development in European Nations*. Exeter.

Asplund, R., Sloane, P. J., Theodossiou, I. (eds.) (1998). *Low Pay and Earnings Mobility in Europe.* Cheltenham, Northampton, MASS.

Baker, J. (1996). *Insertion, Exclusion and Social Factors. Language of Social Policy in Europe*. London.

Beaugrande, R. de, Grosman, M., Seidlhofer, B. (1998). *Language Policy and Language Education in Emerging Nations*. London.

Beitter, U. E. (ed.) (1999). *The New Europe at the Crossroads*. London, Frankfurt/M.

Benda-Beckmann, K. von (1995). *Nationalism, Ethnicity and Cultural Identity in Europe*. Utrecht.

Bifulco, M. (1998). *In Search of an Identity for Europe*. Bonn.

Blotevogel, H. H., Fielding, A. J. (1997). *People, Jobs and Mobility in the New Europe*. Chichester.

Breakwell, G. M., Lyons, E. (eds.) (1996). *Changing European Identites. Social Psychological Analyses of Social Change*. Oxford.

Brinker-Gabler, G., Smith, S. (eds.) (1996). *Writing New Identities. Gender, Nation and Immigration in Contemporary Europe*. Minneapolis.

Carl, J. (1999). *The Question of National and European Identity in Contemporary Europe*. Osnabrück.

CEDEFOP (1998). *Vocational Education and Training – The European Research Field*. Background Report Vol. II. Thessaloniki.

Coleman, J. A. (1996). *Studying Languages. A Survey of British and European Students. The Proficiency, Background, Attitudes and Motivations of Students of Foreign Languages in the United Kingdom and Europe*. London.

Connor, U. (1996). *Contrastive Rhetoric. Cross-Cultural Aspects of Second-Language Writing*. New York.

Convrey, A., Evans, M. Green, S. Macaro, E. (eds.) (1997). *Pupils' Perceptions of Europe. Identity and Education*. London.

Cordell, K. (ed.) (1999). *Ethnicity and Democratisation in the New Europe*. Routledge.

Corrin, Ch. (1999). *Gender and Identity in Central and Eastern Europe*. Ilford.

Delanty, G. (1995). *Inventing Europe. Idea, Identity, Reality*. Basingstoke.

Diana, M. N. (ed.) (1997). *Cultural Awareness. Linguistic and Cultural Training towards Mobility in Europe*. Trieste.

Dunn, J. (1999). *Language and Society in Post-Communist Europe.* Basingstoke.

Erskine, A., Elchardus, M. Herkommer, S. (eds.) (1996). *Changing Europe. Some aspects of Identity, Conflict and Social Justice.* Avebury.

Everett, W. (ed.) (1996). *European Identity in Cinema.* Exeter.

Gastelaars, M. (1998). *United Europe. The Quest for a Multifaceted Identity.* Maastricht

Gowan, P., Anderson, P. (eds.) (1997). *The Question of Europe.* London, New York.

Hedetoft, U. (ed.) (1998). *Political Symbols, Symbolic Politics. European Identities in Transformation.* Aldershot.

Hoffmann, Ch. (ed.) (1996). *Language, Culture and Communication in Contemporary Europe.* Clevedon.

Identity of Non-Dominant Cultures in the Process of European Integration (1996). Bratislava: Ministerstvo kultury Slovenskej rebubliky.

Jenkins, B. (ed.) (1996). *Nation and Identity in Contemporary Europe.* London.

Kazamias, A. M., Spillane, M. G. (1998). *Education and the Structuring of the European Space. North-South, Centre-Periphery, Identity-Otherness.* Athen.

Kriesi, H. et al. (eds.) (1999). *Nation and National Identity. The European Experience in Perspective.* Chur.

Kurti, L., Lagman, J. (eds.) (1997). *Beyond Borders. Remaking Cultural Identities in the New East and Central Europe.* Boulder, COL.

Landau, A., Whitman, R. G. (eds.) (1997). *Rethinking the European Union. Institutions, Interests, and Identities.* Basingstoke.

Leonard, M. (1998). *Making Europe Popular. The Search for European Identity.* London.

Makikalli, M., Korhonen, A., Virtanen, K. (eds.) (1997). *European Identities. Studies in Integration, Identity and Nationhood.* Turku.

Martiniello, M. (ed.) (1995). *Migration, Citizenship and Ethno-National Identities in the European Union.* Aldershot.

Mayo, M. (1997). *Imaginig Tomorrow. Adult Education for Transformation*. Leicester.

Mikkeli, H. (1998). *Europe as an Idea and an Identity*. Houndmills.

Neumann, I. B. (1995). *Russia and the Idea of Europe. A Study in Identity and International Relations*. Routledge.

Neumann, I. B. (1999). *Uses of the Other. "The East" in European Identity Formation*. Manchester.

Oudin, A.-S. (1996). *Immersion and Multilingual Education in the European Union*. Baile Atha Cliath.

Price, G. (1998). *Encyclopedia of the Languages of Europe*. Oxford.

Pynsent, R. B. (ed.) (1996). *The Literature of Nationalism. Essays on East European Identity*. Basingstoke.

Row, Th. (ed.) (1996). *Reflections on the Identity of Europe. Global and Transatlantic Perspectives*. Bologna.

Rychener, F. et al. (eds.) (1998). *Certificates, Skills and Job Markets in Europe. A Summary Report of a Comparative Study Conducted in Germany, Spain, France, Italy, Netherlands, United Kingdom*. Thessaloniki.

Segers, T. (ed.) (1996). *Cultur, Identity, Europe*. Frankfurt/M.

Smyth, A. P. (ed.) (1998). *Medieval Europeans. Studies in Ethnic Identity and National Perspectives in Medieval Europe*. Basingstokekstoke.

Synak, B. (ed.) (1995). *The Ethnic Identities of European Minorities. Theory and Case Studies*. Gdańsk.

Tassinopoulos, A., Werner, H., Kristensen, S. (1998). *Mobility and Migration of Labour in the European Union and their Specific Implications for Young People*. Thessaloniki.

Tonra, B., Dunne, D. (1997). *A European Cultural Identity. Myth, Reality or Aspiration*. Dublin.

Varennes, F. de (1996). *Language, Minorities and Human Rights*. The Hague.

Vermeulen, H. (1997). *Immigration Policy for a Multicultural Society. A Comparative Study of Integration, Language and Religious Policy in Five Western European Countries*. Brussels.

Whitman, R. G. (1998). *From Civilian Power to Superpower? The International Identity of the European Union*. Basingstokekstoke.

Willems, G. M. (1996). *Issues in Cross-Cultural Communication. The Europe Dimension in Language Teaching*. Nijmegen.

Winther-Jensen, Th. (ed.) (1995). *Challenges to European Education. Cultural Values, National Identities, and Global Responsibilities*. Frankfurt/M.

Wintle, M. (ed.) (1996). *Culture and Identity in Europe. Perceptions of Divergence and Unity in Past and Present*. Aldershot.

Wodak, R., Corson, D. (1997). *Language Policy and Political Issues in Education*. Dordrecht.

Wodak, R. (1999). *The Discursive Construction of National Identity*. Edinburgh.

Articles (1997-1999)

Aspinwall, M. (1998). Globalism, Exit and Free Social Riders. A Dysfunctional Integration Theory. In: *European Journal of Political Research*, 33 (3), pp. 323-346.

Audigier, F. (1999). Teaching about Society, Passing on Values. Elementary Law in Civic Education. In: *European Education*, 31 (1), pp. 38-64.

Banchoff, Th. (1999). German Identity and European Integration. In: *European Journal of International Relations*, 5 (3), pp. 259-289.

Beetham, J. (1997). Language, Diversity and Mobility. A European Perspective. In: *American Language Review*, March/April, pp. 29-31.

Cinnirella, M. (1997). Towards a European Identity? Interactions Between the National and European Social Identities Manifested by University Students in Britain and Italy. In: *British Journal of Social Psychology*, 36 (1), pp. 19 ff.

Cormack, M. (1998). Minority Language Media in Western Europe – Preliminary Considerations. In: *European Journal of Communication*, 13 (1), pp. 33-52.

Delors, J. (1999). European Identity. A Political Identity. In: *Balkan Review*, 14, pp. 4-8.

Du Bois-Reymond, M. (1998). European Identity in the Young and Dutch Student's images of Germany and the Germans. In: *Comparative Education*, 34 (1), pp. 19-31.

Grant, N. (1997). Some Problems of Identity and Education. A Comparative Examination of Multicultural Education. In: *Comparative Education*, 33 (1), pp. 9-28.

Hansen, P. (1998). Schooling a European Identity. Ethno-Cultural Exclusion and Nationalist Resonance within the EU Policy of "the European Dimension of Education". In: *European Journal of Intercultural Studies*, 9 (1), pp. 5 ff.

Hayden, M. C., Thompson, J. J. (1997). Student Perspectives on International Education. A European Dimension. In: *Oxford Review of Education*, 23 (4), pp. 459-478.

Koivumaa, K. (1998). Europe. Several Identities, or One Single Identity? In: *Perspectives. Review of Central European Affairs*, 10, pp. 21-37.

Lahav, G. (1997). Ideological and Party Contraints on Immigration Attitudes in Europe. In: *Journal of Common Market Studies*, 35 (3), pp. 377-406.

Lim, R./Pithers, R. T. (1997). A Non-English-Speaking Background in Adult Vocational Education. Breaking through the Barriers. In: *Journal of Vocational Education and Training*, 49 (4), pp. 531 ff.

Luttringer, J.-M. (1997). The Role of the Social Partners in the Development of Vocational Training in Countries in Transition. In: *Vocational Training. European Journal*, 11 (May-August), pp. 48-52.

Menendez Alacron, A. V. (1998). National Identity, Nationalism and the Organization of the European Union. Perspectives from France and Spain. In: *International Journal of Contemporary Sociology*, 35 (1), pp. 57 ff.

Moxon-Browne, E. (1997). Eastern and Western Europe. Towards a New European Identity? In: *Contemporary Politics*, 3 (1), pp. 27 ff.

Nesbit, T. (1999). Mapping Adult Education. In: *Educational Theory*, 49 (2), pp. 265-280.

Neumann, I. B. (1998). European Identity. EU Expansion and the Integration/Exclusion Nexus. In: *Alternatives. Social transformation and Human Governance*, 23 (3), pp. 397-314.

Rusconi, G. E. (1998). The Difficulty in Building a European Identity. In: *International Spectator*, 33 (1), pp. 23 ff.

Safr, V., Woodhouse, H. (1999). Eastern, Western or Pan-European? Recent Educational Change in the Czech Republic. In: *European Education*, 31 (2), pp. 72-95.

Schlesinger, Ph. (1997). From Cultural Defence to Political Culture. Media, Politics and Collective Identity in the EU. In: *Media Culture & Society*, 19 (3), pp. 369-392.

Sluga, G. (1998). Identity, Gender and the History of European Nations and Nationalisms. In: *Nations and Nationalism*, 4 (1), pp. 87 ff.

Svec, S. (1998). Transformation of the Adult Education System in Slovakia. In: *International Review of Education*, 44 (4), pp. 379-392.

Taylor, R. (1997). The Search for a Social Purpose Ethic in Adult Continuing Education in the New Europe. In: *Studies in the Education of Adults*, 29 (1), pp. 92-101.

Thomas, G. (1997). The European Challenge. Educating for a Plurilingual Europe. In: *Language Learning Journal*, 15 (March), pp. 74-80.

Wilson, A. L. (1999). Creating Identities of Dependency. Adult Education as a Knowledge-Power Regime. In: *International Journal of Lifelong Education*, 18 (2), pp.85 ff.

AUTHORS

Cecilia Almlöv

Uppsala University
Department of Scandinavic
Languages
Advanced Studies in Modern
Swedish
Box 1834
751 48 Uppsala / Sweden

Zygmunt Bauman, Professor em.

University of Leeds
Department of Sociology
Leeds LS2 9JT / UK

Etienne Bourgeois, Professor

Universitè Catholique de Louvain
Department of Education / FORG
1348 Louvain-la-Neuve / Belgium
Bourgeois@forg.ucl.ac.de

Agnieszka Bron, Professor

Ruhr-Universität Bochum
Institut für Pädagogik
Lehrstuhl für Erwachsenenbildung
44780 Bochum / Germany
agnieszka.bron@ruhr-uni-bochum.de

Tordis Dahllöf, Ph.D.

Centre for Multiethnic Research
Box 514
751 20 Uppsala / Sweden

John Field, Professor

University of Warwick
Department of Education
Coventry CV4 7AL / UK
cesbl@snow.csv.warwick.ac.uk

Lars Grundström

contact through editors

Wolfgang Jütte, Ph.D.

Universität Flensburg
Internationales Institut für
Management
Erwachsenenbildung/Weiterbildung
24943 Flensburg / Germany
juette@uni-flensburg.de

Christina Lönnheden

Stockholm University
Department of Education
106 91 Stockholm / Sweden
Lonnheden@ped.su.se

Mieczysław Malewski, Professor

University of Wrocław
Department of Education
50-527 Wrocław / Poland

Barbara Merill, Ph.D.

University of Warwick
Department of Education
Coventry CV4 7AL / UK
Barbara.Merrill@warwick.ac.uk

W. John Morgan, Professor

University of Nottigham
Director, Centre for Comparative
Education Research
John.Morgan@nottingham.ac.uk

Tanja Možina

Slovenian Institute for Adult
Education
1000 Ljublijana / Slovenia
Tanja.Monzina@asc-saec.si

Elżbieta Oleksy, Professor

Łódź University
Centre for Women Studies
90-136 Łódź / Poland
Eloleksy@krysia.uni.lodz.pl

Branka Petek, Professor

Centre for Permanent Education
1000 Ljublijana / Slovenia

Marcus Reinecke

Ruhr-Universität Bochum
Institut für Pädagogik
Lehrstuhl für Erwachsenenbildung
44780 Bochum / Germany
marcus.reinecke@ruhr-uni-bochum.de

Kjell Rubenson, Professor

University of British Columbia
Department of Education ?
Vancouver, B.C. / Canada V6T 1Z4
Kjell.Rubenson@ubc.ca

Michael Schemmann, Ph.D.

Ruhr-Universität Bochum
Institut für Pädagogik
Lehrstuhl für Erwachsenenbildung
44780 Bochum / Germany
michael.schemmann@ruhr-uni-bochum.de

Ewa Solarczyk-Ambrozik, Professor

Adam Mickiewicz University
Faculty of Educational Studies
60-569 Poznan / Poland

Janos Sz. Tóth

Hungarian Folk High School Society
1011 Budapest / Hungary
mnthfhss@mail.matav.hu

Albert Tuijnman, Professor

Stockholm University
Department of International
Education
106 91 Stockholm / Sweden
Albert.Tuijnman@interped.su.se

Didaktik

Horst W. Jung; Gerda von Staehr
"Endzeit" und historisch-utopisches Lernen
Didaktische Grundlagen
Bd. 1, 2., unv. Aufl. 1995, 190 S., 19,80 DM, br.,
ISBN 3-89473-920-7

Hans-Joachim von Olberg (Hrsg.)
Porträts und Quellen zur Didaktikgeschichte
Ein Studienbuch von und für Lehrerstudenten
Bd. 2, Frühjahr 2000, 208 S., 29,80 DM, br.,
ISBN 3-8258-2024-6

Horst W. Jung
Katastrophische Lernereignisse
Bd. 3, 1996, 96 S., 16,80 DM, br., ISBN 3-8258-2764-x

Horst W. Jung; Gerda von Staehr (Hrsg.)
Lernreflexionen
Erfahrungen aus Studium und Referendariat
Die abgedruckten Lernreflexionen – eine im Anschluß an ein Magisterexamen, drei nach bestandenem ersten Lehrerexamen und zwei nach Abschluß des Referendariats – stammen sämtlich von Personen, die einen Teil ihrer Examina bei uns abgelegt haben und die uns in der einen oder anderen Weise zu ihren akademischen Lehrern zählen. Gemeinsam ist den Verfassern auch eine – unterschiedlich intensive und unterschiedlich gewendete – Beziehung zur Kritischen Psychologie. Da, wie gesagt, die Anregung zu dieser Reflexion von uns ausging, kann nicht erwartet werden, daß es sich bei dem Unternehmen um die Wirkung eines kritisch-psychologischen "Pfingstereignisses" handelt, bei dem der "heilige Geist" einer bestimmten wissenschaftlichen Position, ohne weiteres Zutun von (Lehr-) Personen, auf die für die Erleuchtung der Selbstreflexion bereiten "Gläubigen" herniedergestiegen ist. Nein: Wir haben die Reflexionsarbeit angeregt und arrangiert. Ja, wir haben sogar, in unterschiedlicher Weise, entweder kaum oder mehr oder weniger, auf die Reflexionsarbeit eingewirkt. Wer daher der Auffassung ist, wir hätten uns – methodisch – "die Hände schmutzig gemacht", dem wollen wir nicht widersprechen. Wir glaubten aber den methodischen Purismus opfern zu müssen – um der Möglichkeiten der Akteure willen. Wer also "klinisch reine" Selbstreflexion zu dem hier gewählten Gegenstandsbereich sucht, dem wünschen wir bei seiner Suche nach entsprechenden Publikationen viel Erfolg! Der Leser wird nach alledem nicht mehr erwarten: – daß er hier verallgemeinerbare Ergebnisse im Sinne von Umfrageresultaten

empirisch-analytischer Forschung vorfindet, – daß in den Lernreflexionen der Anspruch erhoben wird, gültige Aussagen über Studium un Referendariat zu treffen, denen jedermann zustimmen kann, – daß sich im Anschluß an die selbstreflexiven Rekonstruktionen umstandslos mehr oder weniger originelle Hypothesen zur instrumentellen, "kontrollwissenschaftlichen" Weiterverwendung entwickeln lassen. – daß schließlich, in völliger Verkennung kritisch-psychologischer Selbstansprüche, die Herausgeber sich zu über "der Sache" stehenden Interpreten, Kommentatoren oder Beurteilern aufschwingen.
Bd. 4, 1997, 264 S., 29,80 DM, br., ISBN 3-8258-3400-x

Hans-Christian Florek
Leistungsbegriff und pädagogische Praxis
Der "pädagogische" Begriff der Leistung ist ein Kern des Berufswissens der Lehrerinnen und Lehrer aller Schulformen. Das Buch nimmt die gegenwärtige Diskussion über Leistungsforderungen in der Schule auf und stellt sich der Herausforderung, Leistungsmerkmale praxisbezogen neu zu bestimmen. Sie werden als "Orientierungen" für die Gestaltung des Unterrichts, als "Kriterien" der Leistungsbeurteilung und als "Zielvorstellungen" für die Leistungserziehung ausgelegt. Ein neuartiges Verfahren ermöglicht die kompetente Beurteilung und Bewertung konkreter Schülerarbeiten. In einem größeren Sinnzusammenhang aber wird die Bedeutung des Leistungsgedankens für eine professionelle Berufsausübung begrenzt.
Bd. 5, 1999, 128 S., 24,80 DM, br., ISBN 3-8258-4315-7

Horst Wilhelm Jung;
Gerda von Staehr (Hrsg.)
Historisch-politisches Lehren und Lernen
Geschichte – Standpunkte – Erfahrungen
In bewußter Abgrenzung zu marktgängiger didaktischer Begleitung herrschender gesellschaftlicher Trends bietet dieses Buch eine Skizze der geschichtsdidaktischen Diskussion von 1989 – 1997, ein Plädoyer für historisch-politisches Lernen in der Perspektive der Weltgesellschaft, eine Antwort auf die Frage nach der Relevanz des Marxschen Denkens für geschichtsdidaktische Reflexion, einen Vorschlag für gemeinsames historisch-politisches Lernen von Lehrenden und Lernenden im Anschluß an eine entsprechende Schulprogrammentwicklung, eine Anleitung zu kritisch-psychologischem Umgang mit dem Theorie-Praxis-Verhältnis im Lehrerstudium, eine Anleitung zur Bildung kritischen Lehrerselbstverständnisses, einen selbstreflexiven Einblick in aktuelle Probleme des Referendariats.
Bd. 6, 1999, 224 S., 29,90 DM, br., ISBN 3-8258-4474-9

LIT Verlag Münster – Hamburg – London
Bestellungen über:
Grevener Str. 179 48159 Münster
Tel.: 0251 – 23 50 91 – Fax: 0251 – 23 19 72
e-Mail: lit@lit-verlag.de – http://www.lit-verlag.de

Preise: unverbindliche Preisempfehlung